MUSIC
AS
PROPAGANDA

Recent Titles in
Contributions to
the Study of Music and Dance

Music and Musket: Bands and Bandsmen of the American Civil War
Kenneth E. Olson

Edmund Thornton Jenkins: The Life and Times of an American Black
Composer, 1894-1926
Jeffrey P. Green

Born to Play: The Life and Career of Hazel Harrison
Jean E. Cazort and Constance Tibbs Hobson

Titta Ruffo: An Anthology
Andrew Farkas, editor

Nellie Melba: A Contemporary Review
William R. Moran, compiler

Armseelchen: The Life and Music of Eric Zeisl
Malcolm S. Cole and Barbara Barclay

Busoni and the Piano: The Works, the Writings, and the Recordings
Larry Sitsky

MUSIC
AS
PROPAGANDA

Art to Persuade,
Art to Control

ARNOLD PERRIS

Contributions to the Study of Music
and Dance, Number 8

GREENWOOD PRESS

Westport, Connecticut • London, England

Library of Congress Cataloging in Publication Data

Perris, Arnold.
  Music as propaganda.

  (Contributions to the study of music and dance,
ISSN 0193-9041 ; no. 8)
  Bibliography: p.
  Includes index.
    1. Music—Psychology.   2. Propaganda.   3. Persuasion
(Psychology).   4. Control (Psychology).   5. Music and
state.   6. Music and society.   I. Title.   II. Series.
ML3838.P43   1985   781'.15   84-27969
ISBN 0-313-24505-3 (lib. bdg.)

Library of Congress Catalog Card Number: 84-27969
ISBN: 0-313-24505-3
ISSN: 0193-9041

First published in 1985

Greenwood Press
A division of Congressional Information Service, Inc.
88 Post Road West, Westport, Connecticut 06881

Printed in the United States of America

10 9 8 7 6 5 4 3 2

What passions cannot music raise or quell?

John Dryden, *Ode to St. Cecilia's Day*

Music has a great advantage; without mentioning anything, it can say everything.

Ilya Ehrenburg (in a comment on the premiere of Shostakovich's Eighth Symphony, 1943)

"If you have troubles," Valentine declared, "I can give you a piece of advice: Turn on dance music."

Aleksandr I. Solzhenitsyn, *The First Circle*

Contents

Preface

Every author earnestly hopes the title of his book will fascinate everyone who gives it a glance. The author also takes the chance, of course, that it may turn some away. The title of this book may repel some readers who are affronted by the thought of the noble art of music linked with the craft of deception and mind control. But propagandizing is an ancient use for music: not to deceive, necessarily, but to *persuade* (the first meaning of the word). As used here the term embraces a wide range of messages. Many are quite forthright and beneficial, or, at least, not malicious or tyrannical.

Many works of music are named here, many are very familiar. Many composers appear, too, from the anonymous composer of *Yankee Doodle* to Richard Wagner; and several critics are cited, such as St. Augustine and Bob Dylan. The reader is invited to re-listen (perhaps in the mind) and to try to respond to the music as its first audience did when the beguiling ballad, energetic march, or heroic symphony, the political opera or protest song proclaimed a message: a reason for music in addition to its being music.

Ultimately all music survives its first occasion because it is effective as art. If there is, or once was, an extramusical purpose, it too may sound beyond the generation that accepted or spurned the composer's or performer's statement. A long time after, the message may no longer speak to anyone, since the cause is no longer current. Such a variety of examples has yielded this history of music as propaganda.

Many readers scanned these pages in typescript; I thank them all. I must offer my appreciation individually to my colleague at the University of Missouri-St. Louis, Joel Glassman (Political Science) and I also wish to thank Robert Hegel (Washington University, Chinese Literature), Lois Ibsen al Faruqi (Temple University, Islamic Studies), and John Borelli (College of Mount St. Vincent, New York, Sanskrit Literature).

CHAPTER 1

Messages in the Music

> Give me the making of the songs of a nation and I care not who makes the laws.
>
> Andrew Fletcher, Saltoun, England,
> *Convention Concerning a Right Regulation
> of Government for the Common Good of Mankind* (1703)

For Americans who cannot escape our Puritan heritage, music is not to be taken very seriously.[1] It does not shape our daily lives. It is not a profound social issue, like public health or military expenditures, that is to be judged with solemn gravity. It has nothing to do with the government of nations, except for a little pomp and circumstance on national holidays. We could certainly live without it.

But would we? No society yet studied is without music, neither in the tiny, lost tribe of the Philippine Tasaday[2] nor in the rigorously censored lives of the eight hundred million Chinese during the Cultural Revolution. The ultimate mind control that George Orwell imagined and depicted in *1984* included a necessary function for music in the coldly calculated world of Big Brother.[3] We are indefatigably addressed by music, though we are often barely aware of its presence. Music reaches us from the home stereo and in our cars, it is piped into banks, office buildings and supermarkets, and it sounds behind the action of films and television plays, playing subtly with our emotions and our will. We use music to work by, to jog by, to quiet the baby, for aerobic exercise, for ceremonies, and for religion (usually demanded by the ritual); there is music for the President of this Republic and for the Queen of England, for parades on Main Street and on Red Square, in the Buddhist temple and in the village in Papua New Guinea.[4] We may hear music that was composed four centuries ago for the choir of St. Peter's Basilica and music that has just been composed to bring stadium crowds to their feet. Would we respond without the thrust of music in these "messages"? No doubt we would, but the occasion and the intended information and response would be immeasurably duller, less vital, and probably less convincing. The agents and directors inferred in the list above would have no other device as beguiling or as immediately energizing with which to transmit their messages.

Is music, then, a ready tool for propaganda? The thought is disturbing because *propaganda*, defined as information to aid or to injure, has acquired an odious meaning in modern times. To link the beloved art of music with the devices of deception and with the presentation of controlled information that intentionally misleads is distasteful. Can this linkage be true? The concept of a state which controls artists is also offensive to citizens of the Western democracies, who believe that the making of art should be left to artists, according to the principle of free speech, perhaps colored by the nineteenth-century view of the artist's will as paramount and inviolable. We judge that extramusical controls must ultimately inhibit the imagination of the composer and diminish the quality of his work. Can an artistic mind function if it is bound to the strictures of a political ideology? Which must come first—the success of the art (its aesthetic quality) or the success (the accuracy and effectiveness) of the ideological message?

But suppose the creative artists accept the official ideology. Are they then inhibited? Was Haydn, apparently content for twenty-nine years with the system of patronage, inhibited in working out the possibilities of the sonata form? Are his last symphonies, written after he exchanged a closed social situation in Esterhaz for the larger, primarily nonaristocratic audience of London, a striking exhibition of freedom from the constraints of the royal taste? It does not seem that this is the case. But Haydn was a genius who was well appreciated by the Prince, and his daily efforts were part of the "ideology" of the Prince's regime. Fortunate Prince! Happy musician!

Were the great composers of religious music, such as Palestrina in sixteenth-century Rome and Johann Sebastian Bach in eighteenth-century Leipzig, ever inhibited by the official requirements of their respective liturgies? Yes! But they worked within them, most of the time, manipulating their craft within the models of their epoch. With their taste and skill, they fitted together the sacred words and the message, which presumably took precedence in any conflict with their musical criteria.

Propaganda is the "spreading of ideas, information or rumor for the purpose of helping or injuring an institution, a cause or a person," according to the Merriam-Webster dictionary. In terms of such a definition, then, the music that is used to enhance a religious service is an appropriate tool. It is music as propaganda. In fact, sound itself may be a nonverbal statement of clear intent and effectiveness. For example, the sound of a pipe organ will immediately suggest a religious occasion to many Americans, so limited has the venue for hearing organ literature become in this country. Beethoven's choral *Ode to Joy* (titled in the suggestive words of Friedrich Schiller), as used in his Ninth Symphony, was intended to "spread ideas" about the brotherhood of man. Surely no one will disagree that the singing commercials of radio and television belong to an art of persuasion, if not rumor. Songs of protest, satire, praise or scorn from all times fall into the category of music as propaganda. Some examples are *Die Gedanken sind frei* (Thoughts Are Free),[5] which appeared during the German Peasant Wars of the sixteenth century, *Lillibullero*, a satire against the British governor in Ireland appointed by James II, and *Yankee Doodle*, with which the American colonists adapted an English satire against themselves. But such use is scarcely archaic. Arlo Guthrie's chronicle, *Alice's Restaurant Massacree*,[6] written in 1968, is a beguiling protest against an officious and petty village police department, as well as the Viet Nam War draft. Its long text is tongue-in-cheek from beginning to end, but has been clearly understood as social criticism and heard by thousands of people in concerts and from the record album. The vocal style is simple, and the singer's ideas are assimilated effortlessly.

When we hear an old and familiar song that is familiar because it is part of our culture, even a fragment will arouse the established meaning. Words are not necessary, not even the title: They come to mind at once. A couple measures of this tune at once delivers such a message to Americans:

Tempo di Marcia

The Marines' Hymn recalls a patriotic emotion that we have experienced at some time and in some place, initially as a child, perhaps at a parade, on a patriotic holiday, and possibly also as a member of the armed forces. Conversely, the literary element also works; *to read* a line or two of the lyrics in the absence of the melody evokes the same reference: "From the halls of Montezuma, to the shores of Tripoli. We fight our country's battles on the land and on the sea!" And there is still a simpler clue. Read only the titles of a miscellaneous list of songs: *Home on the Range, Some Enchanted Evening, The Marines' Hymn, Raindrops Keep Falling on My Head*. Each one has its message for the reader, each one of a different kind or intensity, for the experiences and social settings that accompanied one's hearing of the music differed. They may have been profound, of little consequence, joyous, or even unpleasant.

Music is *doing* something to everyone who hears it all the time. It is an art which reaches the emotions easily, often (always?) ahead of intellectual awareness. In the film *Jaws*, a melodic motive in the bass arouses our fear of the shark each time we hear it, whether or not the terrifying creature appears before our eyes. Associations are supplied when we turn on our listening skill as surely as we ask a computer to search for a key topic. We use music to change our behavior. We may play a recording or turn the radio dial to match or change our present mood. We go to a concert expecting to be aroused to excitement and pleasure by the music, by the performers' skills, and by their enthusiasm, as well as by that of the other members of the audience. A stronger response is evoked by an uncommon occasion for the performance, such as that of a world premiere, a return engagement of a star, a holiday season, or a performance which will go into the *Guinness Book of World Records*!

To the modern, urban listener, music is most often a passive experience; planting corn as a community task while everyone sings a work song is a scrap of remote folklore. More of us are music receivers; we may become excited by the performance, but only a small percentage of people engages in making music. To be sure, some listeners also perform occasionally as amateurs. Some sing in choirs. Even fewer try to create music for a particular occasion; if one is not inhibited by a lack of professional skill, this is always a strong experience. One states a message to persuade, to beguile, or to inform someone (it may be oneself alone). If the listener accepts the message and is changed by it, then the music-propaganda has functioned as desired. This functions as much as the conclusion of Beethoven's mighty Ninth Symphony functions: there is an emotional response both to the artistic climax and to the literary or verbal meaning. The audience is overwhelmed by Beethoven's skill and by his expressive power, which clothes Schiller's stirring words (even in a clumsy translation into English).

In this book, the past and the present will be scanned for examples of music with this purpose and additional dimension. Some examples were transformed by later composers or performers. Some acquired multiple messages. Some music announces one meaning, while intentionally or inadvertently it evokes a different response.

I do not argue that every piece of music holds a message or that all music is written to persuade the listener to a conscious and explicit response. Some music and musical forms are by definition abstract and nondescriptive. Is the content of the Haydn and Mozart symphonies supposed to lead the listener to some conceptual meaning? It was never thought so. The nicknames of several symphonies ("Miracle," "Military," "Surprise," "Jupiter") were added by their publishers. Haydn's "London" Symphony No. 104 is not his musical picture of the city in the 1790s. A Marxist view of the history of art argues that all art, and certainly a symphony, speaks for a class, the ruling class in every period of history.[7] Since the ruling class up to the modern period was aristocratic, autocratic, and often indifferent to the lower classes, then art spoke for that elite, to the disadvantage of art for other segments of society.

A serious artwork of Western culture, let us say a Haydn symphony, is intended for a class of listeners which is prepared to appreciate it; it is not popular entertainment or folk art. The audience which heard Haydn's music was an aristocratic society; it was joined by an affluent middle class that was modestly educated and had the means and the leisure to turn aside for a time from the chores of making ends meet—a choice not available to the lower classes. This was *their* music. Listening to works like Haydn's symphonies reaffirmed their status in society: They would not be confused with the lower classes. But even Karl Marx admitted that some great art, like the dramas of classical Greece and the plays of Shakespeare, transcends the social and economic setting from which it arose.[8] Some art is perceived as universal and above a class statement. It is not an entirely perfect argument. Marx and his early apostles were generally university graduates and this at once made them the recipients (and the captives?) of middle- or upper-class education and values, which they did not discard, despite their concern for the proletariat. And there are still other viewpoints.

Some composers appear to stand outside the social environment in which they lived and to be innocent of vigorously changing times, or at least not to allow their milieu to be represented in their work. Such apolitical artists are useless in a controlled society, as under the Socialist regime of the USSR, in which the effort of every citizen is expected to fit overtly the political ideology and to "continue the revolution." More daring, then, are those composers through the ages who have recognized the grave social concerns of their time and used the tools of their art to try to bring about improvement. We expect artists today, like everyone else, to be politicized to some extent. This is true not only in the democracies, where we are taught to read, weigh, and then choose sides on public issues, but also in the totalitarian governments which rigorously politicize their citizens toward one viewpoint only.

But our subject here is the study of music, not politics or economics or cultural history. It is important always to keep in mind the aesthetic effectiveness of the art itself. The works which we might easily label as political music—and there are many— endure because of the eloquence of the composer's skill. All the eloquence of the words (if it is a work to be sung), an emotion-wringing title, or awareness of the original tempestuous event

which it memorializes will not be enough to interest later generations if the quality of the music is poor. If the composition is
effective and expressive, *the nonmusical message will endure with
it*, and continue to be restated to succeeding generations. Here is
the unique power of high art. A classic with such a moral or social
or political meaning is restated again and again to later generations,
even when the referential aspect is diluted or perverted by performers or concert organizers. Above all, in the performing arts (distinct
from the static presentation of the visual arts), the message is
heightened by the active presence of human beings reproducing the
music.

Ludwig van Beethoven's single opera, *Fidelio*, is an enduring
work of musical propaganda. It was a difficult task for him and he
was never quite satisfied with it, even after the third version: "This
opera will win for me a martyr's crown!"[9] But it is a mark of his
profound concern for the social issues of his time that his initial
problem was to find a libretto of social significance, worth enhanc-
ing with his powerful vocal and instrumental language—an intensity which few composers before him had the capacity to
generate.[10] *Fidelio* is the story of a political prisoner, Florestan,
who has been falsely accused. His advocacy of civil liberties (as we
would term his action today) has earned the enmity of the director
of a state prison, Pizzaro, who has secretly hidden him in a
dungeon to die of neglect. But the hero's wife, Leonora, has never
given up hope that he is alive, and she has disguised herself as a
man, and called herself Fidelio, so that she might investigate his
whereabouts. Fidelio has become a helper to the jailer, Rocco.

Fidelio contains several stirring musical scenes which demonstrate the composer's skill in rendering the emotional and dramatic
situation of the story more compelling and more suspenseful than it
might be if told in words alone. One of these is the Prisoners
Chorus, the finale of act I. In this quietly moving scene, the
prisoners are permitted a rare few minutes of freedom from their
dank cells to roam the courtyard inside the walls, and they sing *O
welche Lust* (How wonderful, the air and light around us!). We
may assume Beethoven's audiences were aware of the customary
fate of political enemies of a ruler or his henchmen. But a twentieth-
century audience has no difficulty, either, in bringing compre-

hension and sensitivity to the subject of this 1805 opera. The history of authoritarian governments in our time makes the summary imprisonment of political dissidents a very real horror. Here, the musical sound begins with a murmuring, tentative movement, as the prisoners stumble from their cells into the courtyard. It then represents the uncontrollable swell of their emotion at reaching the sunlight, their momentary cry for freedom, and the frightened warning from one voice: "Never speak that word; here we are watched and overheard!" The instrumental and vocal setting emphasize the clear-cut meaning for the audience.

At the Vienna May Festival in 1964, *Fidelio* was conducted by Herbert von Karajan, who also staged the opera, designed the lighting, and suggested the costumes. In this prisoners scene, a tall iron fence was set obliquely across the stage, separating the prison from the courtyard. When the disheveled men stepped through the opened gate, backlighting cast shadows from the spiked posts stabbing across the floor, like long claws reaching out to hold the forlorn creatures there. A line of guards, dressed like Nazi storm troopers, stood motionless. Tight fitting black helmets shielded their heads, and bayonets were at their sides. It was a chilling picture. The musical expression, for its part, suggested the serenity of a free nature, nourished this inspiration for a few minutes, then snuffed it out in the numbing hopelessness of the prisoners' situation. The audience, largely Austrian, seemed to shrink back in their chairs. Beethoven's statement on tyranny had become timeless.[11]

Beethoven and his librettists, Josef Sonnleithner and, for the later revision, G. F. Treitschke, lived under the autocratic ordinances of the Austrian Emperor Francis I, according to which all theater works had to be approved by a court censor. When the official read the text for this opera, which was based on a recent French play by Jean Nicolas Bouilly, he objected to the inference that political prisoners disappear from sight. In a modern democracy with a free press, such an incident would stimulate a news story and perhaps a parliamentary inquiry. In Austria in 1805, only a whisper might be ventured. Sonnleithner, to be sure, pointed out that *Fidelio* was set in another country (Spain), and in an earlier century, and that Florestan was rescued by an upright minister, Don Fernando, who granted mercy and justice in the name of his king.[12] All the prisoners received amnesty in the end; presumably they had been guilty only of angering the tyrannical Pizarro, who was then thrown into the same dungeon.

On September 30, two weeks before the premiere, the opera was banned. Two days later Sonnleithner sent off a letter to the censor protesting that the play "has been most especially revised because the Empress had found the original very beautiful and affirmed that no opera subject had ever given her so much pleasure!" Presumably the Empress had been referring to the safe return of the heroic husband to his faithful wife. Sonnleithner also noted that an operatic version of the play by the Italian Ferdinando Paer had recently been performed in the imperial cities of Prague and Dresden. Further, Beethoven had spent over a year and a half on the project, and rehearsals were already in progress so that the premiere could be presented on the name day of Her Majesty (October 15)! The librettist also argued that the story was about "a private revenge," not a government policy, and that no sedition was intended by the use of such a plot.[13] On October 5, the censor approved the opera after a few "harsh" incidents had been removed. Problems of music copying and rehearsals, however, delayed the first performance for five weeks.[14]

There exists a story (without a solid source) that the real subject of the play by Bouilly was the situation of the Marquis de Lafayette, who had been summarily imprisoned by the Austrians because of his overt sympathy with republican views. These views had included bold support of the conspicuously successful American colonists against the British king many years before. The parallel was striking because Madame Adrienne de Lafayette had carried out a long effort to gain her husband's release, and in fact joined him in prison for a time until he was released. (She did not need to disguise herself as a man.) Whether this reference is true or a coincidence, it is indicative of the political climate of Beethoven's era and his active concern to represent in art true-to-life crises of liberty. Civil rights for all was a principle still rare among the laws of any nation in the world. At age twenty-two, Beethoven had inscribed in his friend Vocke's album: "Love liberty above all things." "Never deny the truth even at the foot of the throne!"[15]

Beethoven did not write *Fidelio* as a specific attack on the Emperor, much less on the composer's aristocratic acquaintances who patiently contributed to his financial support. (His manners with aristocrats were often brusque anyway, and he considered himself and other artists, like Goethe, the only true aristocrats of society.)[16] His opera did not incite members of the audience to run out and march about the Palace or hang up posters of protest, much less to set fire to the imperial prison.

On the contrary. After three performances, it was withdrawn. The mood in Vienna on November 20, 1805 for such a dramatic (and optimistic) work was decidedly unsympathetic. Napoleon had taken the city a week before, without resistance. Many of the seats for the premiere were occupied by the French military personnel. The wealthy Viennese and the nobility, Beethoven's most appreciative audience, had fled the city.[17] Reviewers thought the opera was unbearably long and lacking in imagination. One German critic complained that the melodies "lack that happy, clear, magical impression of emotion which grips us so irresistibly in the works of Mozart and Cherubini."[18]

But *Fidelio* was not buried. There were two further versions. A few months after the discouraging premiere, several of the composer's staunchest supporters met with him in a six-hour session to urge drastic changes.[19] Three acts were compressed into two. His friend, Stephan von Breuning, revised the libretto. Beethoven asked Sonnleithner for permission to print the new libretto under his name again, presumably so that the censor would not see it as a new work and insist on another reading.[20] A few performances were staged in March, 1806. Now it was the composer himself who spoiled the potential success. His suspicious nature (and inexperience in the theatre) caused him to think the manager was cheating him of his percentage of the receipts. In a fit of temper, he withdrew the score.[21] In May of 1814, another version, with the experienced aid of Treitschke, was performed. At last it began to be a repertory piece.

Thayer elegantly pictured the euphoria of "liberation" in Europe at this time:

Nothing presaged or foreboded the near advent and thirty years' sway of Metternichism. No one dreamed that within six years the "rulers" at this moment "of happy states" would solemnly declare, "all popular and constitutional rights to be holden no otherwise than as grants and indulgences from crowned head" [Laybach Circular of May, 1821]; that they would snuff treason in every effort of the people to hold princes to their pledged words; and that their vigilance would effectually prevent the access of any "Leonore" to the Pellicos, Liebers and Reuters languishing for such treasons in their state prisons. At that time all this was hidden in the future; the very intoxication of joy and extravagant loyalty then ruled the hour.[22]

But *Fidelio* was subtly dangerous because it was dressed in an "establishment" style well known to the audience, even though it was charged with more emotion and sheer sound than the operas of Beethoven's contemporaries. His audiences were not composed of radical thinkers, but we may suppose that the impassioned libretto and music reached some sympathetic minds. At its simplest, without politics, it is a thoroughly reassuring morality tale: A virtuous woman rescues her wronged husband and the villain is punished.

Beethoven's protagonists (and Bouilly's) were not commoners, not oppressed peasants driven to revolt. Florestan and his wife, even Pizarro, and obviously Don Fernando, were upper-class subjects who occupied a social status admired and envied by the middle-class members of the audience, and certainly understood by the upper-class patrons. In eighteenth-century literature these were appropriate, responsible characters of the type deemed suitable for a serious drama. The opera in 1800 had not yet absorbed the literary rage for the "simple man"—roughhewn heroes who would revolt against local tyrants and distant kings—as in Rossini's *William Tell* (1829), based on Schiller's play, and Auber's *Masaniello ou la muette de Portici* (1828).

Even the French Revolution was not quite a people's war. The mobs standing before the guillotine watched noisily, but they were not sufficiently literate to write pamphlets, give speeches and promulgate laws for a republic. Beethoven and the literate classes of Europe, however, understood the vast changes which occurred with the fall of the Bourbon kings, and many looked with hope to the rise of the young general, Napoleon Bonaparte, who seemed to promise justice for all. When Napoleon proclaimed himself Emperor of Europe in 1804, Beethoven was outraged, for he had dedicated his new Third Symphony to him. According to Beethoven's student and friend, Ferdinand Ries, the composer tore the title page in two and threw it to the floor.[23] When the score was published in 1806, an inscription was added (in Italian): "Heroic Symphony, composed to celebrate the memory of a Great Man."

The Congress of Vienna, which artfully cut down the sovereign boundaries Bonaparte had devised, heard a performance of *Fidelio* on September 26, 1814. We may suppose that none of the crowned heads in attendance saw himself or herself as a political oppressor; after all, they had just vanquished the most monstrous oppressor of Europe since Attila. It is more to be supposed that this glittering collection of despots perceived that the opera was merely about "Wedded Love," as Sonnleithner had deviously suggested. This was in fact the subtitle of the opera (*Die eheliche Liebe*), taken directly from Bouilly's French play, *Léonore ou l'amour conjugale. Fidelio* tells *us* far more than a noble love story because of our remembrance of the bloody struggles for social justice which have stained history since Beethoven put down his pen.[24]

A very similar collaboration by Beethoven and a German dramatist was his instrumental music for Goethe's *Egmont* in 1810. Again a "freedom fighter," lying in chains, was sustained by a vision of a faithful woman (his fiancée, Clärchen) as the Goddess of Liberty. In this plot, however, the hero was executed, and his death became an impetus for a victory struggle by his followers.

The appearance of *Fidelio* was another stroke in Beethoven's personal campaign against autocracy. It is not one man who is imprisoned in *Fidelio*, but Everyman. With his opera Beethoven penned a powerful statement against all tyrants, both for those who listened in Vienna in 1805 and 1814, and ever after. Today his message is no less a public accusation of political injustice, no less a goad to oppressors, and no less a hope for those who wait for freedom and vindication.

It is perhaps all the more surprising that twenty years before 1805 another French playwright, Pierre Caron de Beaumarchais, had written a trilogy about a servant, Figaro, a barber and jack-of-all-trades who outwits the upper-class schemers around him. Figaro is a hero without any social status, neither nobleman nor petty official (though through a twist of the plot he turned out to have middle-class parents). The second of these French plays, *The Marriage of Figaro*,[25] was likewise turned into an opera by a German (Austrian) composer, Wolfgang Mozart. As *Le Nozze di*

Figaro, it has become one of the most popular in the history of opera.

In Beaumarchais's plots (*The Marriage* is the second of the three) it is the aristocrats, creatures of triviality, who are helpless without the cleverness and strength of Figaro. In Paris, the French play had become a scandal. It was a skillful attack on the frivolous interests and despotic behavior of the aristocracy. Beaumarchais was already famous. He had supporters next to the king, including the Comte d'Artois, the king's brother (later to be the reactionary Charles X). But high members of the Church and the king's Minister of Justice said the comedy "smelled of sulphur."[26] The aristocratic character of Almaviva, the Count, was the shadow of Louis XVI! And the audacious commoner, Figaro? The playwright himself. Like Martin Luther, who had not supposed his recommendations would ignite a revolution, Beaumarchais did not foresee that the monarchy would be overthrown in a few years. His confrontation with the government lasted more than two years; six censors in turn pored over the script.[27] It became a *cause célèbre* in the salons of the nobility. Queen Marie-Antoinette, blissfully secure in her niche, supported the production as an entertaining theater piece, not supposing it predicted the end of her era. The curiosity engendered by the unproduced (but much read) comedy even reached Catherine the Great of Russia, who announced plans to stage it! *The Marriage* was finally presented on April 27, 1784. This began a run of sixty-eight performances, an unparalleled success in the annals of the Comédie Française.[28]

In the musical setting which enchanted Vienna two years later, it is worth a pause to realize how dangerous were the ideas expressed. Grendel epitomizes this political bomb, its fuse already hissing, by the remarks of three powerful men of the time:

Louis XVI: We should have to destroy the Bastille if a performance of this play was not to be a dangerous blunder.

Danton: Figaro has killed the aristocracy.

Napoleon: If I had been king, a man such as he would have been locked up. There would have been an outcry, but what a service it would have rendered society! . . . *The Marriage of Figaro* is already the revolution in action.[29]

Amusing plays about servants besting their masters were not new to this period. In Pergolesi's comic opera, *La Serva padrona* (The maid becomes the mistress) of 1733, a wily servant persuaded her employer to marry her instead of a woman of his own social class. Jean-Jacques Rousseau's *Le Devin du village* (1752), a great favorite, presented the triumph of the honest rustic over the venal and dishonest upper class. But equality of men, much less of men *and women*, was not foreseen or admired by anyone but a few philosophers, such as Rousseau, Montesquieu, Locke, and Voltaire. We take the message of *Figaro* lightly because it is a comedy; we know it will turn out all right. (But *Fidelio* is not a comedy and it also turns out all right; Beethoven's subject and music intentionally elicit solemn emotions.) Spectators have generally failed to perceive the social significance in Mozart's opera, clothed as it was in the conventions of eighteenth-century musical satire, and with such consummate eloquence. Today we are at a long distance from these costumed characters. In 1784 the audience was at no such distance; plot, language and music all bore a contemporary impact. As political propaganda it was all the more seductive, and hence more dangerous, because it was masked in a *nonrevolutionary* musical language. Though it is probably not what Beaumarchais had in mind, Figaro's droll opinion of the *opéras-comiques*, "*Ce qui ne vaut pas le peine d'etre dit, on le chante*" (What is not worth saying you might as well sing),[30] may also have served to deflect the apprehension of the aristocrats toward musical theatre.

The opening scene of *The Marriage of Figaro* commenced the attack. It is not set in the grand salon of the Count Almaviva, Grand Corrégidor d'Andalousie (who is not present), but rather in a nearly empty bedroom just assigned to the count's valet and his bride-to-be, Susanna, maid to the Countess. The opera is about servants! In the crux of the scene, the young couple deduced that the Count has picked this room, with its doors connecting to each of the royal bedrooms, in order to satisfy his private desires and that he will find some excuse to send Figaro off, so that he can invite himself in unseen to flirt with Susanna. More outrageous still, the Count wishes to reinstate the medieval feudal right of the lord to spend the wedding night with every girl married on his estate. This presumably archaic custom angers Figaro, who has served his master honestly and felt that he and his bride deserve respect. The plot then revolves around the Count's habit of chasing women (along with bewildering subplots in the fashion of the time), and how Figaro, helped by Susanna and even the faithful Countess, can outmaneuver the Count.

Mozart was fortunate in the friendship and diplomatic skills of his Italian librettist, Lorenzo da Ponte. The poet was able to counter the machinations against Mozart by jealous musicians at the court. Beaumarchais's play, however, was banned in Vienna. In his *Memoirs* da Ponte records the censor's belief that *Le Mariage de Figaro* was "too liberal for a well-bred audience."[31] Da Ponte pruned the most biting satire from the French dialogue when recasting it in Italian and avoided an outright confrontation with the censor. To be sure, an opera based on a play that no one was permitted to see was irresistible. The librettist slyly involved the Emperor Josef II in the rehearsals, and the work came off as the authors desired. The audience was enchanted by the young composer's delectable melodies and the masterful characterizations which were depicted more through the music than the words. Nearly every number was encored.[32]

With the play clothed in Mozart's musical silks, it is little wonder that Beaumarchais's unequivocal attack on upper-class *mores* was slipped smoothly into the ears, if not the consciences quite yet, of the audiences. It was another prophecy of the French revolution, five years in the future. It is no wonder that Louis XVI's ministers were *en garde* before the insinuation that master and servant might become equals. But now another contrast with *Fidelio* appears.

Does a performance of *The Marriage of Figaro* kindle our social concern in the same manner as *Fidelio*? Is it a prod to social action? Do we feel a moral responsibility? Probably not, even in those societies where the fragments of an aristocracy remain and the opera is known. Further, the persuasive demonstration of equal respect for women is another social issue which may not be consciously perceived. Our passing indignation at the Count's feudal standards (not to mention Marcellina's devious contract and Figaro's one-sided opinion of virtue) is likely blunted by Mozart's beguiling music. Further, the audience's sensitivities are likely blunted by another convention already cited. This is an eighteenth-century comedy; we do not take its preachments seriously.

The propaganda suggested thus far has been explicitly identified by verbal clues: descriptive titles, or words to be sung, although in some the message is by design oblique. Can a symphony—one of Haydn's 104 or Beethoven's nine—carry an explicit message? By definition, a symphony is an orchestral composition constructed with purely musical elements, the form dictated by technical conventions (the establishment of a key, exposition of themes, development, four independent movements, and so on). No literary or programmatic guidelines are expected; it is abstract. A symphony "means" nothing beyond the syntax of its sounds. It was the nineteenth century, the Romantic period, strongly influenced by literary movements and by the theory of the interrelationship of the arts, which turned the abstract symphony of the Classical era into the program symphony and the symphonic poem. Here appeared extramusical statements and clues for listening: the hybrid symphonic-cantata works of Berlioz (*Romeo and Juliet, The Damnation of Faust*); the use of such evocative subtitles as Mendelssohn's "Italian" and "Reformation" and his overtures (*Fingal's Cave*); Mahler's "The Titan" (the subtitle of his First Symphony, which he later deleted) and his vocal and choral symphonies; and the dramatic tone poems of Richard Strauss, some supplied with a detailed scenario, like *Don Quixote* and *Till Eulenspiegel's Merry Pranks*.

Beethoven's innovations in the symphony were a justification for these later literary and descriptive preferences. He used subtitles of his own choosing in his "Pastoral" Symphony. He used words, singers and a chorus in the conclusion of his Ninth and in the mingled styles which make up the Choral Fantasy. His expression was more dramatic, louder and more individualistic than that of the previous epoch. His merger of instruments and voices contradicted the respected models of Haydn and Mozart. Why did he do this? Because he had a verbal message to offer which was more important than the conventions of the orchestral form. The sudden interjection of the bass voice in the fourth movement is but one of several unexpected events which arrive throughout the Ninth Symphony with stunning impact. The solo singer, both with his presence and his words, at once seizes our attention. The ideas of Schiller are stated in unambiguous fashion, intensified by the sonority of Beethoven's large orchestra, the moment prepared by three grandiose movements of power and sublimity. Thus Beethoven took no chance that we might miss his meaning: It is a protest against war and conquest, against the division of humanity into the strong and the weak, of those with rights and those with none. And it is a rejection of despair.

A look at Haydn's world further accentuates Beethoven's contrast with the past. Haydn was a well paid and enormously respected musician, but he was, nonetheless, a servant in livery for twenty-nine years on the staff of the Esterházy Princes. He was a genial, modest man who fulfilled his daily duties year after year, writing for immediate performance symphonies and string quartets by the dozen, piano works, sacred compositions for solemn occasions, and lighthearted operas to suit the taste of his employer. As the years passed, Haydn began to chafe at his servitude, but he did not noisily attack the long-standing customs of his profession.[33] Beethoven, however, makes us painfully aware of his milieu. He was frustrated by his dependence on patrons, publishers and impresarios, traumatized, to be sure, by the early onset of deafness (at age twenty-five), and frequently ready with a belligerent and suspicious response to anyone about him.[34] It is useful to compare these two composers' symphonies as expressions of the artistic, intellectual and psychological thrust of each century.

As examples, consider the last symphony in each one's list: Haydn's No. 104 in D major (1795), and Beethoven's No. 9 in d minor (1823). Even the choice of mode, major versus minor, is of significance.[35] Each work contains the customary four movements, but the order of the movements and their proportions, along with the themes, orchestral color, degree of emotional intensity, and the sheer sound of the symphonies, reveal that an artistic distance inconceivable to Haydn's generation has been traveled. In Haydn's work we can most often surmise what is to come section by section, despite his fertile imagination. In Beethoven's work, we are unable to predict what actually will occur. We are surprised and astounded, now wrapped in a sublime mood, now roughly shaken in our seats. Whimsically, we might visualize Haydn, as he offered his piece, courteously hoping that it would please his listener, but imagine Beethoven seizing his listener by the ruffled collar and thundering, "Pay attention! There's more here than the notes!"

Yet these two musicians were part of the same cultural tradition and used similar techniques of composition. The aesthetic and emotional expectations of Beethoven for his work, and, by extension for his century, were far beyond Haydn's, not excepting Haydn's *Sturm und Drang* period, which was, at the least, prophetic. The comparison of their separate efforts, especially in this abstract medium, reveals the enormous changes which arose. The nearly one hundred years between the birth of one man and the death of the other witnessed an eruption in intellectual freedom and in social change that found its musical equivalent in the heroic statements of Beethoven. He penned a warning to tyrants, and, simultaneously, an inspiration to all others who listened: Join hands; hope lives.

NOTES

1. See Gilbert Chase, *America's Music* (New York: McGraw-Hill Co., 1966, second edition), chapter 1. Chase challenges the belief that American Puritans condemned all music except in the church: for example, "The Puritans' attitude was not antagonistic or intolerant, but it was moralistic" (p. 6).

2. *Time Magazine*, October 18, 1971, p. 59.

3. George Orwell, *1984*, (New York: Harcourt, Brace & Co., 1949), pp. 27, 44, 149, 299.

4. See *Ethnomusicology*, vol XII(3) (1968), pp. 415-18; vol. XV(1) (1971) pp. 91-92; vol. XIX(1) (1975), pp. 67-89.

5. Wanda Willson Whitman, ed., *Songs That Changed the World* (New York: Crown Publishers, 1969), p. 8; *Lillibullero*, p. 10; *Yankee Doodle*, p. 33.

6. Milton Okun, ed., *Great Songs of the Sixties* (New York: Quadrangle Books, 1970), pp. 30-35.

7. Marxist views are discussed further in Chapters IV and V.

8. "Introduction to the Critique of Political Economy," par. 8., tr. in Lee Baxandall and Stefen Morawski, eds., *Karl Marx and Frederick Engels on Literature and Art* (New York: International General, 1974), p. 137.

9. Ludwig van Beethoven, *The Letters of Beethoven*, Emily Anderson, tr. and ed. (London: Macmillan 1961), vol. I, No. 479 (hereafter Anderson, *Letters*); see also No. 481.

10. In November 1803 Beethoven attempted a work on a libretto by Schikaneder—*Vestas Feuer* (Vesta's fire), but became disgusted with the crudities of the text: "Imagine such a Classical subject proceeding from the mouths of our Viennese apple-women," he wrote. (Anderson, *Letters*, I, No. 87a.) He reused some of his musical ideas the following year in *Fidelio*.

See Elliot Forbes, *Thayer's Life of Beethoven* (hereafter Thayer/Forbes) (Princeton: Princeton University Press, 1964), vol. I, p. 340. In the same month he declined a libretto because the topic was "connected with magic" and also because the incomplete book had met resistance from the theater manager who had commissioned it and served as censor. (Ibid.) Sonnleithner's libretto followed on the heels of these, and Beethoven had found his text. (Anderson, *Letters*, I, No. 88.)

Accepting a commission did not violate his artistic principles; he wrote always on the expectation of a monetary return. Both publishers and patrons were eager to be associated with his name. Of his many publishers he bragged, "I state my price and they pay." (Anderson, *Letters*, I, No. 51.) But he would not take a commission if aspects of it offended him. In a letter of April 2, 1802, to a Leipzig publisher he ridiculed an admirer's suggestion that he compose "a revolutionary sonata" in honor of Napoleon. His reason was that "everything is trying to slip back into the old rut, now that Bonaparte has concluded his Concordat with the Pope. . . ." (Ibid., No. 57.)

Léonore, ou l'amour conjugal by Bouilly was set to music in 1798 by Pierre Gaveaux, a popular composer and singer of the Théâtre Feydeau in Paris. The singer's works were well-known (in German) in the German theaters. (Thayer/Forbes, I, p. 346.)

11. In 1952 Rolf Liebermann (b. 1910) composed *Leonore 40/50*, a modern adaptation of the story set during World War II.

12. The "rescue opera" was a popular theme in this period of war, in particular at the Paris Opera. Celebrated examples were Cherubini's *Les Deux journées* (known in English as *The Water Carrier*) in 1800. It should not be overlooked that Bouilly was also the author of this libretto. Cherubini's opera was performed in Vienna in 1805 a few weeks before *Fidelio*. Another was Spontini's *La Vestale* (1807). The subject similar to Schikaneder's play (note 10), *La Vestale* was staged in Vienna in 1814 during the Congress of Vienna shortly after the new version of *Fidelio* was heard.

13. Thayer/Forbes I, pp. 385-86.

14. Ibid., p. 386.

15. Michael Hamburger, ed., *Beethoven: Letters, Journals and Conversations* (Garden City, N.Y.: Doubleday & Co., 1960), p. 3; Anderson, *Letters*, I, No. 4.

16. In the astonishing incident at the Teplitz spa (1812), according to Bettina Brentano, Beethoven showed Goethe how to make the nobility step aside for *him*. (Hamburger, *Beethoven*, p. 108.) Beethoven admired the English, "who knew not only how to value art, but how to reward it [the London Philharmonic Society had sent him a Broadwood piano], and

furthermore, had instituted freedom of speech and writing, even in opposition to the King and the most powerful ministers of state, tolerating neither censors nor tax-collectors."—Letter of Wilhelm Christian Müller, 1820. (Ibid., p. 173.) Even in his later contempt for Napoleon, Beethoven admired the tyrant's ascent from such a humble beginning. "It suited his democratic ideas," recalled a French visitor, Baron Trémont. (Ibid., p. 66.)

17. Thayer/Forbes, I, p. 386.

18. Ibid., p. 387.

19. Ibid., pp. 388-90; 393.

20. Anderson *Letters*, I, No. 128.

21. Thayer/Forbes, I, pp. 397-98; O. G. Sonneck, ed., *Beethoven: Impressions by His Contemporaries* (New York: Dover Publications, 1954), pp. 60-68.

22. Thayer/Forbes, I, p. 596.

23. From the memoirs of his pupil Ferdinand Ries, in Sonneck, pp. 53-54, and Thayer/Forbes, I, pp. 348-50. Stanley Sadie, ed., *The New Grove Dictionary of Music and Musicians*, 6th ed. (London: Macmillan Publishers, 1980. Hereafter, *NG*.) vol. II, p. 363. The title page of Beethoven's copy used for his conducting (not the autograph concerned here) still reveals the words "intitolato Bonaparte" under an erasure. It is reproduced in H. C. Robbins Landon, comp. and ed., *Beethoven: A Documentary Study* (New York: Macmillan and Co., 1970), p. 175.

24. Beethoven considered subjects for operas again and again. "The Ruins of Babylon" and "Romulus" were suggested by Treitschke (Anderson, *Letters*, I, Nos. 310, 311, 317), "Mathilde ou les croisades" by Karoline Pichler (ibid., No. 516), and in his last years, a libretto on the legend of Melusine was suggested by Franz Grillparzer (Sonneck, *Beethoven: Impressions*, pp. 157-59).

25. The full title is *La Folle journée ou le mariage de Figaro*. Pierre-Augustin Caron de Beaumarchais, *Théâtre Complet*, vol. III, G. D'Heylli and F. de Marescot, eds. (Genève: Slatkin Reprints, 1967. Originally published in 1870).

26. Frederic Grendel, *Beaumarchais: The Man Who Was Figaro* (London: Macdonald and Jane's, 1973), pp. 214-17.

27. Beaumarchais, *Théâtre Complet*, III, pp. iv-xxxiii.

28. Ibid., pp. 215, 220.

29. Ibid, p. 220. The United States of America owes Beaumarchais a debt, one seldom acknowledged. His genius made Lafayette's later contribution possible. In his patriotic zeal for France, Beaumarchais brilliantly and successfully persuaded Louis XVI to intervene in the war between England and her colony. It was a timely and disguised means of besting the British power. The French king's intent was not to promote democracy, but rather

to regain some of France's glory. Thus he looked the other way while Beaumarchais created a fictitious trading company to ship arms to the American insurgents. The playwright carried out this daring project from 1775 to 1776; and here and there he jotted down the first lines for *Le mariage de Figaro*. (Grendel, *Beaumarchais*, pp. 157-69.)

30. Beaumarchais, "Le Barbier de Séville," act I, scene 2. *Théâtre Complet*, II.

31. Louis Biancolli, ed., *The Mozart Handbook* (New York: Grosset & Dunlap, 1962), pp. 139-42.

32. Michael Kelly (the first Basilio), "Reminiscences," ibid., pp. 136-38.

33. Karl Geiringer and Irene Geiringer, *Haydn: A Creative Life in Music* (Garden City, N.Y.: Doubleday & Co., 1963), second edition, rev. and enl. See Chapters IV and V.

34. Such observations by his contemporaries are to be found in several collections. For Goethe, see Sonneck, *Beethoven*, p. 106; Ignaz von Seyfried, ibid., pp. 38, 45; Dr. Karl von Bursy, ibid., pp. 141-42; and Bettina von Arnim, pp. 76-79. For Dr. Alois Weissenbach see Thayer/Forbes, I, p. 595. Some of his letters suggest paranoia, as Anderson, *Letters*, I: Nos. 93, 94, 98, 130, 138a, 139, 485. On the beginning of his deafness, see his long, candid letters of 1801 to Franz Wegeler, ibid, I, Nos. 51, 54. The most eloquent and immediate commentary on the composer's frustration and mental agony is his impassioned "Heiligenstadt Testament" of 1802 in Hamburger, *Beethoven*, pp. 31-34.

35. The coloristic, "solemn" minor mode was used with considerable restraint in instrumental music by Haydn's generation; he used it but eleven times in his 104 symphonies. The minor tonality called forth the conventional sentiment of pathos in some subsequent subtitles: No. 26, "Lamentation"; No. 44, "Mourning"; No. 45, "Farewell." As a contrast in late-nineteenth-century taste, note that only one of Tchaikovsky's six symphonies (No. 2) is in a major key. Five of Mahler's nine are in the minor mode.

CHAPTER 2

People without Power: Musical Nationalism in Europe, 1830–1920

The magnificent tone pictures of which "My Country" is composed are the greatest adornment of our [repertoire], and have been these seven years since the first performance . . . in 1875; but now they appear before us as a mighty whole . . . as Smetana's greatest poetic achievement, as the proudest hymn of praise with which the mind of an artist ever glorified his country. . . . Since the opening of the National Theatre there has never been such an exalted mood among any Czech assembly as last Sunday in the Zofin Hall. . . . After the "Vltava" a real hurricane of applause broke loose; his name resounded on every side amidst indescribable cheers, the audience rose to its feet, waving hats and scarves toward the master to whom glorious bouquets with splendid ribbons in national colours were handed, and the same unending storm of applause was repeated after each of the six parts of the cycle.

V. V. Zeleny (1882)[1]

A hundred and thirty years ago or more, the great-grandparents of many present-day Americans left their homes in Europe to come to America. Many hoped to leave long-standing patterns of poverty, and anticipated a life of boundless promise. Some fled arrest or imprisonment for their unsuccessful attempts to gain political freedom. Germany, Bohemia, Moravia, Poland, Italy, Scandinavia, Russia, the Baltic region, the Balkans: Europe was a patchwork of nations, duchies, princedoms, and their autocratic rulers. In many of these lands there were voices which called for freedom, and above all the freedom from foreign rule.

But not all the nineteenth-century subjects who found themselves victims of tyranny or poverty or intellectual oppression fled to the New World. Some in Central and Eastern Europe emigrated to the considerably freer society of France and England. Frédéric Chopin, a young Polish pianist, elected to become an expatriate in France and never returned to his native land. Others, who did not have the means to emigrate, remained at home. Some chose to live within a social system which was distasteful, since it was, nevertheless, located on their native soil; for some artists, native soil has been an irreplaceable element in artistic creation. In this latter group were Bedřich Smetana, Antonín Dvořák, and Jean Sibelius. Richard Wagner's political actions for a time became so militant that he was compelled to flee Germany, but was later forgiven; he put aside his enthusiasm for democracy and political change for the rest of his life. Still other composers were apparently undisturbed by their social and political milieu, working within it with obvious success and efficiency. Here were Schumann, Mendelssohn, Brahms, Bruckner, Tchaikovsky, Albeniz and Granados. And apparently all the French, too: Their individual status had long been tied to their success in obtaining government commissions, from Lully to Berlioz, from the Sun King to the Citizen King.

The overtly nationalistic music of the nineteenth century is chiefly from the "little" countries, the several ethnic entities that dotted the geographical confines of the Austrian Empire, the kingdoms of the Germanies and the buffer zones of Russia. The Bohemians and Scandinavians struggled for ethnic visibility. Patriotic Italians had another purpose: geographical unification of the peninsula and political freedom from Austria. It was not the Germans, nor the French, nor the Italians who were driven to delineate their national cultures; these three had formed an international style, to which every serious musician aspired. Everyone knew of the glories of the Paris opera, the status of the German symphony, and the consummate *bel canto* of Italian melody. A rare, few artists held virtual international artistic passports. Franz Liszt, Hungarian born, was a prodigious pianist, conductor, composer, and writer, and an elegant voice and visage at any salon; he could travel everywhere and receive an hysterical welcome, as well as a platform for his music. For all its aristocratic international sophistication, his behavior still involved social reform on occasion; he published a solo piece (*Lyons*) in support of the silk workers' strike in Lyons, France in 1837. The Germanic technique that he used, however, blurred the identification of his national heritage, even in his twenty *Hungarian Rhapsodies*, which became widely known. His music, like his personality, expressed the broadest of knowledge and of cultural settings: the *Faust* Symphony, the *Dante* Symphony, *Switzerland, Italy*, his twelve *Transcendental Etudes* (for piano), his choral works, *The Legend of St. Elizabeth* and the *Hungarian Coronation Mass*, and his dazzling piano concertos, which were the epitome of the Romantic virtuoso's *métier*.

The nationalistic element in Frédéric Chopin's music—to ignore here his achievement of superlative music for the piano—was apparent in his own lifetime, and was part of his image. Perhaps there is no patriotic fervor which seems so intense as that of the artist who is forever a wanderer outside his native land. Abroad in Germany when the Russians seized Warsaw in 1831, Chopin eventually settled in Paris, a city most receptive to geniuses of all genres. Among his dozens of works for the piano, which dazzle with innovations of keyboard technique and coloristic devices, and a new sense of tonality, are two dance types which acknowledged his Polish heritage. The first is displayed in his fifty-one fascinating mazurkas; the second, in the eight virtuoso pieces inspired by the court dance, the polonaise, its stately movement metamorphosed into noble and fiery concert works. What is nationalistic about them, patriotic, or a gesture of protest? Can a Chopin polonaise (the immensely popular No. 6 in A-flat, for example) not stand just as music? Of course! But imagine the audience of Paris in the 1830s, seeing before them this introverted Pole, who (presumably) could never go home again. A nationalistic inference of political protest was elicited from all but the politically indifferent—and the cosmopolitan Parisians were not politically indifferent. These pieces were Polish art; they were reminders of Poland's plight in contemporary Europe. To keep a perspective on Chopin's total work, we must note that most of his works, including, for example, the sonatas, the scherzos, the preludes, and the concertos, were not constructed on Polish elements. Nevertheless, he was the first Polish composer to be known throughout the concert world.

When martial law was declared in Poland in December 1981, the state radio network was the only source for information to the world, and the news was terse. One foreign reporter was frustrated because all that could be heard was the initial announcement of martial law over and over, "interspersed with maddening snatches of Chopin."[2] Maddening, to be sure, to an international reporter! The music was, to him and to other non-Poles, only an irritation and an irrelevant stream of sound. But to the Poles, it expressed an unambiguous nonverbal statement: This is an hour of national gravity; patriotic devotion and obedience to the national will are expected from all. In Paris, the exiled members of Poland's out-lawed trade union hung Solidarity banners on Chopin's tomb in the historic Père Lachaise cemetery.[3]

The growing ferment for political independence in nineteenth-century Europe was insistently crushed by the military force of the rulers. Some artists took their protests to the streets and to the public print, and some suffered imprisonment or banishment. Verdi, Smetana, Dvořák and others worked out their longing for national identification through art. Their methods and materials were the subtle ethnic elements of music: melody, rhythm, dance forms, and peculiar instrumental preferences. For some, like the Bohemians (the future Czechoslovaks) and Sibelius, the use of the native language was an act of belligerence; in middle Europe the language of the upper class and the educated was German, not Bohemian or Slovenian, and in Finland, it was Swedish, not the obscure and difficult Finnish tongue. Thus for Smetana to compose an opera, like *The Bartered Bride*, about peasant society and with a Bohemian libretto, was an affront to the social hierarchy of Prague.

Smetana himself had been brought up speaking German, and he had had to work to become fluent in his native tongue, which was still being systematized by philologists. The use of social satire in popular farces and the inclusion of folk dances and other nation-alistic elements dressed in trivial styles were innocuous ways of expressing the native culture. Smetana began to push such folk ele-ments toward the level of serious European musical art—that is, the Germanic style, based on the hallowed tradition of Haydn, Mozart and Beethoven. This attempt to elevate folklore into art was perceived as a threat to the status quo and as a political attack through art. As we have seen in the examples of Mozart and Beethoven, social criticism embedded in art of a high quality can break down entrenched barriers. A vivid work of art may persuade indifferent or essentially neutral spectators to a change of mind, or even to overt support of a new order. But such art is dangerous to the present order. Smetana's masterpiece, which became a world famous folk opera, was based on a plot by the rebel patriot writer Karel Sabina.

In *The Bartered Bride* the custom of filling the stage with persons of nobility and authority was discarded. Neither aristocrats nor other upper-class spokesmen appear, nor even servants obeying, or disobeying, their masters. It is a story about peasants and their age-old custom of marrying off a daughter through the offices of a marriage broker. There are several thumping folk dances and a rousing drinking song in which not champagne, but Pilsner, is drunk. There is also a circus troupe of suitably third-rate class and a hero who has a stutter. The provincial characters exhibit uninhibited joy and anger, with impulsive shifts to wistfulness and quiet. (In the music this is often suggested by shifts between a major key and its parallel minor—as C major, c minor—and a sudden modulation from the major key to its mediant or third step in the scale, as C major to e minor.) Throughout the opera, Smetana's dramatic skill blends with his ready supply of folklike ingenuousness.

It would be Romantic to report that his opera achieved an instant artistic success, as well as a political thrust, but it achieved neither. In a political atmosphere oddly like that of the first performance of Beethoven's *Fidelio*, there was a limited audience for the premiere because of alarm over the outbreak of war between Prussia and Austria. Another stroke of bad luck was that several national societies had chosen that very day (May 30, 1866) for an excursion to the country![4] The second performance was not well received either, and the theater manager asked to be relieved of his agreement for six performances.[5] On May 5, 1882, the hundredth performance was given to a packed house, and Smetana had become a celebrated artist.[6]

One unfortunate consequence of the first performance was that five hundred Czech patrons in Prague asked that Smetana be dismissed as conductor of the Czech National Theatre on grounds of treason: His music went beyond the acceptable (trivial) presentation of native music; it was too vivid, too modern, and was subversive to Bohemian art! If this seems incredible, we should remember that the art of a minority is characteristically tolerated by the majority only when it appears to be innocent diversion. Even some Czechs in 1866 considered this to be the appropriate stance! Perhaps some also judged it the safer position for their daily existence under the Austrians. It should not be assumed that all the artists of any minority group were attracted to the nationalist movement. Some were opposed to using indigenous traits, regarding them (much as second-generation immigrants to America sometimes regard things of the "old country") as crudities and as a move backward.

In addition to his eight demonstratively nationalist operas (his favorite was *Libuše*), Smetana also turned to Liszt's innovation, the symphonic poem. A major achievement in terms of both the form and his patriotic ambition was a cycle of six works, *Má vlast* (My country), dedicated to the city of Prague. Numbers 1, 2, and 4 are real travelogues of Bohemia, filled with reminiscences which tugged at the emotions of the Czechs then as they do now. Other poems in the cycle describe symbolically political, religious, or mythical events in the literature and history of the people. The second, the most expressive and thus the most often heard, describes the source of the great river *Vltava* and became known by its German name, *The Moldau*. Such was the stifling domination of the German language over Middle Europe—and music publishing— that the Czech name is seldom used as the title outside Czechoslovakia even today.

The Moldau, demonstrating Smetana's superb skill as an orchestrator, as well as his mastery of the variation technique, succeeds in reaching the listeners' emotions before their intellects. We are given a résumé of the imaginary scenes along or in the river: the source in the two springs, the peasants' dancing, the moonlight idyll, the rapids, the vision of the historic castle, *Vysehrad* (also the title of the first piece in the cycle), and we are quite willing to "see" and to "hear" the events Smetana assures are, or *once were* (nostalgia is a useful tool of propaganda) associated with Bohemia's river, the historic backbone of her people's culture.

Numbers 5 and 6 of the cycle form a pair that depict the heroic battles of the Hussites against the Germanic armies. Smetana's own program notes instructed the earnest listener: "The work [*Tabor*] tells of strong will, victorious fights, constancy and endurance and *stubborn refusal to yield, a note on which the composition ends. . . ."*[7]* In *Blanik*, the defeated heroes hide in Blanik hill, where they are cast into a profound sleep, to await the call to rise again to the aid of the Czech nation.

Some years before, Smetana had written to his friend, Jan Neruda, in praise of the Bohemian troops attached to the Austrian army against the Prussians:

Praise be to God, our nation fights back uncowed and as *one* man. All of us, in Bohemia as in Moravia, five million Czechs. Victory will and must be ours and soon. Until then let each one stay at his post wherever he is, for now, during the struggle, the muses are silent and Prague is unhappily a site of struggle where nothing but struggle is known at present (October 3, 1869).[8]

Neruda (1834-91), a nationalist writer, considered the Czech spirit elegiac. In identifying this basic quality in Smetana, Neruda also noted that the composer was a superb interpreter of the piano music of the expatriate Chopin, whom he had embraced as a kindred soul.[9]

The impetus to bring recognition to Bohemian, Moravian and Slovak music did not spring from a tardy need to initiate a native music. There are Czech works which date as far back as the establishment of Christianity in the region in the ninth century. The oldest known Czech religious song, *Hospodine pomiluj ny* (Lord have mercy on us), had long been used at the coronation of the Czech kings. But the promise of success in the imperial capital of Vienna and other centers of prestige such as Berlin, Paris, and Italy drew many composers away. Jan Vaclav Stamic, better known in history as Johann W. A. Stamitz, developed a far-reaching new style of orchestral writing and performance standards in the middle of the eighteenth century—at the German court of Mannheim.

The brief review of Czech music history explains the frustration of the nineteenth-century nationalists: Their voices were drowned in the mainstream. It was Smetana's ambition to provide music which was the equal of the German style that had been so long in vogue in Prague. After World War II, the Prague German Theatre was renamed the Smetana Theatre; at long last, he had supplanted the foreigner's preeminence.[10] His countryman, Antonín Dvořák, was also a nationalist, but in a far less overt fashion. For one thing, Dvořák was satisfied with abstract Classical forms such as the symphony (he wrote nine) and the string quartet. His operas, though on regional subjects, also were composed on German models.

Dvořák was befriended by another traditionalist, Johannes Brahms, a thoroughgoing German whose brief experiment with folk idioms in his highly successful *Hungarian Dances* led him to urge Dvořák to create a set with Bohemian and Slovak folk elements. Dvořák's *Slavonic Dances*, Op. 46 (1878), originally for piano duet, in turn became a great success. His publisher (and Brahms's), Simrock, commissioned another set a few years later, as Op. 72. These are not arrangements of folk melodies or dances, but original works, which breathe the distinctive lilt of middle European music. None, indeed, sounds like an Italian *tarantella*, a German *Ländler*, an Irish jig, or an English Morris dance. One of the rare instances in which Dvořák used a Bohemian folktune occurs in his concert overture, *Husitska*, Op. 67, an apotheosis of the Hussite battle hymn, which Smetana had used in the last two movements of *Mà vlast*.

The reason the Slavonic dances—the *furiant*, the *kolo*, and so on—are not confused with Italian, German, Irish, English, or other European dances is a matter for highly technical analysis. This demands a minute scrutiny, as the Czech folk idiom is built on the same general musical base and the same historical foundation as these others. Since the end of the sixteenth century, the same system of scales, tonal centers, and vertical blocks (chords) had formed the musical vocabulary and grammar used by Dvořák, Beethoven, and Bach. There *are* distinct traits and patterns in a musical language. One, for example, may be to favor a strong accent on the first beat of a measure, another style prefers to emphasize the second beat or second half of the first beat (syncopation). Another feature one might look for is a preference for forming a melody in the major mode, the diatonic scale of Western Europe, or, conversely, a preference for using many half tones and chromatic intervals, as in the music of Eastern Europe (a borrowing from Asia and North Africa—neither influence very far away). A nonnative listener must acquire highly trained listening capacities to recognize such aspects. This demands repeated listening and analysis to recognize what is there and what is not there. To be sure, we can simply listen, uncurious about the technical differences. For the native musician or listener, the distinctions are familiar and to be taken for granted. An American who is listening for the first time Aaron Copland's *Hoedown* from the ballet suite *Rodeo*, at once recognizes his "own" music. Why? The choices of particular rhythmic patterns, accents, repeated tones, and directions of tones are American. They are not German or Italian or Czech. Whether or not *Rodeo* could have been written *only* by a American is a moot point. Perhaps a contemporary Czech might successfully imitate Copland's folkish music, but the point is that Copland wrote a score about American ranch life which seems utterly convincing to the most critical audience: Americans. It is in the style, with the method and medium, of art music. A symphony orchestra was not heard on the Great Plains, but this is irrelevant to the nationalistic identification of the work. Authentic Bohemian *kolo* and *mazurka* were not accompanied by a symphony orchestra, either. Dvořák composed idealized dances for the enjoyment of concert audiences. What we gain by his stimulating orchestral timbres we lose, alas, from its original function: We remain stuck in our seats; we do not dance.

How then does the outsider recognize and receive, as it were, the nationalistic message intended in the *Slavonic Dances*? As concert listeners, we may not be concerned by this challenge. Dvořák's dances are enjoyable; a few of them are small masterpieces and have become standard works in the genre of concert dances. But if we ignore, or fail to recognize, the message that the composer offers to us through his nationalistic vocabulary, we miss the composer's point. We are usually given a clue, sometimes even in the form of an overt statement, in the title. Since we are here considering music as propaganda, this is the first significant information to observe and make the effort to comprehend.

When the late Baroque composers for the keyboard wrote suites of dances, they employed the pattern laid down by Froberger and his seventeenth-century contemporaries. The preferred *allemande, courante, sarabande* and *gigue* by then had transcended their geographical origins of Germany, France, Spain and England (or Italy). Like virtually all the forms or types used in the Baroque period, dance music had become internationalized. When Johann Sebastian Bach composed French suites and English suites for the harpsichord, he scarcely thought he was offering a nationalistic compliment to his quite distant neighbors. In fact his two sets show very little difference in characteristics; they are generalized dances, not nationalistic, but internationally used stereotypes. They were everyone's property. It is for this reason, in particular, that the smaller nationality groups were conscious of their being cultural captives of the larger and older musical cultures. It also explains why in the search for nationalism all the ethnic peoples of Europe eventually retrieved their distinctively national traits to express in the arts, not only in music, but also in literature, poetry, folklore, drama, and, to a lesser extent, in the subjects of visual arts. In literature, it had begun with the rise of Romanticism at the end of the eighteenth century, an incipient nationalist movement, but also the romantic yearning for the ancient and mysterious past: Brentano and Arnim, the tales of the Brothers Grimm in Germany, the wondrous legends invented by MacPherson in England.

Russia was not one of the "little countries." The Czar was treated as a royal brother by the other monarchs, and alliances were frequent in the historic maneuvering for control of the continent. Since the time of Peter the Great, however, the Russians had considered themselves culturally in the wake of France, Germany and Italy. Professional musicians were imported by the Russian Court. In the era of Catherine the Great, Italians directed the St. Petersburg opera; native-born composers, like Dimitri Bortniansky (1751-1825) and others studied with the Italians and wrote in their style. The first to make a name for Russian music was Mikhail Glinka (1804-1857), who wrote two national operas that were attractive enough to win the respect of European audiences. The first was *A Life for the Czar* in 1836, and *Russlan and Ludmilla* followed soon after. Glinka, like other talented musicians born in the fringes of Europe before and after him, had found it necessary after study at home to go abroad, to Germany, for a professional finish. When he returned to St. Petersburg, he joined a literary group, which included the young writers Pushkin and Gogol, who in time also won respectful attention for a distinctively Russian expression. Glinka's music included some so-called orientalisms, melodic and modal peculiarities, which the other Europeans relished as evidence of the exotic influence of the Eastern provinces of Russia.

In remarks on Russian song, Glinka wrote: "We inhabitants of the north feel differently. With us, it is either mad boisterousness or bitter tears. . . . Our melancholy Russian songs are children of the north which we have, perhaps, taken over from the east. The songs of the orientals are just as melancholy, even in gay Andalusia."[11]

The longing for international recognition culminated in the works of Peter Tchaikovsky, who seemed to have had a foot in each camp. On one side, he wrote symphonic works thoroughly in the Germanic orchestral tradition: six symphonies (with Russian folk tunes in the Second and Fourth Symphonies), chamber works, his ballets, *Swan Lake* and *Sleeping Beauty*, and his concert overtures, *Romeo and Juliet* and *Francesca da Rimini* (after Dante). In the camp of the nationalists were his works for the theater: operas based on Pushkin's dramas (*The Queen of Spades, Eugene Onegin*), the symphonic poems, the *Slavic March*, and the consummate depiction of the military assault and defeat of the enemy (*Overture, 1812*). The stirring Overture depicts the Battle of Borodino at the approaches to Moscow in 1812 and the first defeat of Napoleon, the general who had conquered all of Europe. It was a Russian triumph, never to be forgotten and always to be commemorated. (The field of Borodino was once again to be a cause of pride; it was the location where the Soviet Army began its rout of the Nazi forces.) Tchaikovsky constructed a substantial work in free sonata form, securing a nationalist flavor by the use of traditional tunes such as the Czarist anthem, *God Preserve Thy People*, and, to symbolize the French, scraps of the fervent *La Marseillaise*. But in form and style it was a familiar European Romantic method.

Orientalism is a word that often is chosen to characterize Russian music. This usage is not glib. The borders of Russia touch far more Asian peoples and nations than Western ones, and a host of cultural regions exist within Russia itself, which is home to civilizations of various ethnic stocks and languages. The southern Russians between the Black Sea and the Caspian—the Azerbaijans, Uzbeks, Kazaks—are Asian peoples, and the presence of the

Ottoman Empire from the fifteenth to the nineteenth centuries was close and aggressive. It was Nicolai Rimsky-Korsakov who showed a preference for these sources with a stream of works in all genres. They provided an exotic flavor which fascinated European concert audiences. Unlike his older contemporary, Tchaikovsky, Rimsky-Korsakov seldom turned to German models, though his training (like Tchaikovsky's) had been in the German tradition. He was the most prolific of the avowed nationalist group known as The Five (in Russia they were nicknamed "The Mighty Little Heap"[12]) with nine operas, including *The Snow Maiden, Sadko,* and *The Tale of Czar Saltan,* on native or Eastern subjects. Rimsky's last opera, *The Golden Cockerel (Le Coq d'or)* was such a withering satire about a befuddled monarch that it was banned after its posthumous introduction in 1909. His *Russian Easter Overture* is based on liturgical melodies the composer had found in a collection of old Russian Orthodox Church canticles; these evoke a mood of solemn awe, and, to the Western European listener, a pleasing sense of the "exotic" locale. But Rimsky also generated a raw excitement in this music, suggestive of the springtime celebrations of a pre-Christian people. It is this distinctive color from such a creative artist which proclaims a nationalist spirit to his listeners: patriotism and self-respect at home, as well as respect and a strong image to listeners in other nations.

Rimsky's largest effort in the symphonic genre, though not a traditional symphony, was *Sheherazade,* based on stories from *The Tales of the Arabian Nights.* Other members of The Five who produced vivid contributions to a nationalist music were Alexander Borodin, (the opera *Prince Igor*) Cesar Cui, Mily Balakirev, and Modest Mussorgsky. The next generation continued the thrust: Anatol Liadov, Alexander Glazunov, Mikhail Ippolitov-Ivanov, and many more.

Mussorgsky's opera, *Boris Godunov,* was an original solution to the contemporary musical problems of realist drama. Based on a historical subject, it was grandly conceived, but by the time of Mussorgsky's death in 1881 it had been weakened by repeated revisions. It was reshaped, and in part reorchestrated, by Rimsky-Korsakov.[13] Its flawed hero, Czar Boris, is a man of relentless personal ambition. He usurps the throne of the dead Ivan the Terrible, according to gossip, by the murder of Crown Prince

Dimitri. Boris is unable to push aside the gnawing accusations of his conscience. In the prologue (scene 1) Boris, feigning humility, is persuaded by the court and the public to accept the crown. The opera then relates the false czar's psychological disintegration, stimulated by the ambition of officers at the court and by an impostor, a renegade monk, Grigori, who, posing as Prince Dimitri, presumed dead, gathers an avenging army to march on Moscow. But this is not the only message of the opera. In some versions the stock formula brings the opera to the end with the death of Boris, the leading Character. In Mussorgsky's libretto, however, this was not the conclusion. The curtain descends not on a stage vibrating with excitement (though a mob has appeared), but on a tableau of pathos and a solitary figure, a simpleton, who utters the underlying message of Mussorgsky's opera: the never ending misery of the Russian people under the authoritarian rule. "In place of well made theatrical plots there are cross sections of the life of a whole people."[14]

The opening scene introduces the theme, as police goad a crowd of peasants to demonstrate enthusiasm for Boris and to shout for him to take the crown and be their "father." In their earthy dialogue, very candid for the time, they cynically inform the audience that their lives are meaningless. At the close of the opera, as Dimitri and the mob he had deceived into supporting him depart *en masse*, the simpleton, a *kurodivy* (in Russian, one touched by God), laments the future of the motherland:

Flow, bitter tears.
Weep, unhappy souls.
Soon the enemy will come
And darkness will cover us.
Woe then to Russia!
Weep, Russian people.
Weep, hungry people.

A nationalistic work from one of imperial Russia's enemies was Jean (Jan) Sibelius's *Finlandia*. It was composed as the last section of six tableaux depicting landmarks in Finnish history and titled *Finland Awakes;* the section was later revised as an independent work with its now well-known title. The original program, in

November, 1899, was one of several veiled protests during that year, when the Russians, under the despotic Nicholas II, sent a military administrator to complete the Russianization of the Grand Duchy of Finland. With the February Manifesto Finland had lost her autonomy, all rights of freedom of speech and assembly had been abolished, and Russians had replaced Finns in all positions of authority, including the police.

It is a much told myth that the premiere of this piece caused such a stir that it was banned for several years. Sibelius himself, at age seventy, gave credence to this patriotic exaggeration.[15] The score of *Finlandia*, in fact, was published in Finland in 1900. The work received several performances and made Sibelius famous. With its resemblance to a fiery piece of oratory—eloquent, inflammatory, delivered in a thundering voice—it would stir any audience; if a conductor or concert organizer wanted to turn an audience to a positive emotion, *Finlandia* would surely be one piece to select. For it to become propaganda, only the addition of a label would be needed—*Finlandia* or *America*, obviously enough, but almost any religious or patriotic or communal connotation would do—and no audience could resist the enthusiasm engendered. The tense opening atmosphere, with its barking, brassy chords, chills the listener with foreboding. Then follows a clash of wills, good versus evil. After a moment of suspense, the choral finale appears, or rather, it descends, as if from some celestial realm. All the necessary and expected ingredients of a nineteenth-century rousing finale are skillfully employed; and its energy gathers all before it. The text sung by the chorus has been supplied by many hands for many occasions. But even the language, whether familiar or foreign to the audience, hardly matters; it is music of exaltation and triumph which is irresistible and totally understood. Understood, of course, by everyone within the European musical culture. For the Finns and the whole European community, including their descendants in the New World, it is a musical statement which always strikes its mark.

But Sibelius wrote other works with a defiantly patriotic purpose before and after *Finlandia*. In 1893, he set to music a poem for the labor movement, *A Workers' March*, which was published but soon forgotten. A cantata for men's voices, *The Song of the Athenians*, with a bellicose text by Abraham V. Rydberg, written two months after the February Manifesto, was a far more explicit

attack on the foreign occupation. The ancient story of the courageous Greeks willing to die for their birthright and homeland was
clearly understood by the Finns as an allegory about themselves.
Still another allegory was his 1906 cantata, *The Captive Queen*,
which told the story of a prisoner whose people arose to rescue her.
The original title of the poem by Paavo Cajander, had been *The
Liberated Queen*, but in 1906 the Russians, who had put down their
own violent uprising in 1905, were in no mood to hear of a subject,
not even a mythical queen, who cries to be liberated.

Among Sibelius's other nationalistic works are his program
pieces: *Tapiola*, the *Karelia* Suite, and the four *Legends*, based on
the epic, the *Kalevala*. *The Swan of Tuonela* (1893) is the best
known. He also composed seven symphonies without a clue to any
nonmusical purpose, but by the imaginative (and Romantic-
minded) listener, they are invariably said to evoke fjords and snow
fields. Still, Finnish authorities have noted similarities between
Sibelius's melodies and Finnish folk tunes, and compared his
rhythms with the rhythms and peculiar inflections of the language
itself.[16]

Sibelius achieved national fame early and was given an annual
stipend by the government in 1897—even before *Finlandia* and his
First Symphony. His compositions thus became of extraordinary
patriotic significance to his countrymen, and were broadly interpreted as battle songs of the people. For the tiny nation, so unequal
to her conqueror, every cultural accomplishment which brought
her international attention, as Sibelius's music had done, was a
subtle act of passive resistance to Russia. After achieving
independence, the nation continued its support of its distinguished
citizen. In the 1930's, the Finnish government took advantage of the
rapidly growing medium of the phonograph to contract with foreign
recording companies and orchestras, such as the English Columbia
Graphophone Company, to record the symphonies of its favorite
son. Perhaps no other major composer has been brought to the
world's attention initially and continuously by the medium of
recording, as was Sibelius's good fortune during those years.
Complete cycles of his music were given, and leading conductors—
Stokowski, Koussevitzky and Ormandy—vied with each other to
perform and record Sibelius. He became the voice of Finland to the
world.

Edvard Grieg (1843-1907) stands as the representative of musical nationalism in Norway. Among his characteristic works are the incidental music for Ibsen's drama, *Peer Gynt*, and the distinctive *Lyric Pieces* for piano solo. An unconcealed nationalistic statement is heard in his piano transcriptions of the *Slåtter*, music for the Hardanger folk fiddle (Op. 72); Norwegian elements are vividly projected in the use of an altered major scale and the imitation of a drone on the sympathetic strings of the Hardanger. But his most popular work is neither descriptive nor nationalistic; it is his Piano Concerto in A Minor, from the same cultural stream as those of Chopin, Mendelssohn and Liszt.

Other European peoples who chafed under the domination of a foreign power were the Balkans, the Serbs, the Greeks, and the Romanians. Turkish culture held control of parts of southeastern Europe until World War I, and it was a region, like Russia, repeatedly influenced in musical and religious matters by Asian society, history, language, musical instruments, dance forms, vocal style, harmonic texture, and polyphony (or lack of it). A traveler today in Eastern Yugoslavia, that amalgam of ethnic groups created in 1918, may see in Sarajevo, for one instance, the minarets rising above the seventeenth- and eighteenth-century mosques that are still in use. It is the blending and borrowing of Near Eastern musical elements by the folk and art composers of Romania, Yugoslavia, Greece, Hungary, and Russia which catch our ears; it is not the diatonic melody, the preference of major mode, and symmetrical accents, all of which are the familiar ingredients of western European music. The uncommon ingredients have arisen from the folk music, which has been extensively researched and notated by the twentieth-century Hungarian-Romanian composers Béla Bartók and Zoltan Kodály, both of whom used folk material in quotation or suggestively in many of their works. Bartók distinguished authentic Hungarian folk music from the gypsy music that had been accepted as Hungarian by the generation of Liszt and Brahms.

A tangible achievement in musical nationalism for these European people came late. Perhaps it was, in part, the habitual emulation of the international models of high culture—symphonies, operas, and solo instrumental music. But there was no lack of raw material to express an ethnic distinction: the folk melodies and dance rhythms which all, or nearly all, of Europe had long developed in abundance. These traits were proudly included in the conscious efforts of Bartók and Kodály.

In Romania, the development of a European art music was delayed until the Turkish domination ended in 1822 and German and Italian styles could spread freely in the region. A distinguished nationalist, however, did not appear until the early twentieth century, when Georges Enesco (1881-1955) became internationally known as a violinist, conductor and composer. His *Romanian Rhapsodies* have the colorful, ritual character of the symphonic poems of Liszt and Smetana, but without their explicit images. A distinctively colored work is Enesco's *Sonata No. 3 in A Minor* for violin and piano. To make his point here, and perhaps also to explain the florid, tortuous chromatic lines of the melody, he subtitled it "In the Popular Romanian Style," that is, as a folk singer might ornament a melody in long, chromatic melismas. The pitches, though in the European tuning system, move as close as possible to the narrow intervals of much eastern Mediterranean music. The second movement all but suggests that an alien tuning system is about to break out! The traits of Romanian style are on display throughout the sonata: pitches which slide chromatically up or down to another node, flexible tempos nudged by *rubatos*, an uninhibited use of ornaments, and a mixture of modes beyond the European major and minor scales. It is a successful example of the blend of classical and folk styles, and of the performance practices of the concert hall and the village virtuoso.

The influence of the ancient Byzantine Empire, including the vocal styles of the Eastern Christian churches, dominated the music of some other eastern groups, the Serbs, Montenegrins, Bosnians and Macedonians, now represented in the eastern section of Yugoslavia. Here too the Turkish domination held back the development of art music in the West European tradition. To the north, in modern Bulgaria, the indigenous music also expresses Near Eastern traits. Turkish instruments are a non-Western feature that can still be heard throughout much of the Balkans and Greece: one- and two-string fiddles (*gusla*), reed pipes, the prodecessors of the clarinet (*yarul*) and oboe (*zurna*), and various flutes. A unique sound in many Hungarian and Romanian orchestras and ensemble music is the *cimbalom*, a huge zither (in a box-like frame) played with small hammers, a development of the Persian *santur*. Liszt described the instrument as part of the gypsy orchestra of his time in his book, *The Gypsies and Their Music in Hungary* (1859).[17] It is required in Kodály's orchestral suite, *Háry János*, originally an opera based on a comic tale about a folk hero. (The cimbalom is noticeable in the *Intermezzo*, and the syncopated rhythm in this section is a feature of Hungarian music.)

Kodály, an avowed Hungarian patriot, believed that the works of art which exert the most influence in the world are those which are founded on an artist's national characteristics. This is a stand which could come only from a composer whose life and work had endured the fetters of an unwanted foreign culture. The Hungarians (though they are not alone) are a people whose land has been a battle arena for the contests of alien powers, the site of foreign armies who have marched across its plains from east to west and west to east. Kodály, unlike his compatriot Bartók, remained in Budapest throughout the anguished years of World War II. By then he was an old man and a world figure in music. His monument to freedom of expression is to be heard in his choral work, *Psalmus Hungaricus* (Hungarian psalm).

The composite text of the *Psalmus Hungaricus* comes from Hungarian history. In the sixteenth century, the Turkish Muslim military government of Hungary forbade the clergy to speak to the people except in texts from the Bible. (The prophets of Islam include Moses and Jesus.) A poet and teacher, Michael Veg, selected Psalm 55, with its descriptions of the persecutions of the Hebrews and their hope for a return to a free nation. Veg interpolated his own comments into the Hungarian translation of the scripture, in which the Hebrew psalmist complained bitterly at the faithlessness of his friends, more bitter to him than the cruelties of his enemies. These particular lines held private significance for Kodály because of a painful experience he had had in the years following World War I: He had served briefly as Deputy Director of the National Academy of Music in the short-lived Hungarian Socialist Republic. When the Republic was overthrown, Kodály was accused of various crimes and his patriotism questioned. He was so grieved that he wrote no music for two years. He was later vindicated, and a commission was given him for a work to commemorate the fiftieth anniversary of the joining of the twin cities of

Buda and Pest. The *Hungarian Psalm* was the result. It is a profound lament and prayer which resonates with the anguish of three epochs separated by history but united by the same sorrow.

Kodály's compatriot, Béla Bartók, made an impressive effort to preserve the folk music heritage of his people, but it did not encompass all his compositions. He is best known to the world for his large works for orchestra, which have become staples of the modern repertory: the piano concertos and the *Concerto for Orchestra*. What is Hungarian or Romanian in these works is so sublimated that it is seldom to be recognized outright. Some of his works, however, are clearly constructed with folk elements: The *Romanian Folk Dances* for piano solo, which Bartók transcribed for small orchestra in 1917, is one. His Sonatina for piano (1915) was also transcribed for orchestra in 1931, and then titled *Transylvania Dances*, for the thematic material is entirely Romanian folk tunes. His collection of *Fifteen Hungarian Peasant Songs* came directly from his ethnological research; the source is his treatise entitled *Hungarian Folk Music*. The six volumes of piano pieces he wrote for children (*Mikrokosmos*), a highly imaginative catalog of melodic, modal and rhythmic elements, are culled from his meticulous knowledge of Eastern European idioms. The subject matter of his *Cantata Profana*, subtitled "The Enchanted Stags," is a story from Romanian folklore that is infused with symbolism: nine sons follow a heroic stag into the forest, where they become stags also; despite the pleas of their father, they refuse to return to the life of men, so that they might continue to drink from the pure spring in the forest.

As the twentieth century has continued to unfold, the ideal of nationalism in both established and incipient nations has remained a stimulus to composers and a reason for music. Many American contemporaries of Kodály and Bartók followed the path of the nineteenth-century nationalists and sought the inimitable and the unique through the use of folk tunes and rhythms, native musical genres, and historical and legendary allusions. Among these musicians were Charles Ives, Henry F. Gilbert, Arthur Farwell, Arthur Shepherd, and, in the next generation, Aaron Copland, William Grant Still, and Roy Harris. A respected musical identity is now the goal of many emerging countries of the Third World. Particularly in Asia, it has been a preoccupation of composers and musicologists who wish to emulate the concert world of the West, and thus gain another status symbol of modernity.[18] The conflict between the native style and Western sound (modes, instruments, forms, melody, harmony or the absence of it, function, and so on) have provoked aesthetic, and sometimes philosophical, contradictions that remain unsolved. A nationalist music must generate nationalist imagery, mood, memories, slogans, and overt responses. If it does none of these things, it is not effective, and its message has failed to arrive. The composer should earn, as Smetana did, indescribable cheers, with the audience rising to its feet and waving hats and scarves, "the proudest hymn of praise with which the mind of an artist ever glorified his country."[19]

NOTES

1. Frantizek Bartos, ed., *Bedřich Smetana: Letters and Reminiscences.* (Prague: Artia, 1953), pp. 266-67.

2. *Newsweek*, December 28, 1981, p. 24.

3. Associated Press, reported in St. Louis *Post-Dispatch*, January 17, 1983.

4. Bartos, *Bedřich Smetana*, p. 102.

5. Ibid., p. 103.

6. Ibid., pp. 252-54.

7. Ibid., p. 265.

8. Ibid., p. 114.

9. Ibid., p. 128.

10. For the centennial of Smetana's death in 1984, cycles of his works were heard in Prague, including all eight operas, a fragment of his final incomplete opera, *Viola*, and his lesser-known symphonic works. (*International Herald Tribune*, March 3, 1984, p. 5.) It is also evidence of the contemporary reverence for the national heritage that Edward J. P. O'Connor (University of Connecticut) could locate 45,000 folk songs, dating from 1820 to the present during his research in Czech libraries in 1981. ("Folk-music Practice in Czechoslovakia: Past to Present." Paper read to the annual meeting of the Society for Ethnomusicology, College Park, Maryland, 1982.)

11. Sam Morgenstern, ed., *Composers on Music* (New York: Bonanza Books, 1956), p. 130.

12. Victor I. Seroff, *The Mighty Five: The Cradle of Russian National Music* (Freeport, N.Y.: Books for Libraries Press, 1948), pp. 3-4.

13. For a recent discussion of the several versions see *NG*, XII, pp. 867-70.

14. *NG*, XII, p. 872.

15. Harold E. Johnson, *Jean Sibelius* (New York: Alfred A. Knopf, 1959), pp. 92-93.

16. Ibid., pp. 236-37. For his Finnish sources see pp. 285 and 287.

17. Morgenstern, *Composers on Music*, pp. 164-65, includes this passage.

18. See *Proceedings of the Second Asian Pacific Music Conference, 25 November-2 December 1976, Taipei* (Seoul, Korea: Cultural and Social Centre for the Asian and Pacific Region, 1977).

19. A recent study related to aspects of this chapter is "Social Obligations of the Emancipated Musician in the 19th Century" by Walter Salmen, in *The Social Status of the Professional Musician from the Middle Ages to the 19th Century*, Walter Salmen, ed., annotated and tr. from the German by Herbert Kaufman and Barbara Reisner (New York: Pendragon Press, 1983), ch. IX especially pp. 274-81.

CHAPTER 3

Wagner, Hitler and the German "Race"

There has seldom been a human life presenting such an artistic web of conscious untruth and self-deceiving world conceit. No one understood better than Wagner how to transform petty feelings into bombastic presentations, to inflate lowly and sometimes sordid little interests into matters of national importance, the destiny of the German people. This is a point where both his life and his art assumed a potential danger for the future of German culture.

Paul Henry Lang (1941)[1]

We cannot withhold our acknowledgement that the human family consists of irremediably disparate races, whereof the noblest well might rule the more ignoble, yet never raise them to their level by commixture, but simply sink to theirs. . . . The qualities of the German spirit may be brought to a manifestation such as is possible to no other people.

Richard Wagner (1881)[2]

Richard Wagner stands as one of the most prolific prose writers of European composers. Nonetheless, this extraordinary body of work (twelve volumes), as the reader already knows, is not the justification for his place in history. Wagner's ten stage works, all for the opera house, original in sound, enormous in design, and exalted in aspiration, are his legacy. But the twentieth century has added other meanings and other purposes to his eloquent music dramas. Because of Wagner's published attitudes on race, religion, and German nationalism, there is more to discern in his music than the musical sound, and also in his librettos—all of which he insisted on writing himself. Whether music historians or opera fans wish to accept the fact or not, the perception of his music has been further altered by the political life of a man whom Wagner never knew: Adolf Hitler.

In previous chapters we identified some messages in music as social justice, national unity, or freedom from a foreign tyrant, and used as examples music by Mozart, Beethoven, Smetana, Sibelius, and others. These statements of the past still touch us in the Western democracies because such aspirations are inherent in our social and political creeds. The overriding ideal of Wagner, the moral and political pamphleteer (never mind that he was ponderous, illogical, and paradoxical), was the potential of the German people. On the face of it, this certainly is no less commendable than Smetana's wish for the political integrity of the Czechs. But Wagner's opinion was at once more exclusive, more selfish, and more controversial. He did not hold out his arms to all his compatriots. In fact, he rejected whole segments of Germans: those who were Jewish, and some Roman Catholics ("the Semite-Latin church").[3]

Wagner's anti-Semitism, mingled with his peculiar view of historic and contemporary Christianity, was expressed with an emotional vocabulary that is matched by the vehemence of the other German nationalist cited: Hitler. The insistence by Wagner that the Germans were a "race," and that the Jewish "race" corrupted the purity and potential of the (Christian) German people, was a view Wagner had learned from Hegel. Wagner's notorious essay, *Judaism in Music*, first published under a pseudonym in 1850, is laced with invective, including phrases depicting the Jewish character as vile and disgusting.[4] His abuse continued in such later essays as "Modern," "Shall We Hope?", "Know Thyself," and "Hero-dom and Christendom."[5]

The prolific and unorganized essayist Wagner, as distinct from the deliberately working composer and librettist, displayed opinions fluently on many subjects, including a faulty prediction of the future of musical art: He foresaw that everyone who came after him would compose opera—and in his style. No other composer has left to posterity so much information on how he viewed the world, nor such egotistical judgments of his own work. Since his fixation on the "German race" was insistent and conspicuous, a summary of these opinions is useful, and is provided by Leon Stein in *The Racial Thinking of Richard Wagner*:[6]

1. The German race is superior to all other races.

2. Language in general, and the German language in particular, is an attribute and indication of racial integrity.

3. Music is the particular province of the German people, achieving its highest expression among them, and deteriorating when it is cultivated by other people.

4. The continued pursuit of music as a separate art, after Beethoven, betokens imitation, sterility, and a lack of racial integration.

5. Christianity in general, and Catholicism in particular, have been detrimental influences on the German *Volk* and culture. [For Wagner, *Volk* serves as his mystical definition of the German people, with overtones of racial superiority.]

6. The Jews have exercised a harmful effect on German culture and music, both in general and through the specific works of composers like Mendelssohn and Meyerbeer.

It must be understood that Wagner did not so summarize his views, but that a reader of his prose writings, supplemented by the letters of contemporaries and the candid diaries of Wagner's wife, Cosima,[7] deduces these views again and again. Those who were sympathetic to his ideas (and his operas) often became fanatical supporters. One reason for the extent of the influence of his voluminous writings is the astonishing range of his subjects, any one of which might arouse the enthusiasm of a reader—who might remain in ignorance of contradictions to it elsewhere in his *corpus*.[8] His supporters were not limited to the German reading public. In France, whose culture he often ridiculed as effete, "The whole universe was seen and judged by the thought of Bayreuth."[9] A flourishing literary magazine, the *Revue Wagnérienne* (1885-88), was founded by the Symbolist poets to present "Wagner as the great poet, Wagner as the great thinker, and Wagner as the creator of a new art form"[10]—not in Germany, but in Paris. His logic was praised and his work admired. The French composer, Georges Bizet, wrote in a letter of May 29, 1871, "Wagner is no friend of mine and I hold him in slight esteem, but I cannot forget the immense pleasure I owe this original genius. The charm of that music is utterly indescribable. . . . The Germans, who, unfortunately, are mighty important to us in music, have grasped the fact that Wagner is one of their most solid pillars. The German nineteenth-century spirit is incarnate in that man."[11]

At base, his indefatigable articles and letters began with a ruthless desire to promote or defend his artistic work. With equal intensity, he attacked his critics and his supposed rivals.[12] His opinions changed with his circumstances. His chauvinist view of the exclusive value of the German language, for example, altered when he lived in Paris in 1840. He thought he might need to remain there to build his career, since he was not well situated in his homeland. He could then argue that the German genius, if the artist "kept his birthright pure, could create sublime works in any tongue and in every nation beneath all quarters of the globe."[13]

Wagner's support of the unsuccessful German democratic revolt of 1849 arose from his supposition that a liberal government would welcome his new art. When he returned from exile ten years later to live again under a monarchy, he rejected the ideal of "democracy" as *undeutsch*, for the word was not to be found in the German language![14] He criticized Prussian militarism until the victorious war of 1866, and then embraced it fully after the Franco-Prussian War,[15] because he believed that the new Reich would support his ambitions to regenerate society. The new state fell into his disfavor when Bismarck declined to subsidize the Bayreuth Festival,[16] and when the Kaiser excused himself from the premiere of the *Ring of the Nibelung* cycle in 1876 to attend a military show, Wagner returned to his denunication of Prussia's militarism.

Although his opinion of the supremacy of the German "race" permeated his writings, it is rarely as explicitly expressed in his opera librettos. But there are some specific statements: In *Lohengrin* (act I, scene 1) King Henry the Fowler (an uncommon use by Wagner of an historical figure) reminds his court that the "East" has long threatened Germany and that now is the time to defend the kingdom's honor. In act III, scene 3, again the king faces his knights and exclaims, "With pride I feel my bosom swell. The enemy will not dare attack again. The German sword for German land!" This bellicose stance, however, is not developed; no battle scenes are demanded in the opera! *The Mastersingers of Nuremberg* also has a historical setting with a fictional plot, and in the closing chorus Wagner eulogizes the glory of the German past: Art remains as a solace and hope, but it must be untainted by alien authority.

Beware! Bad times are at hand
For when bow German folk and land
To spurious foreign pomp, ere long
No prince will know his people's tongue,
And foreign thoughts and foreign ways
Upon our German soil they'll raise.
Our native Art will fade from here
If none no longer hold it dear.
So heed my words:
Honor your German Masters
If you would stay disasters!
For while they live in every heart,
Though should depart
The pride of holy Rome,
Still thrives at home
Our sacred German Art!

Wagner's hold on a Germanic national entity or culture is, in fact, vague. *The Flying Dutchman* is not a German legend but Norwegian in locale,[17] though Wagner based his version on Heinrich Heine's story. *Tannhäuser* and *Lohengrin* restate the fascination of the early Romantic period with the medieval world: The subject is the conquest of Christian morality over paganism and witchcraft. (But the voluptuous Venus in *Tannhäuser* does belongs not to the Roman pantheon, but to German folklore.) Wagner's *Nibelung* tribe live somewhere along the Rhine; the medieval setting is a German version of the Scandinavian *Song of the Volsungs* mixed with the Wotan myth. *Tristan and Isolda* takes place in Cornwall and Brittany, and *Parsifal*, Wagner's pious "festival play," is located in the Spanish Pyrenees.

Why did not Wagner compose a realistic "political opera" in the manner of Beethoven's *Fidelio*? Or like Verdi's several allegories of the Austrian subjection of the Italians (for example, *Aida*, in which the Egyptians hold the Ethiopians prisoners, or *Nebuchadnezzar* in which the Babylonians (Austrians) bind the Hebrews (Italians) to years of bondage)? In Germany the political situation was not oppressive, and the German people were not in bondage to a foreign power. Their language, so holy to Wagner, was a major tongue; it was not demeaned, like Smetana's Czech and Sibelius's Finnish, by being outside the main cultural stream. *The Bartered Bride* filled the need for a national opera for the Bohemians, as much earlier Weber's *Der Freischütz* had become the prototype of German national opera. Both these works are patently more nationalistic than anything Wagner ever wrote.

After his early *Rienzi*, Wagner disdained scenarios of mundane persons.[18] *The Mastersingers of Nuremberg* is the sole exception of true-to-life people untouched by irrealism. His preoccupation with the supposed Jewish machinations in his life becomes tedious and irrational in his prose writings, yet he never fashioned a plot in which one or more characters are identified as actually Jewish, as in Marschner's *Der Templer und die Jüdin* (based on Scott's *Ivanhoe*) of 1829, or Halévy's *La Juive* (1836), or the Biblical plots of Verdi's *Nabucco* (1842) or Saint-Saëns's *Samson et Delilah* (1877). Rather, in Wagner's judgment the Teutonic myths were the only literary material of enduring worth and universal significance for lyric dramas, defined as the complete work of art *(Gesamtkunstwerk)* and "The Art Work of the Future."[19] The persons who fill his operas are greater than reality. They are of heroic, mythical dimensions, capable of superhuman strength, evil, goodness, or sacrifice. Their interaction emphasizes the inequality and imperfection of individuals or races, with insistent themes of purification and redemption and the regeneration of an exalted class of leaders.

Wagner's metaphors on stage demand the need for interpretation, especially as they are elements of old myths recast for a contemporary audience. *The Ring* constructs a complex sequence of events in which the actions of the corrupted gods, humans, and a subhuman race (the *Nibelungs*) plot to steal and retain the magic lump of gold resting at the bottom of the Rhine River. The gods are less than noble, but the Nibelung race is vile and repugnant. The dwarf Mime is "gruesome, grizzled, and gray, cramped and crooked, with hanging ears stretching, bleary eyes staring." Wagner's instruction is that the delivery of Mime's Nibelung crew (men's chorus) is to be in "the Jewish manner of speech—shrill, hissing, buzzing, a wholly foreign and arbitrary distortion of our national idiom." Here Wagner dramatizes his complaint of the Jew's defilement of the language of the pure race.[20] (Presumably the German Jews spoke only Yiddish, a crossbreed, to be sure, of Hebrew and German.) Wagner states that the Nibelung tribe represents the Jews who have robbed the world of its gold and are determined to dominate all mankind. Alberich, the Nibelung who initiates this epic of greed and revenge, is shown to crave gold and power more than the elevating quality of love. The selfish and vain gods are led by Wotan, who is depicted as a vengeful Jehovah, not the forgiving father god of the Christians.[21] The redeemer, foretold by destiny, is Siegfried (Wotan's mortal grandson), sinless, generous, youthful, and Christlike (but no teacher). In the composer's preliminary sketch for the cycle (1848), he described Siegfried as "the God become man,"[22] the one who would take upon himself the guilt of the gods to atone for their sins. This point is also discussed in his historical sketch, *Nibelungen*, the basis for his version of the Nibelung drama.[23] The allegorical Christ is, not surprisingly, brought to his untimely death by the tainted Nibelungs. In *The Twilight of the Gods*, the concluding opera of the cycle, Siegfried is treacherously murdered by Alberich's son, Hagen, in an attempt to retrieve the magic gold in the form of a ring worn by the savior-hero. Hagen is willing to sacrifice his integrity, his sister's husband (Siegfried himself, by Hagen's trickery), and his brother to own the gold. Wagner's meaning: Jewish greed inevitably corrupts all.

It may be argued that explaining the *Ring* in terms of Wagner's psychology is unnecessary to enjoy the operas. But myths and legends characteristically espouse cultural mores: It is their purpose as the heritage of a people. When the myth is recast in a modern setting, it is to be expected that the author has done so in order to state, or restate, the eternal morality of the mythical ancestors, thereby to illumine contemporary crises, perhaps to rebuke or laud contemporary leaders or events, and to suggest a solution to the modern dilemma, perhaps through moral fortitude. Therefore, we must identify the message that Wagner expected his audience to recognize and to respond to positively. The allegory was not meant to be so esoteric that it would fail to illumine the world of his day and the future. Without this information, or without the effort to grasp this information, we fail to perceive the whole of Wagner's work. For the listener/reader to be selective—to accept only the exterior, visible events—is to assume the role of censor. To be pleased only with the sheer sound of voices and instruments is too simple and too naive a response to this abstruse art. Wagner's music is not a reflection of folk culture in the way that *Der Freischütz* is. There are no thumping polkas, much less Ländler or waltzes, to set us among sons and daughters of the soil. The middle-class townspeople of *Die Meistersinger* are clothed—by the music—with a sumptuousness rather like that of a Rembrandt painting. Wagner's musical nationalism is the product of his ability to create a feeling of power, and even of arrogance, which was then labeled German nationalism. "*Die Meistersinger* stirred up genuine German feelings," the Grand Duke of Weimar told Wagner in 1872.[24] The composer accomplished this without folk idioms, but through an extraordinary manipulation of musical elements: rhythm, harmony, stunning sonorities and intimidatingly large proportions.

With his indefatigable flow of literary *apologia* before and after his composition of the librettos and music, the operas were soon designated exemplars of the grandeur, the superiority, and the power of German culture. This formidable body of chauvinism and elitism was ready (but not in fact readied) to be installed in the Nazi ideological program.

In defense of Wagner's bias, we must acknowledge a corrective, so to speak. Stein discerns that Wagner "clearly realized the danger of confusing intellectual and cultural dominance with political and military prowess. He foresaw, too, that pride in artistic achievement could easily be transformed and pass into the desire for aggrandizement and for military dominance."[25] In his essay entitled "What Is German?" Wagner warned his countrymen against yearning for German glory in the manner of the Holy Roman Empire.[26] Unfortunately, again, Wagner did not predict accurately the outcome of his arguments. Both Kaiser Wilhelm II and Adolf Hitler had themselves portrayed in paintings dressed in the shining armor of Lohengrin: Each regarded himself as the holy knight destined to rescue the noble Elsa (Germany) from the diabolical Ortrud (the alien forces of evil).[27] *Lohengrin* was the first opera Hitler ever saw, and he committed the libretto to memory during his stay in Vienna.[28] Robert G. L. Waite suggests that the plot of the blonde girl who is menaced by her lecherous guardian, Frederick of Telramund, evoked Hitler's troubled home life during his childhood, and that Hitler saw himself as the knight who rescued his mother (whom he held in extraordinary reverence) from his violent father, who had been her guardian before he married her.[29]

The "Führer concept," the superman and the hero-savior who is to come, had a central place in Wagner's writings. The founder of the First German Reich was Kaiser Frederick Barbarossa (r. 1152-1190), whom Wagner saw as a medieval reincarnation of the mythical Siegfried. Legend had it that Frederick did not die, but lay in an enchanted sleep in a mountain cave, and when the nation was again in dire need, he would awaken.[30] This concept continued into Wagner's late essays, such as "Hero-dom" (1881).[31] The duty of the hero included restoring the lost Aryan purity of the German people. *Mein Kampf*, part one, concludes with Hitler's summary of the first Nazi party meeting: "A fire was kindled from whose flame one day the sword must come which would regain freedom for the Germanic Siegfried and life for the German people."[32]

Still another corrective is that Wagner's anti-Semitism, unlike Hitler's, arose from the composer's religious views, from his virtual obsession with Christ, and from his conviction that Christianity was corrupted by its Jewish antecedents, as already noted. Wagner lived during a period when European societies, including Germany, considered themselves devoutly Christian, particularly amid the revival of religious feeling in the Romantic period.

Wagner's ideas have been termed proto-Nazi,[33] but this term may be applied to only some of his views. In the first place, his life work, from beginning to last, was to create music for the stage; it was not 1) to found a fascist government, 2) to rule the world, or 3) to strike down, with war machines if necessary, other groups of peoples or nations outside Germany. Further, he had absorbed his philosophical and sociological ideas from other nineteenth-century writers, in particular Fichte and Hegel, and, later, Schopenhauer and Gobineau.

There are parallels and associations with Hitler's creed, nonetheless, and they are painful to note. Both men ardently believed in the superior historical richness and capacity of German culture. Each contended that he alone could release the power to restore the people to their greatness, Wagner through the creation of his new musico-dramatic art form, and Hitler through political and social controls and military superiority over the nation's enemies, domestic and foreign. Wagner, like Hitler, vehemently espoused anti-Semitism. Wagner also rejected Jewish artists from any connection with his efforts, yet, as in Hitler's Third Reich, Wagner allowed exceptions if they brought particular success: A few outstanding Jewish artists remained in the Wagner circle, and sometimes the hypocrisy was evident.[34]

When Hitler entered the political scene in the 1920s, *Lohengrin, Tannhäuser, The Ring, Tristan and Isolda*, and the genial *Meistersinger* had attained world fame in the repertoire of Romantic opera and concert music. The works demanded, and received, the most powerful voices of each generation, the most celebrated conductors, the biggest and best orchestras. Wagnerian music evoked the most solemn aura, and presumably carried the most profound "value," since Beethoven. It was indeed constructed with the most complex texture and invention. And it was composed by a German who said that his work (alone!) proved the exalted place of German culture past, present and future. The supreme German egotist of the twentieth century could not fail to embrace the eloquent expression of the supreme German egotist of the previous century.

Thomas Mann, otherwise an ardent admirer of Wagner, noted in a 1949 letter: "There is in Wagner's bragging, his eternal ranting, his *allein-redenwollen* ["solo conversations"], his desire to enter every discussion about everything, a nameless insolence which foreshadows Hitler; clearly there is much "Hitler" in Wagner."[35]

There is indisputably a link between Wagner's polemics and the ideology of Adolf Hitler, and there is also the influence of Wagner's passionate prose style.[36] The first link is through the writing of the English historian Houston Stewart Chamberlain, who married Wagner's daughter, Eva, in 1908 and became Wagner's ardent vindicator, apostle and biographer. Chamberlain's monumental *Foundations of the Nineteenth Century*,[37] published (in German) in 1911, was read avidly by the Kaiser to his son, and the monarch ordered the work to be circulated among the officers of the German Army and in schools and libraries. By the start of World War I the sale of the work had reached 100,000.[38] Another link with the oncoming creed of Hitler was the work of Karl Grunsky, particularly *Wagner and the Jews,* published in 1920.[39] Grunsky praised Wagner's works as "a paean of all things German, and therefore a continuous offense to Jewish nature." He declared that Wagner was "a religious discoverer . . . far on the road to the future."[40] When Hitler, early in his public career, embraced Wagner's operas as an expression of German nationalism, he did so with the politician's awareness that he could draw about him the renown of this theatrical art like the mantle of a crown prince.

When the Nazi party took control of Germany on January 30, 1933, the State Opera was ordered to give a performance of *Die Meistersinger von Nürnberg.* In 1932, Josef Goebbels had witnessed this opera and eulogized "the giant Wagner" in his diary: "As the great 'Awake' chorus begins, you feel the stimulation in your *blood.* Germany, too, will soon feel the same and be called to an awakening. We must *attain* to power!" The following year he could gloat that Wagner's closing "Awake" chorus had "regained its true significance," as Hitler became dictator with the slogan, *Deutschland erwache!* (Germany, awake!).[41]

Hitler's early ideals were German nationalism, and, allied with it, the nineteenth-century view of the supremacy of the Aryan race. Dietrich Eckart, a Munich poet and one of the founders of the original Nazi party, is credited with instructing Hitler in the Chamberlain-Wagner theory of Aryan racial purity. (The close of Hitler's *Mein Kampf* is dedicated to Eckart.) Eckart also introduced Siegfried Wagner's wife, Winifred, to Hitler, in the circle which met at the home of Edwin Bechstein, the piano manufacturer.[42]

After Hitler's seizure of power in 1933, the rich and vigorous flow of musical life in Germany was rapidly disrupted, as he appropriated all means of communication for his dogma.[43] Everything modern in musical style was condemned. (Political dictators, right and left, seem to arrive with a built-in reactionary taste in the arts.) The new dissonances, especially atonality, as well as jazz or jazz-influenced works, were censured: They smelled of revolution, of independent thinking; they were not Aryan.

The Nazis laid down the rules for popular music. Musicians were admonished to use the major key, to sing words "expressing joy in life rather than Jewishly gloomy lyrics," and to use brisk tempos not to exceed an allegro "commensurate with the Aryan sense of discipline and moderation." Strictly prohibited were the use of "instruments alien to the German spirit (so-called cowbells, flexatone, brushes, etc.), as well as all mutes which turn the noble sound of wind and brass instruments into a Jewish-Freemasonic yowl (so-called wa-wa, hat, etc.)." Plucking of the strings was also prohibited, "since it is damaging to the instrument and detrimental to Aryan musicality. . . ."[44]

In the concert world the state of new music was also in chaos. Honegger could be performed; most of Bartók could not. Stravinsky's *Firebird* was approved, but his *Rite of Spring* was placed on the "index."[45] Arnold Schoenberg's radical twelve-tone method was savagely attacked: "[He] is a fanatic of Nihilism, of destruction. He places himself outside of all community. . . . Even Jews reject this music."[46]

There were a favored few composers. During the 1936 Olympics in Berlin, commissions were given to Richard Strauss, Carl Orff and Werner Egk to compose brilliant background music to dazzle foreign public opinion.[47] Like much art created in fulfillment of a political assignment, it was promptly forgotten.

More narrow-minded, and without even a judgment of artistic taste, was the arbitrary ban on Jewish musicians and music by Jewish composers living or dead. Artists of all kinds, pianists, singers, conductors, who were Jewish were prohibited from public performance. (The "Nuremberg Laws" of 1933 deprived Jews of their citizenship. In November 1938 a proclamation by the Foreign Ministry also banned Jews from attending theatres and concerts.[48]) Many departed, as did some non-Jewish artists who were outraged over the new laws. Arturo Toscanini refused to return to the summer festival at Bayreuth, despite a personal invitation from Hitler. In 1934 Germany's premier maestro, Wilhelm Furtwängler, suffered humiliation when he attempted to defend the "dissonant" music (and sometimes earthy stage works) of Paul Hindemith.[49] The Furtwängler-Hindemith case had nothing to do with the "Jewish question."

But Furtwängler also tried to persuade Bronislaw Hubermann, an eminent violinist, to continue his concert appearances in Germany. In a letter of September 13, 1933, Hubermann replied:

You try to convince me by writing, "Someone must make a beginning to break down the wall that keeps us apart." Yes, if it were only a wall in the concert hall! It is not a question of violin concertos nor even merely of the Jews [who were dismissed from their posts]; the issue is the elementary preconditions of our European culture, the freedom of personality unhampered by fetters of caste or race.[50]

The extremism reached absurdity. To sustain "the unshatterable laws of racial purity," two now forgotten composers were commissioned to write a new score in 1934 to replace Felix Mendelssohn's incidental music for *A Midsummer Night's Dream*.[51] This curiously suggests that the Elizabethan playwright's comic fantasy about imaginary Greeks was irreplaceable in the German theater![52] Handel's oratorio, *Judas Maccabeus*, based on Jewish history (not the Bible), was provided with a new text on a Teutonic subject, *Wilhelm von Nassau*, and *Israel in Egypt*, the story of Moses and the Exodus, was transformed into *Mongrel Fury*. Even Mozart received some harsh words, because he had accepted Lorenzo da Ponte, a Jew, though baptized, as librettist for *The Marriage of Figaro, Don Giovanni* and *Cosi fan tutte*.[53] Richard Strauss, who received autographed framed photographs of *der Führer* and Dr. Goebbels on his seventieth birthday, was less openly criticized for his collaboration with a Jewish librettist, Stefan Zweig.[54]

The omnipotent triumvirate of Hitler, Goebbels and Hermann Goering became the patrons and protectors of the prestigious cultural institutions. Goebbels's interest, as propaganda minister, was in the radio and film studios, but also in the German Opera House in Berlin—where Hitler went to see his favorite operetta, Franz Lehar's *The Merry Widow* (with its setting in Paris!). Goering controlled the other opera houses and major theatres of Berlin. Hitler was the patron of the great houses of Munich, Weimar, Bayreuth and Nuremberg.[55]

Hitler's attraction to the glamour of Bayreuth had begun in the 1920s, when Siegfried Wagner's wife had invited the compelling, and almost religious, figure to be her house guest.[56] Hitler seemed to Winifred Wagner (as to a growing number of other Germans) to be the one man who could revive Germany after its humiliation in

World War I. Hitler became a family friend. Among the four Wagner grandchildren, only Friedelind recognized his sinister potential and his occasional irrational behavior.[57] On the day that Hitler had paid his first visit to the Wahnfried, Wagner's home, he had also made a pilgrimage across the street to meet Houston Stewart Chamberlain, the revered historian who was called the "prophet of the Third Reich."[58]

In Friedelind's memoirs, *The Royal Family of Bayreuth*, published after she escaped to the United States in 1941, she recorded in detail her observations and conversations with Hitler in Bayreuth and in Berlin. When Hitler became Chancellor in 1933, his next visit to Bayreuth initiated a propaganda program of worldwide potential. The annual visit of *der Führer* became a highlight of the calendar of the Third Reich.[59] For his appearance, the theater was decorated with swastika banners. With the attention of the international musical world already on the renowned festival, Hitler's presence, his genuine appreciation of the operas, and the extravagant public adulation which surrounded him produced a vivid image that was sent around the world. Friedelind Wagner, who worked as an assistant stage director from her eighteenth year, believed" everything about the Festspielhaus was . . . polluted by Nazism, by false emphasis and false values. . . ."[60]

Notes in the festival program book attained doctrinal significance. In 1938, this "information" was read by all:

Wagner's work teaches us hardness in the figure of Lohengrin. . . . Through Hans Sachs it teaches us to honor all things German. . . . In the *Ring of the Nibelungs* it brings to our consciousness with unexampled clarity the terrible seriousness of the racial problem; . . . in *Parsifal* it shows us that the only religion Germans can embrace is that of struggle towards a life made divine.[61]

During the Festival, the Reich command post moved to the opera house. In 1934, from the family box, Friedelind Wagner witnessed two aides relay long-distance phone messages to Hitler during *Rheingold. Der Führer* grew very excited as the messages continued. Later he told the family the horrible news, barely concealing his pleasure: Chancellor Engelbert Dollfuss of Austria has been assassinated in his office (by Nazi storm troopers, dressed in Austrian army uniforms). Hitler then added, "I must go out for an hour and show myself, or people will think I had something to do with this."[62] After a Bayreuth performance in July, 1938, Hitler received an urgent emissary from Francisco Franco. The insurgent leader desperately needed planes. Hitler at once summoned Goering, and the decision was made that evening to support the Spanish rebellion.[63]

Jacques Barzun identifies Alberich as an allegorical figure of the nineteenth-century industrial magnate[64] who hoards gold (in *Rheingold*) like the stereotype of the Jewish financial lord. Paradoxically, Windell suggests that if any character in the *Ring* foreshadows Adolf Hitler, it is Alberich, who, "consumed by hate, consciously renounces love for power, and pursues his objective with a fanatic singlemindedness of purpose."[65]

It is not irrelevant to observe that Hitler might have ignored Wagner's operas as well as the composer's didactic writing, but he did not. He admired the Wagnerian repertoire as much as other German music lovers did. None of the operas was ever censored. During the war *Parsifal* was omitted, presumably because the symbols of the Christian church, or church mythology, conflicted with the official direction toward a neo-pagan set of values—as *Mein Kampf* replaced the crucifix and the bible on every altar.[66] Yet *Parsifal* did hold a peculiar suggestion in the Wagner-Hitler thinking: the formation of an elite class.

Waite tracked this early influence of racism on Hitler,[67] and cited two Viennese authors, Guido von List and Lanz von Liebenfels, whose pamphlets were attracting attention in Vienna during the years when Hitler lived there (1908-1913). Liebenfels supplied Hitler with some back issues of his articles. In one the author called for a new order of the racially elite, used the oriental swastika as a symbol of racial purity, and promised that when his new order arrived, stringent laws would be passed against "the mongrelization of the Aryan race." In 1913 Liebenfels declared that "the Holy Grail of the German blood" must be defended by an elite bodyguard of the racially pure, a brotherhood of knights, in fact, who would seize the lesser races of the world and wipe them off the earth by means of mass execution and sterilization.[68] There is no evidence that twenty-five years earlier Wagner's esoteric brotherhood of knights in *Parsifal* had possessed such a violent assignment. But twenty-five years later Adolf Hitler thrust such a program into action with horrifying precision.

The ultimate tragedy of Wagner's bigotry and egotism is that its maliciousness still fulminates. The moral authority he implied by his operas was arrogated by Hitler, and intensified with unending propaganda. It is unending propaganda because Wagner's music has come to be synonymous with Nazism to more than a few persons today, a generation after the dissolution of the Third Reich. The judgment began as World War II broke out. "If Hitler likes Wagner's music, it is all the more reason why every non-Nazi should shun and loathe it," wrote the German-American musician Carl Engel in 1941.[69] Engel assumed that since Hitler had an evil mind, he was attracted by the same qualities in Wagner's music; hence, the music must exude the same poisonous quality. He also argued that even as the Nazi censors banned Schumann's beloved song cycle, *Dichterliebe*, because the poems were by the Jewish poet Heinrich Heine, so should the West be willing to give up what it treasured. But he declared that Wagner's music had been hoodwinking us all along.

What we are giving up is the music of Klingsor [the satanic magician and fallen knight in *Parsifal*] who for one hundred years has numbed our senses with his witchcraft. . . . We should retaliate and ban and burn every scrap of Wagner's music and writings and every book written about the amazing wizard, beginning with the [newly published] books of the Anglo-Wagnerian Ernest Newman. What a small price it would be to pay, if it could help to fight and finally extinguish the Wagner's fanned fire of Nazism.[70]

This was the truth for Engel, as it was for some other critics, historians and spectators then—and still is now.

In 1981, when Zubin Mehta announced selections from Wagner's music for a concert in Tel Aviv, he was prevented from playing them, even from adding a piece as an encore, by vociferous protests by some concertgoers and members of the Israel Philharmonic. Fistfights disrupted the concert. Leonard Bernstein, who often conducted the Israel orchestra, wired his support to Mehta: "The music of Wagner is in the world repertoire and if the Israel Philharmonic wants to play on a world level it must include his works."[71]

At the performances of *Das Rheingold* and *Die Walküre* by the San Francisco Opera in 1983, Andrew Porter noted that the political connotation still aroused strong feelings: The opera house was picketed by people who charged that the music promulgated Hitlerism.[72]

Neither the bigoted views of those nineteenth-century philosophers whom Wagner admired nor Hitler's crimes against humanity have disappeared into the shadows of history. Thus both actions resound in Wagner's music for some listeners who cannot separate Wagner from Hitler, or *Lohengrin* and *Walküre* from the Brown Shirts and the Third Reich. Is this not what Hitler wished? His propaganda has conquered those listeners! It must be clear from the foregoing discussion that the association of Hitler's *Kultur* with Wagner's music dramas cannot be ignored, for it truly exists. But two *can* be separated. If they are not, the musical glory of Richard Wagner cannot be enjoyed. This, too, truly exists.[73]

NOTES

1. *Music in Western Civilization* (New York: W. W. Norton, 1941), pp. 878-79.

2. Richard Wagner, *Prose Works*, 8 vols., tr. by William Ashton Ellis (New York: Broude Brothers, 1966. Reprint of 1897 edition), hereafter *PW*, VI, pp. 275-76 ("Hero-dom and Christendom").

3. Ibid., p. 280; "What Is German?" *PW*, IV, p. 157; *Cosima Wagner's Diaries*, ed. by Martin Gregor-Dellin and Dietrich Mack. Translated with an Introduction by Geoffrey Skelton. (Hereafter *CWD*.) Vol. I, 1869-77 (London: William Collins & Sons, Co., 1978); Vol. II, 1878-83 (New York: Harcourt Brace Jovanovich, 1980), vol. I, p. 852.

4. *PW*, III, pp. 75-122. See also his letter to Liszt dated April 18, 1851, admitting his authorship, in Gertrude Norman and Miriam L. Shrifte, eds., *Letters of Composers* (New York: Grosset & Dunlap, 1946), pp. 178-79. Wagner reissued the article under his own name in 1869.

5. *PW*, VI.

6. Leon Stein, *The Racial Thinking of Richard Wagner* (New York: Philosophical Library, 1950), pp. 3-4.

7. *CWD*, I, pp. 120, 225, 891-92, 915; II, pp. 68, 1031 (the "4 J's—Jews, Jesuits, journalists and jurists"); also 579, 657, etc.

8. Stein, *Racial Thinking*, pp. x-xii.

9. Romain Rolland, *Musicians of Today* (New York: Henry Holt & Co., 1915, second edition), p. 253. For Wagner's views see "German Art

and German Policy," in which he contrasts German and French civilizations, *PW*, IV, pp. 37-63.

10. For a résumé and bibliography on this literary effusion see Albert Goldman and Evert Sprinchorn, *Wagner on Music and Drama* (London: Victor Gollancz, 1964), pp. 30-31, and n. 11, 12. There was also a German periodical, *Bayreuther Blätter*, devoted to the master's ideas on all subjects, which he founded in 1878 and which continued vigorously into the Nazi period.

11. Norman and Shrifte, *Letters of Composers*, p. 240.

12. "The Vienna Opera House," *PW*, III, pp. 366-68; "Music of the Future" (on Italian Opera), III, pp. 332-33; The *Tannhäuser* ballet for the Paris Opera, III, pp. 351-58; "Opera and Drama" (on Meyerbeer), II, pp. 24-48, etc.

13. "On German Music," *PW*, VII, p. 94. Wagner by no means disdained the charm of foreign travel. He went to those cities and countries where his operas were sung, and where his indulgence for physical comfort was satiated. He had a delightful Swiss home on Lake Lucerne. His death came during a stay in Venice.

14. *PW*, IV, p. 166. He also said that "large cities should cease to exist since they produce mobs, and mobs are unGerman. . . ." *CWD*, I, p. 335.

15. See Wagner's plan for a triumphal march and hymn to be sung by the public for the troops' return to Berlin in 1871, and the actual composition, *Imperial March*, played for the new Emperor, in *The Diary of Richard Wagner 1865-1882* ("The Brown Book"), annotated by Joachim Bergfeld, tr. by George Bird (London: Cambridge University Press, 1980), pp. 186-89.

16. *CWD*, I, pp. 852-882; II, p. 33. See *PW*, IV, pp. 167-68, the 1871 postscript to "What Is German?"

17. See Wagner's instructions on performing the opera in *PW*, III, pp. 209-17.

18. But Wagner admired the mastery of Balzac's realist novel, *Père Goriot*. *CWD*, I, p. 443. When he and Cosima visited Vienna they were incessant theater patrons and willingly witnessed many styles. In November, 1875, for example, they saw the German production of Bizet's new *Carmen*, inspired by Merimée's lusty novel. Ibid., p. 874.

19. *PW*, I, pp. 69-213.

20. "What Is German?" *PW*, IV, p. 152; "Opera and Drama," II, pp. 357-58; "Judaism in Music" (beginning), III; "A Word of Introduction to Hans von Wolzogen's 'Decline and Rescue of the German Tongue,'" VI, pp. 28-29; "Modern," VI, pp. 43-49.

21. *PW*, VII, pp. 287, 289.

22. Ibid., pp. 308, 274.

23. Ibid., p. 275.

24. *CWD*, I, p. 455. Goebbels reported in his memoirs that Hitler had seen *Die Meistersinger* a hundred times. *Von Kaiserhof zur Reichkansler* (Munich, 1937), cited in Peter Viereck, *Meta-politics: The Roots of the Nazi Mind* (New York: Capricorn Books, 1965), p. 133.

25. Stein, *Racial Thinking*, p. 210.

26. "What Is German?", *PW*, IV, p. 154; see also p. 164.

27. The orchestra conductor, Sir Ernest MacMillan, in 1939 described this prize-winning painting of Hitler in the Munich House of German Art and remarked that "Hitler identified himself in his own mind with many a Wagnerian hero." Quoted in Viereck, *Meta-politics*, p. 136.

28. August Kubizek, *The Young Hitler I Knew* (tr. of *Adolph Hitler, Mein Jugendfreund*, Graz: 1953, by E. V. Anderson), (Boston: Houghton Mifflin Co., 1954), p. 188. Adolf Hitler, *Mein Kampf*, tr. by Ralph Manheim (Boston: Houghton Mifflin Co., 1943), p. 22.

29. "Adolf Hitler's Anti-Semitism: A Study in History and Psycho-analysis," in Benjamin B. Wolman, ed., *Psychoanalytic Interpretation of History* (New York: Basic Books, 1971), p. 200; Kubizek, *The Young Hitler*, pp. 229-33; Friedelind Wagner and Page Cooper, *The Royal Family of Bayreuth* (London: Eyre and Spottiswoode, 1948), pp. 110-11.

30. The Prussian empire erected by Bismarck for the young Kaiser Wilhelm II was called the Second Reich: It was advantageous to link the new empire with the glorious past. By the same reasoning, Hitler's empire became the Third Reich. The glorious past also supplied the code name for Hitler's surprise attack on the USSR: "Barbarossa." See William Shirer, *The Rise and Fall of the Third Reich* (New York: Simon and Schuster, 1960), p. 810.

31. *PW*, IV, pp. 12, 16. See also *PW*, VI, p. 279.

32. Hitler, *Mein Kampf*, p. 370.

33. George G. Windell, "Hitler, National Socialism, and Richard Wagner," in John Louis DiGaetani, ed., *Penetrating Wagner's Ring: An Anthology* (Cranbury, N.J. Associated University Presses, 1978), p. 222.

34. Some close associations were with soprano Lili Lehmann, pianist Josef Rubenstein, impresario Angelo Neumann, and Hermann Levi, King Ludwig's court conductor who came with the Munich court orchestra needed for the premiere of *Parsifal*. See Stein, *Racial Thinking*, pp. 81-84. *CWD*, II, pp. 254, 893. See also Theodor Adorno's analysis of Wagner's toying with Levi in *In Search of Wagner*(*Versuch über Wagner*) tr. by Rodney Livingstone (London: NLB, 1981), pp. 18-20.

35. "Wagner und kein Ende," translated (incompletely) in Windell, "Hitler, National Socialism, and Richard Wagner," p. 221.

36. "Hitler's love for Wagner's prose also had stylistic consequences. It is

not only the model for the political ideas of *Mein Kampf* but also for its turgid, orgasmic, and grammatically involved prose. . . . Hitler's book and speech inherit Wagner's stylistic faults: painful repetition, crank tangents, offensive grandiloquence, emotion to the point of hysteria. But Hitler's book and speeches equally inherit Wagner's stylistic assets: a vigour and energy ('dynamism') sweeping along impressionable listeners, especially when *en masse*; vague mystic soaring and striving, making readers and listeners feel heroic and uplifted, especially youth reared in the tradition of German romanticism—and both Wagnerism and Hitlerism are most magnetic as youth movements." Viereck, *Meta-politics*, p. 135.

37. *Die Grundlagen des 19. Jahrhunderts*, tr. by John Lees (New York: H. Fertig, 1968). (Originally published by John Lane, London, 1911). Two volumes.

38. Shirer, *Rise and Fall* pp. 107-09.

39. Karl Grunsky, *Wagner und die Jüden* (Munich: Deutscher Volks Verlag), cited in Stein, *Racial Thinking*, pp. 134-36, 98, 199, etc.

40. Translated in Stein, p. 134.

41. Josef Goebbels, *My Part in Germany's Fight*, tr. by K. Fiedler (London, 1935), pp. 131, 268; cited in Viereck, *Meta-politics*, p. 138.

42. Viereck, *Meta-politics*, pp. 91-92; F. Wagner, *Royal Family*, p. 9.

43. See Shirer, *Rise and Fall*, p. 242.

44. Josef Skvorecky, *The Bass Saxophone* (New York: Alfred Knopf, 1979), pp. 3-4. Skvorecky grew up in the Nazi protectorate of Bohemia and Moravia. He adored American jazz and formed a band with his school chums.

45. Richard Grunberger, *A Social History of the Third Reich* (London: Weidenfeld and Nicolson, 1971), pp. 407-8. Chapter 27 is devoted to music.

46. Nicolas Slonimsky, *Music Since 1900*, 1st ed. (New York: W. W. Norton & Co., 1937), pp. 382. This reference is not found in the 4th edition.

47. Grunberger, *Social History*, p. 416; Shirer, *Rise and Fall*, pp. 232-33; F. Wagner, *Royal Family*, p. 139.

48. Robert Edwin Herzstein, ed. *Adolf Hitler and the Third Reich* (Boston: Houghton Mifflin Co., 1971), pp. 86-87. See Shirer, *Rise and Fall*, pp. 232-44.

49. Slonimsky, *Music Since 1900*, 1st ed. (1937) pp. 385-87, 391. The 4th ed. of this volume abridges these references, p. 597.

50. Ibid., (1st ed.), p. 367.

51. Ibid., p. 384.

52. Shirer, *Rise and Fall*, pp. 242-43, judged that without the perform-

ances of classical plays by Schiller, Goethe and Shakespeare, the Nazi-controlled theater in Berlin was ludicrous.

53. Grunberger, *Social History*, p. 408.

54. Slonimsky, *Music Since 1900*, 1st ed., pp. 381, 393; and ibid., 4th ed., pp. 590, 608. See also F. Wagner, *Royal Family*, pp. 113-14.

55. F. Wagner, ibid., p. 93. Grunberger, *Social History*, p. 411.

56. F. Wagner, *Royal Family*, pp. 5-8, 9.

57. Ibid., pp. 79-80.

58. Ibid., p. 40.

59. Ibid., pp. 88-94, 125-26, 181-84.

60. Ibid., pp. 187.

61. Translated in Grunberger, *Social History*, p. 412.

62. Friedelind Wagner and Page Cooper, *Heritage of Fire* (New York: Harper Brothers, 1945), p. 109; Wagner and Cooper, *Royal Family*, pp. 112, 116.

63. Shirer, *Rise and Fall*, p. 297.

64. Jacques Barzun, *Darwin, Marx, Wagner* (Boston: Little Brown and Co., 1941), p. 264. Bernard Shaw saw the whole story as a symbol of nineteenth-century capitalism in *The Perfect Wagnerite* (New York: Dover Publications, 1967. Reprint of fourth edition), pp. 26-28.

65. Windell, "Hitler, National Socialism, and Richard Wagner," p. 225.

66. Grunberger, *Social History*, p. 412; Shirer, *Rise and Fall*, p. 234-40.

67. "Adolf Hitler's Anti-Semitism," in Wolman, *Psychoanalytic Interpretation of History*, pp. 196-97.

68. Ibid.

69. "Views and Reviews," in *The Musical Quarterly*, XXVII (April, 1941), p. 244.

70. Ibid., pp. 244-45.

71. St. Louis *Post-Dispatch*, October 19, 1981 (UPI).

72. *The New Yorker*, June 13, 1983, p. 103.

73. It is salutory to learn from the diaries of Theodor Herzl, the founder of modern political Zionism, that he found comfort in the operas of Richard Wagner. He embraced the music despite his youthful humiliation by members of his dueling fraternity who had participated in an anti-Semitic commemoration of the death of Wagner (1883). In 1895 during the writing of *Der Judenstaat* (The Jewish State) he wrote:

I worked at it daily, until I was completely exhausted. My one recreation was on the evenings when I could go to hear Wagner's music, and particularly *Tannhäuser*, an opera which I go to hear as often as it is produced. And only on those evenings when there was no opera did I have any doubts as to the truth of my ideas.

The pageantry of the opera house he fantasized into his grand picture of the future Zionist nation. "We too shall have such splendid lobbies, the men in formal dress, the women as luxurious as possible. Yes, I will exploit the Jewish love of luxury, as everything else." From Peter Loewenberg, "Theodor Herzl: A Psychoanalytic Study in Charismatic Political Leadership," in Wolman, *Psychoanalytic Interpretation of History*, p. 165.

CHAPTER 4

Music for the Totalitarian State: Marx, Lenin and Soviet Russia

There can be no music without ideology. . . . We, as revolutionaries, have a different conception of music. Lenin himself said that
"music is a means of unifying broad masses of people." It is not a
leader of masses, perhaps, but certainly an organizing force! . . .
Even the symphonic form, which appears more than any other
divorced from literary elements, can be said to have a bearing on
politics. . . . Music is no longer an end in itself, but a vital weapon in
the struggle.

Dmitri Shostakovich[1]

late 19th
ear 1960's

To put it briefly, we are for melodic music, rich in content, which
stirs the souls of men, generating strong feelings. We are against
cacaphonic music. . . . We are not against all jazz music. . . . But
there is music which makes one feel like vomiting, and causes colic in
one's stomach.

Nikita Khrushchev[2]

Are we to understand quite simply that truth is what the government
ordains?

Karl Marx[3] *19th*
cen

This chapter and the next analyze the function of music in a
contemporary society founded on one ideology and one alone; not
an authoritarian rule, as that of Emperor Joseph of Austria, but
totalitarian: the single-minded ideology of modern Marxism in
Josef Stalin's Russia and Mao Zedong's China.

The examples in the previous chapters have sprung from the

epochs of monarchies and incipient democracies, societies with a plurality of social and artistic standards. In the totalitarian state, the content of the musical work is not left to the composer's free choice, nor to the practice of censorship—whether explicit or by prevailing morality—which may not, in fact, always mirror the doctrine. This music, like all art produced in a totalitarian society, must affirm the state ideology and the theory and practice of a sociopolitical program. The ideology of the European monarchies was only vaguely enunciated, if at all, to the composer. The artist was not told what to write, only what he could *not* write. As distinguished from censorship (a ban) in a totalitarian regime, an official doctrine is developed to instruct and direct, as well as delimit, composers, performers, and audiences. Depending on the strictness with which the doctrine is interpreted or put into practice, however, there may also be present in such a society a variety of artistic expressions or styles, old-fashioned, antirevolutionary, even presumably innocuous—but the rulers' intent is to control *all* thought. The policy is intolerant and illiberal toward other sociopolitical principles and intolerant of experimental artistic methods, for these imply dissent.

The systematic use of music for mind control was scarcely founded in contemporary Marxism. An accepted tenet in Plato's *Republic* stated that only appropriate songs in affirmative modes must be included in the education of the future elite.[4] In ancient China, the Confucian belief held that melodies were an indicator of the ethical level of a people: "The melodies of an age of good order indicate composure and enjoyment. . . . The airs of a state going to ruin are expressive of sorrow and [troubled] thought. There is an interaction between the words and airs [of a people] and the character of their government."[5] We may deduce a parallel with the didactic music in the modern authoritarian state: "In the well-governed Confucianist state, music meant for pleasure does not exist."[6] This implies that there can be no "innocuous" music. Art must ever be positive and purposeful.

Lenin and Stalin, and subsequently Mao, discerned the potential of the arts for their new and vulnerable societies.[7] They early commenced control of "negative" music and of those who taught it and performed it. The complementary need was also perceived: Music of high quality and correct ideology must be created to replace music that in any way, overt or subtle, suggested a counterculture or might become a vehicle for public criticism. Further, the early leaders stated that all art must appeal to the masses, the primary consumers, a new audience not prepared—like the bourgeois class—to listen, much less to read. For Karl Marx and his twentieth-century disciples, art of all periods defined a social purpose—with the exception of the universal appeal, regardless of the socioeconomic conditions in which they were created, of such works as classical Greek drama and Shakespeare's plays. According to the Marxist analysis, art has always served one class or another. In Europe, ceremonial music and other art music had served the ruling class. The medieval Christian Church, the Renaissance patron, the German burghers and the fashionable theatergoers identified classes who made possible, and thus shaped, the music of their periods. Public music making was a means to maintain social stability. In a Marxist state such bourgeois art must be purged, remade or replaced by revolutionary art for the proletariat. Lenin wrote: "Art belongs to the people. . . . Our workers and peasants deserve something better than spectacles. They are entitled to real great art. That is why we put foremost public education and training on the biggest scale."[8] Lenin also wanted the theaters, including the Bolshoi opera, to be "purged of any filth," but Anatoly Lunacharsky, his friend and the first Commissar of Education, persuaded him that a sudden dissolution of the repertory would leave nothing, as the revolutionary music of the future was not yet at hand.[9]

For a theoretical foundation we begin with Marx and his associate, Frederick Engels, and then examine the writings of V.I. Lenin, the first executant of Marx's principles to hold control of a national government. The overriding attention of Marxist-Leninist (and also Maoist) thinking was not on art, or even culture, but on economics and political control; only insofar as music and the other arts could serve the revolution were they discussed. Marx's writing chiefly analyzed the humanistic impact on capitalism, the alienation of society and the rise of the bourgeois economics.[10] It appears, however, that he never got around to setting out a systematic policy for the arts;[11] nor did Lenin.[12] I do not find the word "music" in indexes of the works of Marx or Lenin, although biographical anecdotes indicate that both men enjoyed some of the art music of their times. Lenin confessed that listening to music like Beethoven's "Appassionata" Sonata, which he called "amazing, superhuman music," affected him with sentimental feelings which he could not afford to hold with his responsibilities.[13] In Stalin's period, the concept of Socialist Realism yielded criteria for correct art, though applications were changeable and ambiguous. The term "Socialist Realism" first appeared as the title of an essay by the Soviet writer Maxim Gorky in 1933. The following year, at the All Union Congress of Soviet Writers, the USSR Communist Party spokesman, Andrei Zhdanov, set forth the aims of Soviet artistic expression, "to depict reality in its revolutionary development," and called for works "attuned to the epoch." As a national cultural policy, Stalin further defined the dimensions of Soviet art as "cultures, national in form and Socialist in substance."[14]

Marxist theorists, including Lenin, held a contempt for music, such as European opera, which existed solely to please the middle class.[15] Similarly, they condemned music that is experimental or composed for the interest of an esoteric circle or as private expression (art for art's sake) and music, such as vocal or theater music, which through its texts lauds a privileged class or depicts behavior that Marxism would label immoral or selfish. In both Russia and China, these views became codified as artistic policy. It is a passing irony, however, that Marx, who never faced the day-to-day administrative responsibilities of Lenin, Stalin or Mao, could once defend "art for art's sake," when it meant the artist was striving to free himself from a narrow censorship. He ridiculed the "New Instructions to Prussian Censors" (1842), which decreed, as he perceived them, commanding "but one mode of expression—moderation; and one color—gray on gray; one truth—what the government ordains, the sole rationale in the state. . . . Are we to understand quite simply that truth is what the government ordains?"[16] What a plea for liberalism! What a dangerous position for one to hold in any modern state built in Marx's name!

But his was a defense by a radical against a reactionary regime. There were other calls for tolerance, if not liberalism. Marx, as an historical materialist, would not discard artistic monuments of the past, including those of elitist Greece and imperial Rome, if such ancient accomplishments might direct people's minds to socialist construction.[17] Revolution must stamp out feudal, imperialist and capitalist oppression, but revolution need not stamp out the past totally. In 1919 Lenin voiced this principle by pointing out that the young USSR had an irreplaceable need for the experts trained under Czarism, "men and women who grew up under capitalism, were depraved and corrupted by capitalism, but steeled for the struggle by it. . . . All the agronomists, engineers and school teachers were recruited from the propertied class; they did not drop from the skies. . . . Science and technology exist only for the rich; capitalism provides a culture only for the minority.[18] And in 1920: "We know communism grows out of capitalism and can be built only from its remnants; they are bad remnants, it is true, but there are no others. Whoever dreams of a mythical communism should be driven from every . . . conference. . . ."[19]

In Lenin's Draft Resolution, "On Proletarian Culture" (1920), he wrote: "Marxism has won its historic significance as the ideology of the revolutionary proletariat because, far from rejecting the most valuable achievements of the bourgeois epoch, it has, on the contrary, assimilated and refashioned everything of value in the more than two thousand years of the development of human thought and culture."[20]

Perhaps this respect for the past is but the reflection of an educated mind. It also seems to have been necessary as a defense against the extreme leftist opinions of the purists among Russian and later, Chinese, party members. But past achievements, including high art, are still viable and attractive, and may be counter-revolutionary unless interpreted according to the new ideology. The cultural values of the proletariat, as well as those of the surviving bourgeoisie, bear the imprint of history. Indigenous education, both institutional and folk, contains cultural flaws that are tenacious and may be seductive. A deep affection for specific musical works, such as folk and popular music and the social setting in which such music is typically performed, may be inimical to the new society. The musicians, including composers, however, are experts needed for leadership. In the early years of the new society, these experts are yet the products of the old society. Their routines of instruction and models may be again handed down to the next generation. Apolitical artists are useless; those hostile to the new ideology are dangerous. There must be extensive and permanent artistic controls, but these are redefinable, depending on changing political objectives.

These concepts may probably apply to any Marxist or totalitarian state, though indigenous customs and other local factors will qualify the ideology, and underline the arts, of the society. The regime constructed by Adolf Hitler endured for but a short period, from 1933 to 1942, when his ideology became dominated by World War II. The Communist Party of Soviet Russia took control of Russia in 1917 and it still rules. The theoretical basis of Communism, unlike German National Socialism, had an established philosophical basis. Lenin, Stalin, Mao Zedong, and their associates could take direction from the interpretation of history and a prediction of the future, as enunciated by Marx and Engels. The national leaders could justify their response to daily exigencies by references to Marx's writings. In turn, Lenin became the source for later Soviet resolutions.

And so it was that in Soviet Russia the aesthetic criteria became one with the welfare of the proletarian society. Resolutions and directives initiated, supported, corrected, and, when necessary, halted the ambitions of musical artists and everything required for the production of their music: the education of the composer, the publication of musical scores, or the prevention of publication, and their distribution, the employment of musicians to perform concerts, the managers, the halls and theaters, information about programs, and prior approval of all public concerts, especially by such large state musical bodies as the philharmonics. And the State held control of the last word: Critical reviews and Russian music histories were fashioned and refashioned according to the current political winds in Moscow.

The command was for revolutionary art with a message, simple to grasp, but also of high quality. But it is never an easy task to create art which is at once accessible to a general audience (the masses) and also profound. Songs were preferred, for their words would be direct and explicit and their melodies could be simple; symphonies were not needed. But pre-Soviet, non-Communist music, glorious models that they were, remained in the memories, ears, and hands of musicians. The treasured examples of the Romantic period were foremost in their training and concert repertory. The monuments of Russian music most admired in Europe and America were just such works: Tchaikovsky's symphonies and ballet scores and the colorful music of Rimsky-Korsakov, Borodin and Mussorgsky.

Lenin's death in 1924 closed the first period of the Bolshevik revolution. Josef Stalin adroitly and ruthlessly assumed the leadership of both Party apparatus and the state, both of which were securely in his hands by 1927. His personal views and taste now commanded the political actions, and also the necessary literary and philosophical trappings, of an ideological system. Stalin's private paranoia also required that his ego be flattered.[21] Like a despot of past eras, his word was feared and his requests fulfilled at once. His mood was gauged daily, his displeasure feared.[22]

The year 1932 began a crucial period. The first Five Year Plan for agricultural improvement was about complete, and collectivization was a reality. The concept of collectivization now extended beyond agricultural and industrial labor to all workers. A Communist Party resolution of April 23, "On the Reconstruction of Literary and Artistic Organizations," signalled the end of the individuality of artists. The 1920s had been a decade of comparative open-mindness in Soviet music. Experiments by Soviet composers and the new music of European composers was commonly heard. Alban Berg attended the Leningrad premiere of *Wozzeck* in 1927; Nikolai Malko conducted the Leningrad Philharmonic in Arnold Schoenberg's *Gurre-Lieder*. Paul Hindemith, Darius Milhaud, Franz Schreker and Alfredo Casella came to the USSR to conduct their own music. Bruno Walter took compositions by the astonishing young composer, Dmitri Shostakovich, back to Berlin. (But in Moscow, Walter was refused permission to conduct Mahler's Fourth Symphony because of the soprano soloist's lines about heaven and angels![23])

In 1932 this exchange of ideas slowed sharply. Regimentation began by the establishment of unions for the various fields of the arts. It was expected that every musician, every writer and other practitioner of the arts would join the appropriate union. There remained but the promulgation of a creed for Soviet art. This appeared the following year, when the First All-Union [national] Congress of Soviet Writers was held. Its dominant personality was Andrei Zhdanov, chief of the Party in Leningrad, the spokesman for public policy. "Art must depict reality in its revolutionary development,"[24] he said. Art must help propel the revolution forward with subjects which presented, according to the medium, a positive, always victorious view of the Soviet people. The art of music, without visual or literary expression (except in vocal music), struggled to make clear this explicit dogma. How does an instrumental form, such as a symphony, "propel the revolution forward?" What is to be made of piano pieces with purely musical reasons for being? Is chamber music, the connoisseur's delight, ever to be of value again? There was no composer who might stand and speak for music as Gorky had for the literary world. The Union of Soviet Composers was established, and the members discussed, argued, and hesitated. All were intimidated by the inherent danger of failing to echo the Party ideologues. Their response was obvious. If the composers wanted their music performed, it must be simple and conspicuously melodic, and must somehow describe, or at least intimate, the happy life (or the supposition of it) in New Russia. Their demoralization, and its tragic effect upon Russian music, was succinctly described by Boris Schwarz: "Advanced composers turned conventional, and conventional composers became commonplace. Young composers endeavored to be inoffensive, and conservatism became a cherished virtue, while musical nationalism experienced a revival. . . ."[25] Multiformity turned into conformity, and bland uniformity followed.

In the season of 1935, London audiences heard the monumental Symphony of Yuri Shaporin, a highly respected Soviet composer of Prokofiev's generation. Gerald Abraham then noted, "There was a curious sense of disillusionment at the discovery that Revolutionary Russia could produce such far from revolutionary music."[26] In the USSR, the new music of the capitalist West was adjudged regressive and decadent. The senior musicologist, Boris Asafiev, wrote about *Wozzeck* in the new journal *Sovietskaya Muzyka* (Soviet Music) in 1934:

Berg's opera, born of tragic consciousness of reality, and grown out of expressionist transformation of living tissue, reflecting the hopelessness of human suffering in the clutches of the monstrously inhuman capitalist culture, reveals the helplessness of the Western-European petty-bourgeois intelligentsia before oncoming fascistization, and demonstrates the crisis not only in the individual consciousness of the Western-European bourgeois composer, but in Western-European musical culture in general.[27]

By 1936, Russia's musical language had retrogressed to that of the nineteenth century. Soviet Russia became a strange paradox: The most radical experiment in government in modern times had promulgated a reactionary style for the arts.

Sovietskaya Muzyka had commenced publication in January, 1933, and was a means for the exchange of ideas between composers and other writers on music, but the views published could not stray very far from the Party dictum. An editorial by N. Tcheliapov in the first issue declared unanimity with Comrade Stalin and the Central Committee of the Party (the *de facto* executive department of the USSR). The journal announced it would be vigilant against deviations from the 1932 decree. "Under the pretense of study of Western-European technique, the rightist musicians are smuggling in the ideological baggage of the rotting bourgeois world, all these 'atonalities,' jazz harmonies, etc. . . . With the same conviction our periodical will fight all kinds of 'leftist' distortions of Marxism-Leninist vulgarization, and pseudo-simplification. . . ."[28]

Nationalism as an artistic device was all but an accident; it should have been irrelevant according to Marxist theory. By the 1930s the Soviet leaders realized that their expectation of world revolution had not occurred. Great Britain, Germany, France and the United States had not collapsed through revolts by the proletariat as Marx's theory had predicted that they would. The USSR planners now turned inward to nurture their Communist movement and to protect it from the rest of the world. The glory of old Russia was resurrected, and the Czarist period, with all its contradictions to Socialist Realism, now stimulated dozens of stories, films, and vocal and instrumental music. Peter the Great, Ivan the Terrible, Duke Alexander (called Nevsky), and less notable names in Russian history became heroes, their actions and means explained according to Socialistic principles. Tyrannical acts of the old regimes were forgiven; they were evidence of the Czars's unswerving devotion to the Motherland.

National identification also encouraged the minority composers, especially from the non-Russian provinces (Ukraine, Uzbek, etc.), to use a simpler, more songful musical language without feeling that they would be called backward by their Moscow peers. Another result was the preservation of much folk music, but the Russification of it damaged its genuineness. Dilution was unavoidable, since all the musical schools in the vast nation used the same music textbooks, usually written by the Moscow pedagogues.[29] The approved folk tune devices, however, became a crutch for unimaginative composers. It may be deduced that to write about a "folk" subject was a safe substitute for more blatant Socialist topics.

Into this intensely politicized musical climate Sergei Prokofiev returned. In 1918, at age twenty-six, he refused to become involved with the revolution and went to America. He had visited the USSR occasionally, and his work had variously received praise or censure. He now held a world reputation in the West as a radical composer and a brilliant pianist. In 1933 he felt compelled to return to his native soil,[30] which now supported a closed society, and came to terms with the Soviet creed. During 1937, he wrote in a notebook: "The time is past when music was written for a handful of aesthetes. Today vast crowds of people have come face to face with serious music and are waiting with eager impatience. Composers: take heed of this, if you repel these crowds they will turn away from you to jazz or vulgar music. . . . The masses want great music, great events, great love, lively dances. They understand far more than some composers think, and they want to deepen their understanding."[31]

His first works were diplomatic; no abstract symphony lacking a clear propaganda statement, but music for highly nationalistic films. He composed the background score for *Lieutenant Kije*, a satire on Czar Nicholas I and his court. This tuneful, comic, even sassy score also exhibited a brilliant orchestration, but neither the music, nor the story of the insignificant lieutenant, held up a heroic image of Socialist life. Prokofiev's music for a subsequent film, *Alexander Nevsky* (1938) displayed more serious goals. It was solemn, arresting, passionate and triumphant. The film dramatized the thirteenth-century defense of Russia by Alexander Nevsky against alien armies. After the successful film premiere, Prokofiev recast the music as a dramatic cantata. It was the time of the national Party meeting. In the February, 1939 issue of *Sovietskaya Muzyka*, he announced, "I am very happy to have completed this work, dedicated to one of the most glorious episodes in the history of the Russian people, on the event of the Eighteenth Party Congress." With this slavish reference—which had not been the inspiration for either Eisenstein's scenario or the composer's music[32]—Prokofiev dutifully tied his professional service to the current political priority. In fact, he had celebrated not the Soviet revolution, but Russia's heroic past.

Prokofiev achieved a lasting place in world music history with many other works that have transcended the exigencies of political art. He died on March 5, 1953, but the announcement was all but overlooked; on the same day Josef Stalin also died. In the April issue of *Sovietskaya Muzyka*, Prokofiev's obituary was published on page 117. An obituary of Stalin occupied page 1.[33]

Shostakovich, born in 1906, was of the next generation, a musician who grew up in the Soviet system and whose outlook in his formative years was daily directed, informed and bounded by this vigorous ideology. His works from first to last received official discussion, approval or censure. At age nineteen, he graduated from the Moscow Conservatory (1925) and astounded the public with his electrifying First Symphony, which is still in the repertory of world orchestras. He was a rapid worker: By 1935 he had composed five symphonies, a piano concerto, several ballets, music for six films, a performance of *Hamlet*,[34] piano pieces, songs, and still more. Much of his music was promptly issued by the state music publishing house. He had also been admonished regarding his use of modernist affectations—certain dissonances, a sarcastic touch, even impudence, which did not fit the conservative style of his elders.[35]

In 1934 his opera, *Lady Macbeth of Mtsensk District*, cast him from the pinnacle of admiration at home and abroad to the terrifying position of one who had offended Stalin. On January 16 the opera was premiered in Leningrad. The story was highly dramatic, violent, and frank in its preoccupation with sexual attraction. The music was vivid, satirical, violent, and, in a bedroom scene, pornographic—or "pornophonic," as one foreign critic termed it.[36] The subject was a well-known story by Nicolai Leskov from nineteenth-century Russian literature: Katerina Ismailova, the lonely, bored wife of a town merchant, murders her husband and father-in-law to take a lover into her home. But it offered no uplifting lessons, except on the self-centered society of Russia's bourgeois past.

The opera was an extraordinary success; it played for two years in the USSR, and quickly reached Europe and the United States. The score was published in 1935 (Op. 29). In January 1936, two years after the premiere, Stalin saw a performance. His taste in opera was for pompous patriotic spectacles with tuneful arias.[37] *Lady Macbeth* revolted him. The opera was withdrawn from the Moscow stage, and a few days later a devastating review appeared, not in a music journal but in *Pravda*, the organ of the Communist Party. The article, "Confusion Instead of Music," was unsigned and carried the tone of an official pronouncement. Every composer in the nation read the judgment as a timely warning.

From the first moment, the listener is shocked by a deliberately dissonant, confused stream of sound. Fragments of melody, embryonic phrases appear—only to disappear again in the din, the grinding, the screaming. . . . The danger of this trend to Soviet music is clear. Leftist distortion in opera stems from the same source as the leftist distortion in painting, poetry, teaching and science. . . . All this is coarse, primitive, and vulgar. The music quacks, grunts, and growls, and suffocates itself, in order to express the amatory scenes as naturalistically as possible. And "love" is smeared all over the opera in the most vulgar manner.[38]

With some prodding from *Pravda*, other journals and newspapers attacked Shostakovich. Artistic groups expressed their solidarity with the official criticism: "Down with Formalist Chaos in Art, Long Live Music for the Millions."[39] Despite the castigation, Shostakovich's other music was not banned, though his name disappeared from many programs. Even *Lady Macbeth* was heard occasionally in opera houses outside the capital, sometimes with its alternative title, *Katerina Ismailova* (as the composer named the revised version in 1963, as Op. 114). He kept his teaching post and his other privileges. But his public status in the USSR was severely injured. His youthful daring and his gift for satire and shock no longer fitted the revolutionary pattern. Many of his colleagues avoided him.

Shostakovich's response was contrite; he accepted the "just criticism," and presented a heroic and profound Fifth Symphony.

His status now rose again. (The later part of his career is discussed in Chapter 9.)

In 1948 a second reign of terror commenced. The cause was again a new opera and the personal effect it had upon Stalin. The composer was Vano Muradeli (1908-1970), a minority or "national-ity" artist from the province of Georgia. He was not a first-rate composer, although he had earned honors for some compositions. The new opera, *The Great Friendship*, was expected to serve as a grand tribute to Stalin, who was also a native of Georgia, and the style was tailored to his taste. The story glorified a Georgian Communist Commissar, Sergo Ordzhonikidze, who had led in the Sovietization of Georgia and supposedly died later of a "heart attack." The opera was given a spectacular premiere simultane-ously in twelve cities on September 28, 1947. There was a lavish production at the Bolshoi Theatre in Moscow.[40]

The patriotic subject of the opera made for success, but that success was short-lived. Three months later, the work was pulled from the stage and the composer humiliated. Once more the musical world was in a state of hysteria. What had gone wrong? What was now the correct "method"? Zhdanov had witnessed a private performance and was angered by both the music and the libretto. It is supposed that Stalin, too, had seen a performance about this time. The attack seemed to be over the music: "It has not a single memorable melody or aria, . . . it is built on continuous dissonances, and ear-splitting combinations of sounds, . . . noise alien to a normal human ear. . . . The composer did not take advantage of the richness of folk melodies [and] song abundant in . . . the nations of the North Caucasus . . ."[41] (Muradeli's own homeland!). This was not the real "fault" of Muradeli's opera: In later years it was learned that Stalin and Ordzhonikidze had been not friends but rivals! When Premier Khrushchev downgraded Stalin in the 1950s, it was insinuated that Ordzhonikidze's death had been suicide, forced by Stalin.[42]

If the judgment of *Lady Macbeth* or *The Great Friendship*, or of any new work, was directly measured by the personal offense it gave to Josef Stalin, then art for the masses had been denigrated into entertainment for one person, of no more broad social value than compositions for an emperor or prince or czar of the past. It is reasonable to suppose that the ruling elite in a Socialist-

Communist state possess a complete and accurate knowledge of the correct behavior for the society. As an individual, the party chairman or the premier (here, of course, joined in one personality), must also be acknowledged as a significant authority. In so vast and evanescent an art as a national music repertoire, it seems untenable to admit that this single personality is a reliable judge of all contributions. To demand a musical style which fits the narrow definition that Stalin desired is an impossibility. The composer of popular songs is not likely to function within the same mental framework as the composer of symphonies. Surely all kinds of music are needed in the large and mixed society of the Soviet Union. But the Party continued to expect, or maintained in theory, that "one mode of [musical] expression . . . one truth—what the government ordained" would suffice for all music, all composers.

This view was not left to supposition. Shortly after the Muradeli scandal, Zhdanov called Moscow composers and musicologists to a meeting. It lasted three days. Zhdanov set the tone: The professionals were encouraged to express their opinions of the new opera and the state of music. There were few who offered words of moderation, though Shostakovich was one who did. Most of the thirty who rose to speak took the opportunity to be a toady to the Commissar while adding spiteful remarks about their colleagues.[43] Poor Muradeli beat his breast but shifted the blame onto his years spent at the Moscow Conservatory: When he was a youth he had sung folk songs, while his brother strummed the mandolin; higher education had spoiled his natural expression. He also complained that his First Symphony had pleased Leningrad factory workers, but the critics in the papers and journals called the piece poor and unoriginal. "To whom was I to listen? Naturally to the [government] press.[44] Shostakovich had once suffered the same contradiction between factory workers—the people!—and professionals over his early ballet, *The Nose* (1929).[45]

It became clear that Muradeli's opera was only a side issue of the meeting Zhdanov had called. It was time to draw the cords tighter. The lesson of 1936 had been forgotten; the Composers Union had not exercised due care in guiding its members.[46] The Commissar listened and indicated that he would carry their views back to the Central Committee. Zhdanov added, ominously, "The creative workers must also take account of the results of this discussion.[47]

The scathing document which was issued soon afterward by the Committee revealed a witch hunt for followers of "modernist tendencies." This criticism extended to the Big Four: Prokofiev, Shostakovich, Khatchaturian and the distinguished symphonist Nikolai Miaskovsky, all musicians of world renown.

The Composers Union could not maintain its status in world music without continuing activity from the censured composers. The composers knew they could not fight the regime. Accommodation shortly came about, the erring composers offering apologies and pledging to write in less complex musical language, with more vocal works that would unmistakably proclaim Soviet topics. Stalin Prizes were the rewards for good behavior. One went to Prokofiev for his cantata, *On Guard for Peace*, and another to Shostakovich for his oratorio, *Song of the Forests*.[48] Ten years later a different Central Committee recanted some of the unjust accusations, but the personal and national scars remained.[49]

In 1957, a quarter of a century after the 1932 resolution, a second national policy for music was promulgated. In 1956 the Twentieth Party Congress had met. The death of Stalin in 1953 at once ignited a power struggle, as Malenkov, Bulganin, and finally Khrushchev rose to ultimate control. The Party meeting set out a calculated program to discredit Stalin and the "cult of personality." Everything and everybody associated with the past regime waited to see how they would be ranked in the change of administration.

For musicians, the mandatory response was to convene a Second All-Union Composers Congress. Preceding the conference *Sovietskaya Muzyka* opened its pages for discussion, and a stream of articles exposed diverging and uncertain views in the musical world. Their concerns were the same anxieties that unsettled the rest of Soviet intellectuals. The keynote address was delivered by Tikhon Khrennikov, a composer who had been elected secretary of the Composers Union by the First Congress in 1948. Khrennikov's ardent promotion of the status of music had won him the respect of the composers, while his conservative taste and his ridicule of "formalism" ("modernism") made him disliked by many among the younger generation. Through the years, with each shift in Party direction he adroitly leaned with the current and held his powerful position through the Sixth Composers Congress in 1979 at the age of sixty-six. In 1957 his speech, unlike the hard line of 1948, was moderate; it was his job at this hour to secure Socialist Realism as the national aesthetic creed and to shield it from the taint of Stalinism. His address included a statistical report on new Soviet works: It was a record of growth, but not of quality. Since 1948, 120 operas had been written, yet fewer than half had been accepted for the stage. Of these, only six had won sufficient admiration to be performed at more than one theater. (One of these was Prokofiev's *War and Peace*, but this was not strictly a work composed since 1948.)[50]

The Party spokesman in 1948 had been Zhdanov, who had died six months later. In 1957 the spokesman was Dmitri Shepilov, once editor of *Pravda* and recently the foreign minister for a few months. His was not the authoritative, nor fearful, voice of Zhdanov. His address was routinely titled, "To Create for the Welfare and the Happiness of the People." Socialist Realism was to be the guiding line, yet he held out some hope to the liberal minded by suggesting that the rigid rules of "arithmetic and the apothecary" were "not suitable for works of art." "The Leninist style of guidance requires a high adherence to principle, and essential flexibility, and patient care when it deals with cultural workers who honestly and unselfishly fulfill their patriotic duty and essential sensitivity; such a style precludes high-handed commands and petty talent tutelage."[51] The future, or the immediate future, of Soviet music was clear. Socialist Realism would be sustained as the aesthetic guideline, but the "tutelage" might allow some flexibility.

In his turn Khrushchev also put his personal dictum on Soviet music. Like other radicals in politics, he was a reactionary in music. He offered written essays and spoken remarks, the latter sometimes too gross to be seen in print.[52] Ties with the West were reformed, and some artists from the 1920s and 1930s, as well as foreigners, who had been banned were rehabilitated. Shostakovich, the victim of past censures, was singled out for public honors. His earnest response was his Eleventh Symphony, subtitled "The Year 1905," a large programmatic work memorializing the first people's revolution. Schwarz observed that despite "the tendency among Western critics to sneer at this timely work . . . the '1905' Symphony represents to the Soviet people the fulfilment of the dream of a great Socialist art."[53] It has survived the occasion of its composition.

Soviet music has never achieved, and perhaps could never

achieve, a national repertoire that was consistently "revolutionary."
A total control of all music is surely an impossibility. Yet we should
recall that during the Chinese Cultural Revolution (1966-1976),
such control apparently occurred to the extent that only eight
works alone, in one form or another, were heard in public for
nearly ten years! (See Chapter 5.) No such drastic censorship or
control ever existed in the USSR. The prerevolutionary music
survived in great quantities. The beloved works of Tchaikovsky—
most of them—and other staples of Russian Romanticism were
studied, practiced, performed, recorded and listened to with
continuing affection. Conservatory students practiced the B-flat
minor concerto of Tchaikovsky, not to mention Beethoven
sonatas. Singers learned Russian operas and others from Italy,
France and Germany. Philharmonics played Haydn, Mozart and
Beethoven.

There were conspicuous omissions. Church music, both Russian
Orthodox and Roman Catholic, and Protestant repertoires received
rare hearings. In the "liberal" 1970s Handel's *Messiah*, Beethoven's
Missa Solemnis, and some liturgical pieces of Tchaikovsky and
Rachmaninov were sung. Rimsky-Korsakov's *Russian Easter Overture*, banished for decades, was programmed under its old name,
Bright Holiday, the Russian name for Easter. But in 1974 Schwarz
found a Melodiya recording of Tchaikovsky's *Overture 1812* in
which the quotation of the old czarist hymn, *God Save the People*,
was excised and a Russian tune which happened to fit the harmonic
scheme was substituted![54] It is incredible that sixty years after the
revolution, the Soviet hierarchy was still nervous about a public
reference to the church! It is improbable that expatriate
Stravinsky's *Symphony of Psalms* (with a Latin text) was sung in
the USSR in the 1930s when it was new, but Shostakovich's composition pupils studied it at that time. Shostakovich stressed fluency
in score reading by means of playing four-hand piano arrangements, often of a Haydn or Mozart symphony. When there was no
arrangement of an instructive score, he made one. On one
occasion, the class read through the *Symphony of Psalms*.[55]

Lazar Gosman, who played first violin for more than twenty
years in the Leningrad Philharmonic, knew Handel's *Messiah* only
from a foreign recording, and had never participated in a performance until he emigrated to St. Louis in 1977.[56] When Robert Shaw

took his famous Chorale on a 1962 tour of the USSR, his was the first Western group to receive permission to sing a religious work, Bach's B minor Mass.[57]

Domestic policy in the arts also served as a tool for foreign policy when the Kremlin decreed. In July 1972 the biennial meeting of the International Society for Music Education met in Tunis, Tunisia. Composer Dmitry Kabalevsky, Honorary President of ISME, presented a paper entitled "The Glinka Tradition."[58] This was an attempt to show the outside world that Russia—represented by Russian composers—was always sympathetic toward the cultures of the rest of the globe. The evidence began with the father of Russian music. Glinka was found to have "assimilated the music of foreign nations" by writing his two Spanish overtures. (He had lived in Spain for two years in the 1840s.) Name then followed name as evidence of a "splendid international musical tradition." The examples included "The Dance of the Persian Women" in Mussorgsky's *Khovanshina*, Rimsky-Korsakov's *Sheherazade*, his Capriccio Espagnol, the "Polish opera," *Pan Voyevoda*, and others. Glazunov's *Finnish Fantasia* and *Karelian Legend* were also cited. Vasilenko's cycle of oriental scores, as his *Hindu Suite*, "opened a new, post-revolutionary period in the history of Russian and multinational Soviet music." This was not a passing trend, Kabalevsky insisted, as witness Balasanyan's Indian ballet, *Sakuntala*, which won a Nehru Prize in 1963, and Vladimir Fere's symphonic and vocal works on Vietnamese songs. To demonstrate that the USSR shared the concerns of the new African states, there were three pieces: *Africa Fights On*, a symphonic poem by Vasif Adigezalov, an Azerbaijan composer; *African Sketches* by the Lithuanian Julius Juzeliūnas; and *Mahagoni*, an oratorio by the Latvian Marger Zarins on the subject of Patrice Lumumba's struggle for the liberation of the Congo. The text for Zarins's oratorio came from Langston Hughes and a Latvian poet, A. Kruklis. A tape recording heard after the talk revealed rhythmic influences from Afro-American folksongs.

In 1976 at the Bolshoi Opera I witnessed a strong performance of Puccini's *Tosca* (with an unexpected nonrealistic stage set). Here is a libretto loaded with antiestablishment commentary: the terrorist tactics of unscrupulous police, the capture and execution of a "freedom fighter" and the torture of his friend, not to mention other violence. Where is the positive Socialist message here? It is not here, and *Tosca* is neither Socialist Realism nor from the ever-acceptable Russian school. But it is effective operatic art. The prestigious company was permitted to stage it and the public was permitted to buy tickets to see it. Subversive messages in *Tosca* (or the B Minor Mass) were overlooked, or considered not dangerous, or perhaps the censor perceived but trivial consequences to listening to this music.

During the same period I also saw the Bolshoi Ballet dance *Spartacus* to a thoroughly Romantic score by Khatchaturian. The music might have been written a hundred years earlier, but for a few elements. The story is not intended to glorify the modern Socialist state either. It is the tragic tale of a Grecian slave who led a rebellion for freedom; this presumably justified the effort of the artists who conceived and performed the ballet. But such a scenario about individual freedom and sacrifice would earn equal approbation in a Western democracy and be interpreted as an historic antecedent for democracy and civil rights, without the need of a Marxist interpretation. *Tosca* and *Spartacus* are familiar works in the USSR, and the spectator may well read into the performances more than the surface meanings: *Tosca* and *Spartacus* are allegories of an underground campaign for freedom! Veiled attacks on the Communist Party, the KGB, and the tyranny of a rigid clique! We may not assume that anything of the sort happened in these Bolshoi productions, nor that the singers or dancers or conductors were sending a code. Artists enjoy these works; the flawless execution of the music (or dance) is the dominant objective.

In the Soviet system, however, all artists are employees of the state, and prompt, unconditional response to state directives is obligatory. It is impossible to remain untrained in Party doctrine. Indoctrination begins in early childhood and continues through the school years. The curriculum of the national conservatories (and other collegiate institutions) includes required classes in Communist theory and history of the Party. Lazar Gosman, the émigré violinist mentioned earlier, recalled for me that at the Moscow Conservatory the students might cut a music class or even their private lessons without a fuss, but to miss a political class at once brought an inquiry; absences there could bring dismissal from the school. The students read the works of Marx, Engels, Lenin, and

Stalin so often that some passages were virtually memorized. The students hated these classes and shared shortcuts for memorization of the assignments.[59] Some of these conservatory graduates—Rostropovich was in Gosman's class—struggled under the politicization of their work for years and finally found an opportunity to leave. It is reported that since 1970 about 36,000 Russians have emigrated to the United States.[60] Enough emigrant musicians came to form the Soviet Émigré Orchestra in 1979, and Gosman became the leader. (A few Americans were engaged to complete the necessary instrumental balance.) Maxim Shostakovich and Dmitri Shostakovich II, the composer's son and grandson, defected while on a concert tour in West Germany in 1981. In New York Maxim declared, "There is no such thing in the West as a composition that is not allowed—and that is wonderful." Such prominent artists as these and others—Baryshnikov, Kondrashin, Barshai—while in the USSR lived in a pampered world. That was not enough.

In 1972 Seiji Ozawa led the San Francisco Symphony in packed concerts in Moscow. A Soviet music critic complained at the "showoff" manner in the performances of Soviet and Russian works. (Andre Watts played Tchaikovsky's First Piano Concerto.) But the critic admitted that the extraordinary public response to the American concerts was due to "their joyous, holiday atmosphere," while Soviet concerts, he confessed, "are often grey and dull."[61] The reason may be that in the USSR the conductor and the musicians routinely perform works they do not want to play. The emphasis in programming is always on national compositions; artistic worth or appropriateness fall into a second criterion.[62] The ideological imperative spoils the primary matter of enjoying the concert.

Still, music has often been successful as propaganda in the USSR. In the field of education, it was no small accomplishment to inculcate the same principles in so gigantic an educational system for so long, and to promulgate standards for composing music aimed at mass inspiration and edification rather than the nineteenth- and twentieth-century concept of art for art's sake. For the first time in history, a single consciousness enveloped a national musical life. It is futile to conjecture that positive differences would have resulted (if we could agree on "positive differences") had any or all of the Soviet composers been free to create as Western artists do (though there are boundaries in any art). It is foolish to suggest that their total work would have been "better." It is unarguable that Shostakovich did not wish to work outside Russia.[63] Neither did Prokofiev, who had the freedom to do so again and again. And these two artistic minds tower above the rest. Among all the defections to the West, it is not composers who fled in droves, but performers. What this may say about the creative mind as opposed to the re-creative mind I cannot determine. In the field of literature, however, it has been writers noticeably (not actors, for comparison) who cut their ties with the homeland and departed. To be sure, the writer (and the actor) must learn a new language to communicate his art in a new land. The Soviet composer, conservative, even old fashioned in style, speaks a language understood in the West. With or without the propaganda, it functions on both sides of the Iron Curtain.

Far across another boundary of the USSR the Communist movement swept into power in China in 1949 and borrowed for a time some of the intense experience of the Soviets. After several years the Chinese also turned inward to their indigenous knowledge in order to make the alien ideology survive. But the Chinese had far older views of government and the place of the arts than the Russians, and a longer line of tyrants to exorcise. Yet a similar series of crises over the control of music appeared. Were these coincidences of Marxism, world conditions, or art?[64]

NOTES

1. Rose Lee, "D. Szostakovitch", in *The New York Times*, December 20, 1931; cited in Boris Schwarz, *Music and Musical Life in Soviet Russia, Enlarged Edition, 1917-1981*, (Bloomington: Indiana University Press, 1983), p. 130.

2. A declaration of his views on music (1963), translated in Nicolas Slonimsky, *Music Since 1900*, (New York: Charles Scribner's Sons, 1971), fourth edition, p. 1379.

3. Lee Baxandall and Stefan Morawski, eds., *Marx/Engels on Literature and Art* (New York: International General, 1974), p. 60.

4. Plato, *The Republic*, tr. by Paul Shorey (Cambridge: Loeb Classical Library. Harvard University Press, 1930), vol. I, pp. 174-75, 247, 292-93.

See also Introduction, xiv, n. "C", and Plato's remarks on the selection of proper harp songs for youth in *Protagoras*, tr. by R.M. Lamb (Cambridge: Loeb Classical Library. Harvard University Press, 1924), pp. 143, 145.

5. Ch'u Chai and Winberg Chai, eds., *Li Chi* [The Book of Rites], tr. by James Legge [1872] (New Hyde Park, N.Y.: University Books, 1967), vol. II, pp. 93-94. This theme is discussed further in Chapter 5.

6. Rovert van Gulik, *The Lore of the Chinese Lute* (Rutland, Vt. and Tokyo: Charles E. Tuttle, 1969), p. 27. Presumably Gulik is avowing the ideal; there was certainly music among the people that was produced for pure entertainment, but the Confucian "ideal" is no less similar to the modern Socialist ideal.

7. Lenin viewed literature as a superior means of molding thought, more useful than any of the other arts, but he wanted to see the visual arts used promptly in public education with huge posters and monuments of revolutionary heroes, according to Anatoly Lunacharsky. V. I. Lenin, *On Literature and Art* (Moscow: Progress Publishers, 1967), p. 257.

8. Quoted by Clara Zetkin, "My Recollections of Lenin" in ibid., p. 253. Compare the views of Mao Zedong in his seminal "Talks at the Yenan Forum", cited below.

9. Ibid., pp. 260-61. In 1913 Lenin wrote an article, "The Development of Workers' Choirs in Germany," praising the effectiveness of their songs as propaganda both in the quality and the message against "wage-slavery" in the great cities. Ibid., pp. 78-79.

10. Compare Baxandall, *Marx/Engels on Literature and Art*, Introduction, pp. 3-47, esp. 5-8. Note also p. 44 on the official preference for a Romantic style in music in the USSR (and also in the Westernized Chinese music): "In a broad sense, Marx and Engels were cradled by Romanticism." They read the Romantic authors, who were their contemporaries.

11. Ibid., p. 47.

12. Lunacharsky, in Lenin, *On Literature*, p. 256.

13. Quoted by Maxim Gorky in Lenin, *On Literature*, p. 247. See also Lunacharsky, ibid., pp. 259-60; Krupskaya (Lenin's wife), ibid., p. 235; Ulyanov (his brother), ibid., pp. 231-33; Baxandall, *Marx/Engels*, p. 154, and Marx's remarks on pp. 51, 82.

14. Boris Schwarz, *Musical Life*, p. 110. The term *Socialist Realism*, like many Soviet expressions, was adopted and adapted by the Chinese Communists. During the emotionalism of the Cultural Revolution in the People's Republic of China, the aim of art (particularly on the stage) was to be "a combination of revolutionary realism and revolutionary romanticism." Hua-Yuan Li Mowry, *Yang-Pan Hsi/New Theatre in China* (Berkeley: Center for Chinese Studies. University of California, 1973), p. 46.

15. Lunacharsky in Lenin, *On Literature*, pp. 259-60.

16. Baxandall, *Marx/Engels*, pp. 59-60.

17. Ibid., pp. 42, 136-37 (Marx, from "Introduction to the Critique of Political Economy").

18. "The Achievements and Difficulties of the Soviet Government," in V. I. Lenin, *On Culture and Cultural Revolution* (Moscow: Progress Publishers, 1966), pp. 64-65.

19. Ibid., pp. 121-22.

20. Ibid., p. 148.

21. See Gustav Bychowski, "Joseph V. Stalin: Paranoia and Dictatorship" in Benjamin B. Wolman, ed., *The Psychoanalytic Interpretation of History* (New York: Basic Books, 1971), pp. 125-33.

22. See Roy A. Medvedev, *Let History Judge*, tr. by Colleen Taylor (New York: Alfred A. Knopf, 1971); also Anton Antonov-Ovseyenko, *The Time of Stalin: Portrait of Tyranny*, tr. by George Saunders (New York: Harper & Row, 1981). For the recollections of a Bolshoi singer, see Galina Vishnevskaya, *Galina: A Russian Story* (San Diego: Harcourt, Brace, Jovanovich, 1984), pp. 93-100.

23. Schwarz, *Musical Life*, pp. 44-45.

24. Andrei Zhdanov, *Essays on Literature, Philosophy and Music* (New York: International Publisher, 1950), pp. 7-15.

25. Schwarz, *Musical Life*, pp. 115, 110; see also pp. 205-8 and 333.

26. Gerald Abraham, *Eight Soviet Composers* (Westport, Ct.: Greenwood Press, 1970. Reprint of 1943 edition), p. 90.

27. Slonimsky, *Music Since 1900*, 4th ed., p. 425.

28. Ibid., p. 358.

29. Schwarz, *Musical Life*, pp. 260, 381.

30. Sergei Prokofiev, *Materials, Articles, Interviews* (Moscow: Progress Publishers, 1978. English edition), p. 78.

31. Ibid, p. 42 and also 36.

32. Ibid., pp. 34-36. See also Jay Leyda, *Eisenstein: Three Films* (New York: Harper & Row, 1974), pp. 7, 89-90, 143.

33. Schwarz, *Musical Life*, p. 271. See also Vishnevskaya, *Galina*, p. 100.

34. The struggle of Shakespeare's young intellectual also appealed to Prokofiev, who wrote music for a production. See his remarks in Prokofiev, *Materials*, pp. 33-34. Shostakovich composed music for *Hamlet* a second time for a film version in 1964.

35. Schwarz, *Musical Life*, p. 80 (by Shostakovich's teacher, Maximilian Steinberg), for the ballet, *The Nose* (1930), ibid., pp. 70-71; see also Dmitri and Ludmilla Sollertinsky, *Pages from the Life of Dmitri Shostakovich*, tr. by Graham Hobbs and Charles Midgley (New York: Harcourt, Brace, Jovanovich, 1980), p. 53 (on *The Nose*). Another censured ballet, *The*

Age of Gold, was a prize winner on the Leningrad stage; it was not performed in Moscow until 1981, in commemoration of the deceased composer's 75th birthday. Reported in *Soviet Life*, March, 1982, p. 39.

36. Schwarz, *Musical Life*, pp. 119-26; Slonimsky, *Music Since 1900*, 4th ed., pp. 579-80. Shostakovich's analysis of the complex heroine (perhaps his apologia) is found in Sollertinsky, *Pages from the Life*, pp. 66-67; and *Modern Music*, XII:1 (November-December) 1942, pp. 23-25. For a detailed description of the opera by a Soviet writer, see Ivan Martynov, *Dmitri Shostakovich: The Man and His Work*, tr. by T. Guralsky (New York: Greenwood Press, 1969. Reprint of 1947 edition), pp. 37-47.

37. Schwarz, *Musical Life*, p. 122.

38. Excerpts in translation are in Slonimsky, *Music Since 1900*, 4th ed., pp. 618-19.

39. Nicolas Slonimsky, "Dmitri Dmitrievitch Shostakovitch," in *The Musical Quarterly*, XXVIII:4 (October) 1942, pp. 415-21.

40. Schwarz, *Musical Life*, p. 213. Slonimsky, *Music Since 1900*, 4th ed., pp. 1358-60.

41. Slonimsky, *Music Since 1900*, 4th ed., p. 1359.

42. Medvedev, *Let History Judge*, pp. 193-96.

43. Alexander Werth, *A Musical Uproar in Moscow* (Westport, Ct.: Greenwood Press, 1973. Reprint of the 1949 edition), pp. 47-86, contains excerpts of Zhdanov's speech and verbatim remarks from the participants. Slonimsky, *Music Since 1900*, 4th ed., pp. 1362-69, contains Zhdanov's complete speech.

44. Ibid., p. 52.

45. Sollertinsky, *Pages from the Life*, p. 53.

46. The appropriate method for a composer was to play a piano version of his work to a committee of the Composers Union. If the collective judgment was encouraging, the composer made the improvements suggested and proceeded to orchestrating his work, if needed. See Stanley D. Krebs, *Soviet Composers and the Development of Soviet Music* (New York: W. W. Norton & Co., 1970), p. 190, n. 3.

47. Werth, *Musical Uproar*, p. 86. For Muradeli's formal apology, see Slonimsky. *Music Since 1900*, 4th ed., pp. 1369-70.

48. Schwarz, *Musical Life*, p. 228. After Stalin these awards for major works were renamed State Prizes.

49. Slonimsky, *Music Since 1900*, pp. 1376-77.

50. Schwarz, *Musical Life*, pp. 300-301.

51. *Current Digest of the Soviet Press*, IX:13, pp. 15f.; and IX:14, pp. 11-13.

52. Ibid., IX:30, pp. 3-10. For Schwarz's summation of the "thaw," see *Musical Life*, pp. 307-10.

53. Schwarz, *Musical Life*, p. 310.

54. Ibid., p. 594. Visiting conductor Igor Markevitch was given permission to conduct Haydn's *Creation* on condition that the word God be eliminated from the text! Vishnevskaya, *Galina*, p. 180.

55. Sollertinsky, *Pages from the Life*, p. 92. The Soviets' attachment to some Western customs seems beyond the hand of the censor. At Shostakovich's burial (August 14, 1975) the Red Army Band played music not by the composer himself, nor another Russian, but Schubert's *Unfinished Symphony* and Chopin's *Funeral March*, well-worn Western musical sentiments for such an occasion. See Schwarz, *Musical Life*, p. 574. For the *Pravda* obituary, see *Current Digest of the Soviet Press*, XXVII:32 (September) 1975, pp. 21-22.

56. Personal conversation, 1982.

57. RCA Victor recording, No. LSC-2676 (jacket notes), 1963.

58. In Tunis it was announced that Kabalevsky was ill in the USSR and his paper was read by another delegate. My quotations are from the English transcript which I secured at the conference.

59. Shostakovich remembered an all-embracing examination on Marxism-Leninism which his friend Ivan Sollertinsky (a musicologist) faced before he could begin graduate study in 1926. Sollertinsky, *Pages from the Life*, p. 43.

60. *Newsweek*, December 8, 1980, p. 64.

61. Schwarz, *Musical Life*, p. 643.

62. Ibid., p. 530-31.

63. See Maxim Shostakovich's remarks (1981) in Schwarz, p. 645.

64. There have been curious lapses in the militant control of the Soviet media. Large portions of music fill the daily radio and television programs, and the selection is presumably a component in official communications of the day. On June 22, 1941 Hitler abruptly declared war on his ally, the USSR. Aerial attacks began. The Soviet people were shocked at the treachery. Writer Ilya Ehrenburg, like millions of citizens, sat by his radio all day, waiting for more information about the catastrophe. "But Moscow was broadcasting gay, lighthearted songs which in no way corresponded to the mood of the people. No speeches, no articles had been prepared: they were playing songs." *Memoirs 1921-1941* (New York: Grosset and Dunlap, 1966), pp. 507-8.

In February, 1984 the news of President Yuri Andropov's death was withheld by the Kremlin until the following day. But an American correspondent, Dusko Doder, filed a story in which he reported sudden changes in television and radio programming and unusual late-night activity in the defense ministries and KGB offices. Television had switched from jazz to classical music at 8:15 p.m. and the radio stations followed suit three hours later. To the alert reporter these signs indicated that "the country was being placed on an emergency footing." These clues were not recognized by the American Embassy until the next day. Meanwhile Doder's story with its hint of Andropov's demise appeared in the *Washington Post* several hours before the official announcement came from Moscow. (*International Herald Tribune*, February 14, 1984. *Washington Post* Service.) Similar clues were reported by Reuters News Services on November 11, 1984 when the death of Defense Minister Dmitri Ustinov was rumored. The anchormen on Soviet television wore black, and solemn music replaced the scheduled festive songs for Police Day. But no information about Ustinov was released.

CHAPTER 5

More Totalitarian Music: Confucius, Marx and Mao Zedong

The bourgeoisie always shut out proletarian literature and art, however great their artistic merit. The proletariat must similarly distinguish among the literary and art works of past ages and determine its attitude towards [such works]. . . . The more reactionary their content and the higher their artistic quality, the more poisonous they are to the people, and the more necessary it is to reject them.

Mao Zedong (Mao Tse-Tung), *Talks at the Yenan Forum*[1]

[When the correct, harmonious music is sounded] then plants and trees will grow luxuriantly; curling sprouts and buds will expand; the feathered and winged tribes will be active; horns and antlers will grow, insect will come to light and revive; birds will breed and brood; the hairy tribes will mate and bring forth; the mammalia will have no abortions, and no eggs will be broken or addled—and all will have to be ascribed to the power of music.

Li Chi (The Book of Rites)[2]

An army without culture is a dull-witted army and a dull-witted army cannot defeat the enemy.

Mao Zedong[3]

The Soviet experience and world Communist leadership in the 1920s became the model and mentor for China's Communist move-

A substantial part of this chapter originally appeared in *Ethnomusicology*, XVII:1 (January, 1983), pp. 1-28, and is used by permission of the Society for Ethnomusicology.

ment. The two nations are bound together in "indestructible friendship"; so reads the Preamble to the first Constitution of the People's Republic of China in 1954.[4] The crises of the formative years of both Soviet Russia and the People's Republic of China (hereafter PRC) are curiously similar. First came the closing of theaters and the censorship of negative works. Then followed increasing control of educational institutions, including the conservatories. Under both regimes, artists were pressured to form great national congresses to promulgate sanctioned cultural goals and policy. Particularly striking to review is the initiation of a devastating purge a generation after the founding of each government, wrenching the cultural life of the country. In the USSR this took place in 1946-1948, and in the PRC it occurred as the now discredited Cultural Revolution of 1966-1976. Also parallel are ideological experiments in the form of a "thaw" in artistic strictures—and an about-face directive which soon followed: in the USSR, the Resolution of 1932, and in the PRC, "The Hundred Flowers Campaign" of 1956.[5] In both instances, the flood of artistic multiformity was swiftly compressed into one stream of uniformity.

And there are parallel crises which became *causes célèbres*: the condemnations of Shostakovich's opera, *Lady Macbeth of Mtsensk District* in 1936, and Wu Han's opera (that is, the libretto, for the music was traditional), *Hai Jui Dismissed from Office*, in 1965.[6] In later years, when the authority of Stalin and of Mao had receded, the ban on each work was lifted. And Mao himself observed a parallel in the two nations' revolutionary histories in his essay, "On the People's Democratic Dictatorship," written in commemoration of the twenty-eighth anniversary of the founding of the Chinese Communist Party, June 30, 1949.[7]

The most serious artistic problem in China was the reeducation of the artists and concomitantly of their public—a new public for most of these artists. Mao, whose first public writings appeared in 1917,[8] readied his followers for over twenty years before winning complete control of the country in October 1949. But China was even less the nation that Marx had envisioned as the inevitable setting for socialist revolution than Russia had been. Marx, however, and later Lenin, had noted the enormous potential for social change in the crowded populations of Asia.[9] Like Lenin, Mao early faced stubborn opposition from composers and writers and their preference for the entrenched repertory. In China, there were the enormously popular genres of opera with their stories of court life, ghosts and magical beings, Buddhist and Confucian moralities, sentimental romances, and the accepted depiction of the common people as servants or fools.

Lenin had scarcely begun his national tenure before he died in 1922. Mao was Party Chairman for forty-one years. He was a fluent, trenchant and instructive writer, and he often called up the thoughts of the revolutionary fathers. In Mao's major essay, "On New Democracy" (1940), he cited Marx, Lenin and Stalin a total of nine times—and also Sun Yat-sen, father of the Chinese Republic of 1911.[10] In turn, his writings became dogma for his followers. The five volumes of his *Selected Works*, that is, his writings from 1926-1957, in the official English edition (published in Beijing (Peking) 1961-1977), number nearly twenty-one hundred pages. He also left a volume of poetry.[11] It is from these translations that some of his most significant statements are quoted here.

A basic view of the status of the arts in "New China" is found in his major policy statement of 1940, "On New Democracy," written for the premier issue of a magazine entitled *Chinese Culture*. In it we find his confirmation of the value of the past. In a section titled, "We Want to Build a New China," he wrote: "The new society and new state will have not only a new politics and a new economy but a new culture."[12] In another section he wrote: "The new political force of the proletariat and the Communist Party entered the Chinese political arena, and as a result, the new cultural force . . . has made great strides in . . . the social sciences and arts and letters, . . . including the theater, the cinema, music, sculpture and painting."[13] From the section entitled "A National, Scientific and Mass Culture": "To nourish her own culture China needs to assimilate a good deal of foreign progressive culture, not enough of which was done in the past. We should assimilate whatever is useful to us today not only from present-day socialist and new-democratic cultures but also from the earlier cultures of other nations, for example, from the various capitalist countries in the Age of Enlightenment. . . . Similarly, in applying Marxism to China, Chinese communists must fully and properly integrate the universal truth of Marxism with the concrete practice of the Chinese Revolution. . . .

Chinese culture should also have its own form . . . national in form and new democratic [i.e., socialist] in content."[14] Here he affirmed Stalin's slogan of Socialist Realism. In one of Mao's distinctions between the Russian model and his own, however, he declared that Chinese art, music and literature must edify three groups: not only the workers, but also the peasants and the army.

Mao awarded status to artistic effort by saying: "Revolutionary culture is a powerful revolutionary weapon for the broad masses of the people. It prepares the ground ideologically before the revolution comes and is an important, indeed, essential fighting front in the general revolutionary front during the revolution. . . ."[15]

In 1937, at the central base of the Communist Party and army in Yan'an (Yenan), an academy for the arts was established and named for the late revolutionary author Lu Xun (Lu Hsun). The school's purpose was the "rectification of people in the arts."[16] He called a conference of literary and art workers to expound the objectives of Communist art and suggested methods for achieving them. In this context such workers included musicians. His two speeches (at the commencement and the close of the three-week conference) were published as "Talks at the Yenan Forum on Literature and Art." They became the oracle for artistic "workers" in the PRC virtually to the present day, amended versions appearing as major shifts in party policy arose.[17]

Mao's first point was (consciously or not, one of the eight Buddhist principles): Adopt the right attitude. He scolded some artists for not having grasped or accepted clearly basic Marxist concepts. He chided his listeners for being unacquainted with the people or with the variety of audience levels before them. "The cadres, party workers of all types, fighters in the army, workers in the factories, and peasants in the villages, all want to read books and newspapers once they become literate, and those who are illiterate want to see plays and operas, look at drawings and paintings, sing songs, and hear music."[18] Here Mao introduced a view in a discussion of revolutionary art not noted in Marx or Lenin: The audience's needs must be recognized.

The first question to be asked, he said, is: "Literature and art for whom? . . . This problem was solved long ago by Marxists, especially Lenin. As far back as 1905, Lenin pointed out emphatically that our literature and art should 'serve . . . the millions and tens of millions of working people."[19] Mao's reference is Lenin's article on "Party Organization and Party Literature." Lenin also wrote: "It will be a free literature, because it will serve not some satiated heroine, not the bored 'upper ten thousand' suffering from fatty degeneration, but the millions and tens of millions of working people—the flower of the country, its strength and future. . . ."[20]

Mao was concerned that there was so much popular taste for the operas of old China—a taste that has in fact outlived him.[21] Despite this, he restated his argument that the past still had much to offer and would provide necessary models of excellence. "We should take over the rich legacy and the good traditions in literature and art that have been handed down from the past ages in China and foreign countries, but the aim must still be to serve the masses of the people.[22] It makes a difference whether or not we have such examples, the difference between crudeness and refinement, between roughness and polish, between a low and a high level, and between slower and faster work."[23]

Mao also acknowledged a transcendent function of the arts:

Although man's social life is the only source of literature and art and is incomparably livelier and richer in content, the people are not satisfied with life alone and demand literature and art as well. Why? Because, while both are beautiful, life as reflected in works of literature and art can and ought to be on a higher plane, more intense, more concentrated, more typical, nearer the ideal, and therefore more universal than actual everyday life. [The Romantic creed of the nineteenth century is echoed in that statement.[24]] Revolutionary literature and art should create a variety of characters out of real life and help the masses propel history forward.[25]

Mao also discussed the dilemma in raising the cultural standards of the masses while creating art that they could immediately understand. "Popular works are simple, and plainer, and therefore more readily accepted by the broad masses of people today. Works of a higher quality, being more polished, are more difficult to produce and in general do not circulate so easily and quickly among the masses at present. It is possible to popularize some works of higher quality even now. [That is, during the War of Resistance against Japan.[26]] . . . Our specialists in music should pay attention to the songs of the masses. . . ."[27] He urged that the gifted writers and artists "must go among the masses for a long period of time, unreservedly and wholeheartedly, go into the heat of the struggle . . . to observe, experience, study and analyze all the different kinds of people, all the classes . . . the raw materials of literature and art. Only then can they proceed to creative work. . . ."[28] Presumably Mao was recommending that the composers and performers learn from folk and other popular forms, village operas, song and dance shows—*yangge* (*yangko*, see below), types that his professional audience would have disdained.

In one passage Mao, as the pragmatic Marxist, identified two criteria for judging art, the political and the artistic. He maintained that all classes in all times have such criteria:

All classes in all class societies invariably put the political criterion first and the artistic criterion second. The bourgeoisie always shut out proletarian literature and art, however great their artistic merit. The proletariat must similarly distinguish among the literary and art works of past ages and determine its attitude towards them only after examining their attitude to the people and whether or not the art had any progressive significance historically. . . . The more reactionary their content and the higher their artistic quality, the more poisonous they are to the people, and the more necessary it is to reject them.[29] . . . Works of art which lack artistic quality have no force, however progressive they are politically. Therefore, we oppose both the tendency to produce works of art with a wrong political viewpoint and the tendency towards the 'poster and slogan style,' which is correct in political viewpoint but lacking in artistic power.[30]

He ridiculed the zealots who urged artists to substitute Marxist dogma for artistic method.[31]

During the Cultural Revolution the "Talks" were one of the six works to be studied "over and over again."[32] Bonnie S. McDougall made a meticulous comparison between the first editions published and the 1953 and 1966 revised (Chinese language) versions.[33] A notable difference in emphasis, though not in substance, was Mao's position toward accepting prerevolutionary artistic models. In 1943 he spoke of the works of "dead people and foreigners," advising that they were to be used with discrimination. In the later versions they became "the ancients and foreigners" whose works are instructive. Writers were urged "to take over all the excellent tradition in literature and in art." The attitude changed as the Communist leaders changed from existing as a band of rebels

fighting the regime to becoming the new ruling class themselves—and the heirs to this ancient legacy of culture.[34]

The immediate response to the "Talks" was the conspicuous use
of folk material in musico-dramatic entertainments.[35] The initial
version of *The White Haired Girl* appeared, using folk tunes, as a
dramatic tale that went through various forms to become one of the
dominant works of the Cultural Revolution. It was also in Yan'an
in 1940 that the Liberation forces began the organized use of music
for propaganda to the populace by broadcasting revolutionary
songs and choruses over its 300-watt transmitter.[36] A revolutionary
song was composed with the text of Mao's early instructions on
conduct for the Red Army: "The Three Main Rules of Discipline
and the Eight Points for Attention." The Communists were determined to show the people in the farms and villages that the Red
Army men were not like the brutal, pillaging troops of the past.[37]
The text dates from 1928 and 1929; the date of the anonymous
melody is unknown, but as late as 1971 Mao was urging the troops
to sing this song, as well as *The Internationale*.[38]

In his talk, "The United Front in Cultural Work" (October 30,
1944), he said: "In the arts, we must have not only modern drama,
but also the Ch'in operas [that is, the old style opera of Shensi
province, which formed the main part of the ancient state of Ch'in,
or *Qin* in the Chinese transliteration] and *yangko* [*yangge*] folk
dance programs with songs popular among the peasants. We must
not only have new Ch'in in operas and new *yangko*, but also utilize
and gradually remold the old dramatic troupes and the old *yangko*
teams that comprise 90 percent of the total *yangko* teams."[39] And
underscoring the importance of instructive art for the People's Liberation Army, he declared, "An army without culture is a dull-
witted army, and a dull-witted army cannot defeat the enemy."[40]
(Perhaps Mao's early reading included fragments of Plato's
Republic, such as the following: "'I have observed,' he said, 'that
the devotees of unmitigated gymnastics turn out more brutal than
they should be and those of music softer than is good for
them.' ")[41]

The next pertinent, published document by Mao is a talk
specifically addressed to "music workers," August 24, 1956. There
was no official transcript of the speech, and apparently it never
received final editing by Mao, but is a compilation by those

The Three Main Rules of Discipline
and the Eight Points for Attention

Tempo di Marcia

1. Rev- o- lu- tion'ry ar- my men must know,
2. Sec- ond, don't take a sin- gle needle or thread,
3. Dis'- pline's Three Rules we must car- ry through.
4. Sec- ond, pay fairly for what we buy,
5. Fourth- ly, if we dam- age an- y- thing,
6. Sixth, take care, don't dam- age peo- ple's crops,
7. Eighth, don't ill- treat pris- on- ers of war,
8. Know rev'- lu- tion'ry dis'- pline's ev'- ry point,

1. Dis'- pline's Three Rules, Eight Points for At- ten-tion:
2. Peo- ple will sup- port and wel- come us;
3. Eight Points for At-ten- tion we must bear in mind:
4. Buy fair, sell fair, and be reas'- na- ble;
5. Pay the full price, not a half cent less;
6. Eith- er on march or in bat- tle;
7. Don't hit, swear at or search them.
8. Peo- ple's fight- ers love the peo- ple e'er,

1. First, o- bey or- ders in all of our ac- tions,
2. Third- ly, turn in ev'- ry- thing we cap- ture,
3. First, we must be po- lite when we're speak-ing to the mass- es,
4. Third- ly, don't for- get to per- son'- ly re- turn,
5. Fifth, don't hit peo- ple or swear at them,
6. Sev- enth, do not take lib- er- ties with wo- men,
7. Ev'- ry- bod- y must con- scious- ly ob- serve the dis'- pline,
8. De- fend the moth- er- land and for- ev- er march a- head,

1. March in step, to win vic- to- ry;
2. Strive to light- en peo- ple's bur- dens.
3. Re-spect the peo- ple, don't be ar- ro- gant;
4. Ev'- ry sin- gle thing that we bor- row;
5. To- t'-ly o- ver- come war- lord- i- s- m;
6. Get rid of all its de- ca- dent;
7. Mu- tu'lly su- per- vise, and not vio- late it.
8. Peo- ple o'er the land support and wel- come us.

present, circulated among party workers. Perhaps it is spurious, but it is not a contradiction of his views. It was not released officially in English until 1979.[42]

There is little new in these statements. He stressed again a need for a national music, the implication being, as in other matters, that the Chinese must not slavishly follow the Soviets' lead. It is a paradox that both Russia and China accepted the need for a nationalist framework to carry on their revolutions, though Marx's presumption was that communism was an inevitable world movement, one which would supersede national boundaries (though not necessarily national traits and cultural traditions). In 1938 Mao had written: "Contemporary China has grown out of the China of the past; we are Marxist in our historical approach and must not lop off our history. . . . Being Marxists, Communists are internationalists, but we can put Marxism into practice only when it is integrated with the specific characteristics of our country and acquires a definite national form. . . . Any talk about Marxism in isolation from China's characteristics is merely Marxism in the abstract, Marxism in a vacuum."[43]

In 1956 Mao instructed the musicians: "In music you may apply appropriate foreign principles and use foreign musical instruments. But still there must be national characteristics. . . . The arts are inseparable from the customs, feelings and even the language of the people, from the history of the nation. There is a large measure of national conservatism in the arts which can persist for even thousands of years. Ancient art can still be appreciated by later generations. . . ." He cemented his argument with the most venerable reference: "Confucius was an educator and a musician. He ranked music second among the 'six courses.'"[44] Mao did not hesitate to cite this most ancient curriculum in other educational settings also.[45] He noted the systematic organization of musical styles during the Sui and Tang dynasties, and the many styles which came from Central Asia, Korea and India. "The playing of foreign music hasn't meant the loss of our own music. . . . The indiscriminate rejection and the wholesale absorption of Western culture are both wrong. . . ."[46] Mao accepted the fundamental premise that Marxists are historical materialists and the present is built on the past.

There were occasional documents on the function of the arts from other high party leaders during the time period of this study. Premier Zhou Enlai (Chou En-lai) supported the principles of the Yan'an Forum in his talk "On Literature and Arts" in 1961,[47] but he also defended as harmless the performance of some traditional Peking style operas, which he was known to enjoy. Another party document, by the Vice Minister for Propaganda, Zhou Yang (Chou Yang), "The People's New Literature and Art," in 1953, supported traditional opera.[48] Even more liberal a mood appeared, a short-lived one, in early 1956 with the party slogan, "Let a hundred flowers blossom, a hundred schools of thought contend." (The line is a reference from classical Chinese literature.) These directions, primarily in literature, need not be discussed here.[49]

The official, statutory basis for the practice of the arts was the first Constitution of the People's Republic of September, 1954 (nominally in effect until 1975), which stated in Chapter 3, Fundamental Rights and Duties, Article 95: "The People's Republic of China safeguards the freedom of citizens to engage in scientific research, literary and artistic creation and other cultural activities. The state encourages and assists the creative endeavours of citizens in science, education, literature, art and other cultural pursuits."[50] Since it was the Party which drafted the national Constitution, we should note therefore the ideological foundation implied in these rights. In September 1956 the Constitution of the Communist Party of China was adopted by the Eighth National Congress. Its Article 50 states that it is the responsibility of Party organizations to "carry on propaganda among the masses, to raise the levels of their ideology and political understanding . . . and to lead the masses so that they can give full play to their initiative and creative ability. . . ."[51] The fourth and last national Constitution (1982) confirmed these rights (Article 47).[52]

In this short summary of the Marxist and Maoist direction of music in China, some of the complexities and problems of this ideological artistic control have been identified. But there is an inherent factor which must not be overlooked: the force of prerevolutionary musical traditions in China. There are three factors that could not help but shape the acculturation of an alien political, social and aesthetic ideology.

First, there is historical precedence in China for a national music office, for example, in the great Han dynasty (202 B.C.-120 A.D.), the Sui Dynasty (589-618), and the Yuan Dynasty (1279-1368).[53] The Music Bureau of the Han had as its functions the composition of music for court entertainment and the systematic collection of folk songs by which the court might judge its efficacy; according to the theory, the songs would reveal the mood of the times. The correct "mood" was set by the chief of state, the emperor and the son of heaven whose wish was law. The Confucian precepts which long served the court and educated class continued this custom of looking to the capital to affirm society's values.

In the fragments of the lost *Book of Music* (*Yueh Chi* or *Yue Chi*) included in the *Li Chi*, we read: "When the early rulers formed the *li* [rituals] and *yue* [music] their purpose was not to satisfy the mouth, stomach, ear and eye, but rather to teach the people to moderate their likes and hates, and bring them back to the correct direction in life."[54] The classic *Shih Ching* (Book of Odes), among its 305 lyrics, includes folk and court poems and forty temple hymns, dating presumably from 1200 to 700 B.C. Another classic, *Li Chi* (Book of Rites), describes the royal regulations for musical education, for dances in civil court ceremonies, for an annual grand concert, and even for the requisite musical ceremonies when two rulers meet.[55]

Mao himself in many respects played the role of emperor and by the period of the Cultural Revolution (1966-1976) was passionately deified, with his picture hung in places of honor in public buildings and squares and in peasant homes where images had once stood.[56] The Chairman became an object of obedience and veneration. His writings became the modern Classics, cited for official guidance and inspiration in all matters. Mackerras believes that to the Chinese, "politics, ethics and morality are almost synonymous . . . and Maoism is a body of ethics as well as a system of thought."[57] And Mao had prepared a plan for social controls. Unlike the Russian revolutionaries, the Chinese took over the government with an experienced hierarchy in place, including a large army, and ninety million supporters in the Liberated Areas. The Party cultural program was ready, with artist organizations and touring drama (opera) companies, to take the message of New China to the whole country.[58] (This is still the case.) The expectation and acceptance of an official authorized function for the arts had been passed along, with different criteria, from antiquity to the twentieth century.

Second, the Confucian view accepted an ethical power in music, and considered "good" music, properly performed, necessary to maintain a stable society. While we do not find a systematic, continuous program for good music over bad, this concept was in place by the Han Dynasty, when Confucianism became the official creed. "Virtuous songs" from the *Shih Ching* (Book of Odes), as well as correct musical instruments, were identified in the imperial councils as antidotes against evil tendencies by both the ruler and the councillors, and are so cited in the Book of Rites.[59]

The Western reader is cautioned to allow sufficient value to this traditional concept: It was not the Confucian view that music held ethical meanings, more or less vague, and ever open to personal opinion—as in the West we designate music as "cheerful" or "sad" or "spiritual." Rather, the tradition held that *all* music expressed ethical qualities and that music incited concrete behaviors, good or bad. This is a belief alien, and even specious, to most Western musicians, who hold the rational and secular view that (most) music exists for its own sake, without utility and also without metaphysical significance. To the modern Marxist music is not metaphysical either, but it is suggestive and emotion-laden, and must be managed as a popular means of communication.

I do not argue that many early twentieth-century Chinese musicians or audiences held to such Confucian ideals. On the contrary, the onslaught of both the Republican revolution of 1911 and Westernization by education and other contact forced many cultural changes. The Literary Revolution of 1919 in particular attacked the old classical education. The ensuing years saw similar objection to the association of music with official and ethical parameters. Western style conservatories were established and fomented a familiarity with and an adulation of Western styles and art for art's sake. This led to a Chinese-Western art music, which easily admitted more European training when Soviet Russian specialists dominated the conservatories and other agencies following 1949.

Music in the schools, like all aspects of Chinese education, after

1949 was and still is didactic. In the Shanghai district "decadent and unhealthy sentimental songs from abroad, popular among teenagers" in recent years were replaced by "alternatives" by local composers. These were "beautiful, healthy and lively songs which were welcomed and soon sung by students everywhere."[60] Shanghai was also a model during the national campaign for moral education. Rules of conduct ("Love the motherland, the people and the Communist Party of China. Do homework conscientiously. . . . Keep clothes tidy and clean. Do not spit. . . .") were set to music to help young students remember them.[61] As a cultural outlet, music is promoted by national contests in various genres, vocal and orchestral, and broadcast by the Central Broadcasting Service in Beijing, which devotes one third of its programming to music. Hymns are to be heard in Protestant and Catholic churches, which have now been reopened.[62]

The third tradition that supports state control of music is the Chinese anticipation of a verbal message, either suggestive or explicit, in an overwhelming proportion of their music. In many respects, the Chinese are "title lovers."[63] Nearly every piece in the instrumental repertory, primarily based on putative folk songs, has been given a title. Whether or not the musical substance appears programmatic, much less naturalistic, the listener's attention has been guided; one is not left to muse on one's own. Further, the verbal meaning often appears to offer an ethical statement and to be a refining influence. Pictorial references, such as *The Spring River in the Flowery Moonlight*,[64] characteristically state an age-old reverence for nature that abounds in the classics, especially in the Analects and obviously in the Book of Odes.[65] Chinese literature is centered around the celebration of the seasons, and song titles and other musical titles, such as the one above, are allusions to classical models. Possibly they suggest a spiritual mood or gesture; for example, rivers and mountains were primeval holy places or divine entities in themselves.[66]

The Phoenix Searches for Its Mate (Feng Ch'iu Huang) is a *ch'in* (zither) composition whose literary traditions begin with a Han dynasty poet and extend 1700 years to the Ming. It is a classical piece, and in discussing it Lieberman states that a performance even today "calls into play a wealth of allusion which can only enliven the music in the perception of the educated Chinese, for whom all of these references are familiar through poetry, prose and drama. . . . For the modern scholar [i.e., scholar-musician] . . . the music resonates not only in his heart, but also across the ages."[67] In Gulik's *The Lore of the Chinese Lute*, he identifies explicit and didactic programmatic intent of ancient ch'in melodies (pp. 88-100) and the symbolism of terms and names (101-5) and of tones (106-11), for example: "Sometimes even to every bar there are appended explanatory remarks. For instance, we find in a tune describing a beautiful mountain landscape, under a bar in the first part, the remark, 'Here one thinks of high mountains,' and under another, 'Here one thinks of flowing streams'" (88).[68]

Mao's education, though it had not reached a formal university program, had been a classical one. He was ambivalent about such a foundation, but he called upon it time and time again.[69] It was clearly a ready reference for him and his reading public at the time. Despite his acceptance of Marx's view that such mythology is erased by scientifically informed thinking,[70] Mao was unable to compose one poem without the traditional use of a mythical allusion from classical writings and other similar sources.[71] Note the religious grounding assumed to understand his editorial from Xinhua (*Hsin Hua*) News Agency, August 14, 1949: "Imperialists Will Never Become Buddhas Till Their Doom."[72] More irony. It was not Chiang Kai-shek, whom many Westerners perceived as the defender of traditional China, but Mao Zedong who preserved the most ancient of literary arts in his public statements. It was the Communist Party chief, not the Nationalist leader, who expressed himself in the old poetic forms, with classical allusions, and also by the most personal and traditional means of Chinese communication—fine calligraphy.

In another indigenous form, the ubiquitous theatre music, the message was obvious. Plots were infused with reaffirmations of traditional behavior—filial responsibility, respect for the elderly and those in authority, self-sacrifice for family or state—and the words sung were, of course, explicit.[73] At the court, the city theatre or the itinerant shows in the villages, the listener absorbed a moral system while being entertained.

The habit of supplying descriptive titles to instrumental pieces continues down to the present moment. In 1980 I witnessed a solo piano recital in St. Louis by Professor Zhou Guang-Ren of the Central Conservatory of Music, Beijing. Without exception, the ten selections played, all composed since 1949, offered descriptive titles, and all were said to be based on traditional melodies, for example, *Autumn Moon over a Silent Lake, an Ancient Cantonese Instrumental Melody*, in a setting by Chen Pei-Xuan (1973). It was no surprise that the American audience at once set to listening, amidst the keyboard clichés, for aural elements which would depict the scene or event presented by the title—or by the virtuous tale attached to some pieces, offered, it appeared, to justify a non-Socialist (and thus "useless"?) ascription like the title above. In fact the selected composers were exploring the several pianistic styles extant from Liszt and Chopin to Debussy, Bartók and others. But piano composition is still a youthful genre in China. The titles appeared to suit custom, and were all but irrelevant to form and content. If, indeed, the articulated "message" was irrelevant, then most of these pieces were a form of protest, possibly quite unconsciously so: They were art for art's sake.

The result of this long custom, it seems to me, is that Chinese listeners *expect* some direction for their thoughts in listening to music. Abstract titles and terminology were not characteristic: there was no equivalent of the sonata, for example, to dominate the Chinese concert repertory in the last two hundred years. This is not to say that there are no examples of absolute forms; variation was used, and also a kind of suite. Rulan Chao Pian cites "textless melodies" to which texts might be given, and a "dance suite with vocal accompaniment."[74] The literary factor is still tenacious.[75] The overwhelming evidence is that even instrumental compositions were provided with descriptive titles that evoked literary and pictorial responses. Program notes, as in the publication of ch'in music, were expected, and this practice continues into socialist publications now.[76]

I do not suppose that listeners in the past or present found no enjoyment if they ignored the title given. Neither do I assume that they dutifully contemplated each topic. But the tradition of a literary representation in the nonvocal music, and patently in the theater and vocal music, was conspicuous and remains so. There is never a need to ask the question that the Western listener asks in some contexts: What does this music mean? Everyone knows what the music "means."[77] In the People's Republic a public musical performance is never an esthetic or recreational experience alone; it must always demonstrate ideological value, and this must be verbalized lest the listener fail to participate fully in the performance, which is always an official occasion. In a 1980 concert the Central Philharmonic Society of Beijing performed "a symphonic epic, *Ambush from All Directions*" and also "a capriccio, *Tour to a Yi Village.*"[78] (The Yi are one of the fifty-odd conspicuously protected minorities in China.) Didacticism is unmistakable in the libretto of a revolutionary opera like *Taking Tiger Mountain by Strategy* or *The Red Lantern*,[79] but also in a traditional opera, expurgated or otherwise provided with a doctrinaire interpretation, for example, *Monkey God Turns Heaven Upside Down*, an episode from the classical sixteenth-century novel, *Journey to the West*.[80] Indeed, it may be impossible to cite a Chinese composition in a public performance which lacks an objective reference. There are exceptions to be found in traditional instrumental pieces composed on stock rhythmic tunes, such as "Three Variations on Six Beats".[81] This is a practical piece of information for the performer, but such an abstract title is useless for a socialist message. Han found that "the habit of writing program notes for a musical composition was well established around 170 A.D."[82] Perhaps the cultural habit of seeking images from musical sound is a parallel to the Chinese preference for picturesque words. Studies in early Chinese Buddhism show that most abstract Sanskrit words were changed into concrete terms; for example, "nature" became "eyes," "real manner" became "original face."[83] Certainly abstract painting was alien to the tradition of visual arts, and it remains so up to the present in the PRC because (again) it offers no explicit didactic meaning.

Chinese tradition supports the twin functions of aesthetic enjoyment and ideological instruction as a familiar condition of music. Whether or not the verbal message achieves its desired result must be the concern of both art and politics. And these concerns may be antagonistic. If the musical language is agreeable, the music composition will be accepted, and with it the political message, at least *pro forma*. If the music is boring or puzzling, the ideological message will be lost, for no one will care to listen. Mao clearly knew this, as did Lenin, and spoke for the necessity and the power of artistic quality.[84] A positive message clothed in shoddy art was not condoned.

Mao's objectives for art, we may deduce from his writings, were threefold. One purpose was to promote nationalism. The second was a kind of artistic populism, the creation and presentation of music and the other arts for the masses. Surpassing these two was a third value necessary in a proletarian society: a culture that would support socialism and the dictatorship of the Communist Party in the name of the proletariat. Mao had the weight and the habits of the Chinese past to assist him in promoting the first of these two objectives. The growing appeal of democracy and socialism also argued for the second. The third is ever demanded by the aggressive vitality of a Marxist-Socialist movement. The private aims of the artists will support or blend or conflict with any or all of these objectives. The contemporary author-composer who revises *The Jade Bracelet* and retains the old musico-dramatic forms provides entertainment, but his message is trivial and probably counterproductive. In the tenuous climate of reaction to the Cultural Revolution, some older theater works that also display the party line have been staged and the effort well publicized. In October, 1981 a festival in Beijing offered ten operas in various traditional styles with topical plots. *Cai Jiu Compensates for the Ducks* was praised because it "vividly portrays the reconcilation after the 'cultural revolution' and the implementation of the new rural policy."[85] The opportunity to hear several new operas was immediately appealing, and the familiar musical styles carried the message persuasively.

In July 1984 the festival of the arts in Beijing included the premieres of spoken dramas as well as the familiar opera format. Recent socialist achievements were the basis of the dramatic conflicts and again praised. What I witnessed nightly after the festival concluded, however, were the old operas, well attended in large theaters. *The Bottomless Cave*, an episode about the mischievous but brave Monkey God, was an example. It was staged with modern lighting effects and quick, realistic scene changes, but the text and music remained traditional. The standard elements of broad humor and acrobatic battle scenes delighted the audience, which included many children. Other Monkey God operas were frequently presented. *The Romance of Jade* (the heroine's name), and *Romance in a Wardrobe Trunk* were pure entertainment. The nightly television opera was also a classical work—no different from the programming across the straits in Taipei! If there was a political or didactic objective to be learned from this repertory, it seemed to this spectator that it was to hand down the heritage of the national theater to the next generation.

What of the PRC composer whose curiosity prods him, perhaps after a brush with an *avant-garde* Japanese or Western musician, to explore atonal or other nontraditional Western sounds, whether in opera or in another genre? Such music is revolutionary and progressive in the history of the art, but it contradicts artistic popularism, the second objective and simultaneously the indispensable third; it is at once subversive. Under the open attitude of the mid-1980s this situation has in fact occurred, and without censorship. A new opera in the Beijing style, *The Medicine Saint Temple*, was staged in the capital and elsewhere by the Hubei Provincial Opera Troupe. The plot concerned an invalided overseas Chinese woman who comes to the motherland for treatment when all efforts abroad have failed. A youth self-taught in native medicine finds a cure, but he is accused of illegal practice. The musical elements included lines from a Japanese song and some electronic music! The director and co-author, Yu Xiaoyu, aged fifty, declared that Beijing opera is in a crisis and to survive it must attract young adults with relevant plots and modern stage techniques. Yu won a prize in 1979 for his opera, *Sweet Honey*.[86]

At the height of the Cultural Revolution, only eight "model works" of music were permitted for performance or study from the primary schools to the professional theaters, including film,[87] and all other musico-dramatic works were measured against them. Seven of these were for the stage: five operas, such as *The Red Lantern* (in traditional music style), and two ballets, *The Red Detachment of Women* and *The White Haired Girl* (European ballets with offstage singing and Western harmonic style and with orchestrations including some Chinese instruments). The eighth was the *Yellow River Piano Concerto*, based on the last part of a cantata composed by Hsien Hsing-hai in 1939 in Yan'an.[88] The national conservatories (and all schools) were closed and many of the faculty, students, and artists assigned to farm labor. To oppose the reform of the national (Beijing) opera style became a political and cultural crime.[89]

It was likewise dangerous for anyone to perform Western music. During those years some children furtively practiced their Chopin behind curtained windows, according to PRC cultural officials visiting the United States in March, 1980.[90] During this period *The East Is Red*, a historical pageant that appeared in 1949 and was later expanded and much performed, was banned because it did not include enough praise of Mao. It is still banned in the 1980s because it now implies deification of the late chairman.[91]

In the behind-the-scenes factional struggle for national control, there were contradictions and discrepancies, which were exposed in the arts. In 1973 the Philadelphia Orchestra was invited to perform, and did so to great acclaim. After their departure, the Party newspaper, *The People's Daily* (*Renmin Bao*), excoriated the concerts as examples of bourgeois decadence: The orchestra had included Beethoven's *Pastorale* Symphony, Respighi's *Pines of Rome* and Dvořák's *New World*.[92] They also performed the *Yellow River Concerto* with a noted Chinese pianist.

Until 1976 the populace was compelled to hear the model works over and over again, on the stage, in films, on television, over radio and via loudspeakers in public spaces.[93] All traditional operas and even other revolutionary operas composed since 1949 were banned. One of the latter was *August First Storm*, in which the respected premier, Zhou Enlai, was the hero in a 1927 incident—a subject that would have deflected attention from the ambitious radical leaders, who became known as the Gang of Four. The most conspicuous of the four was Jiang Qing (Chiang Ch'ing), who claimed credit for revising all the scripts of the model works to exemplify the correct party line.[94] The plots invariably placed a heroic woman in final command, not a new theme during the post-1949 years (nor unheard of in the great repertory of Chinese operas), but one which blatantly and tenaciously suggested that Mme. Jiang was the only appropriate successor to Mao. The Gang of Four was arrested after the death of Mao in 1976 and the cultural direction promptly changed, accompanied by vigorous propaganda.[95] Perhaps at no time in the history of music, Eastern or Western, has a society endured such an extreme censorship of the performing arts: For nearly ten years, eight hundred million people were required to hear one of a group of eight compositions, in whole or in part, on virtually every musical or theatrical occasion.

All cultural controllers are ultimately dependent upon the will of the artists under their jurisdiction. Only to the extent that all its artists can be persuaded to express political objectives in an effective way will the music in a culturally controlled state be true to the ideology. But the will of the twentieth-century artist is vastly different from that of artists in past societies. No modern nation can long keep its culture sealed off from the ideas of the rest of the world. Today's musicians are informed and politicized to a degree not known in any earlier society. After the Cultural Revolution a hunger for the classical from the Western stream returned with the desire for the native repertory. There was a revival of Verdi's *La Traviata*, performed at first cautiously "to solicit opinions of the workers" in Beijing,[96] but produced with no such equivocation in 1981, and conducted by Sarah Caldwell![97] Bizet's *Carmen* has also been revived—with sharp criticism of the portrayal of smuggling on stage.[98]

The artists of a totalitarian state must be brought to a uniformity in the face of artistic individuality. But cultural and political awareness continue to stimulate the artists' desires for control of their craft. In a doctrinaire government the artists, like all citizens, are explicitly and systematically politicized. The more dogmatic and autocratic the state censorship, the more the artists—or some artists—will struggle, disguise and compromise their artistic judgments and preferences. Is it possible that an authoritarian regime can long mold all artists into "one mode of expression . . . one color, gray on gray, one truth—what the government ordains, the sole rationale in the state," and manage to prohibit all alternatives? Mao observed that a people cannot be satisfied by the phenomena of their daily routine; they crave art to lift them outside themselves. Artists are among these same people. Their aesthetic needs, by the nature of their uncommon talent, are more vivid and more imaginative than those of the masses.

In recent discussions with intellectuals from the PRC I have heard no protests against the concept of art for art's sake, but rather admiration for high artistic quality and invention. There is great respect for the universality of the art of Beethoven and

Shakespeare. Current PRC public programing supports these attitudes. On the other hand, some hold firmly to the view that all art expresses a social message. But the intelligentsia were angered by the Gang of Four's fanatical censorship, which made art politics. "They turned opera into a lecture," one professor remarked to me.[99]

In 1984 the PRC's three radio networks in Beijing daily broadcast many hours of Western classical music, interspersed with folk music of China and, occasionally, of other communist nations, such as North Korea and Yugoslavia. On one morning the stereo radio channel (No. 3) programed works by Haydn, Wagner, Dvořák, and Saint-Saëns (*The Carnival of Animals*). There was a half-hour segment of Chinese songs followed with duets by Luciano Pavarotti and Joan Sutherland! The evening period offered similar "balanced" programming, with a tape from the 1984 Hong Kong Arts Festival (primarily European artists) and Stravinsky's *Rite of Spring*. The station signed off at 10:00 p.m. with waltzes by Waldteufel.[100] Again one may deduce that neither a pro-Socialist ideology nor an anti-Western capitalistic posture appeared in this government-controlled, Party-approved programming.

In the current review of all Mao's theories a new "Guiding Ideology for Literature and Art" has been promulgated. Authority declares that the "Talks at the Yenan Forum" contains "incorrect formulations"; art is *not* subordinate to politics, and to use the political criterion as the primary method of judging the merits of an artistic work is wrong.[101] Ideology, it seems, now accepts the autonomy of the creative artist. For the good of Chinese art, this is a fortunate direction. History indicates that the artist is highly individual, varied, exploratory, and sometimes apolitical and antisocial. I submit, therefore, that in an authoritarian setting, even one with a long history of autocratic rule, the artist at some point inevitably becomes the adversary of the state. We may expect that Chinese musicians will continue to use music as propaganda for their own ends, as ideology, as art, or both.

NOTES

After January 1, 1979 the Chinese government decreed that all proper names, including names of cities, were to be spelled in the modern

Romanization called *pin yin*. Thus, Mao Tse-tung became Mao Zedong; Peking became Beijing. Both styles of transliteration are used here, consistent with the publication of the source cited.

1. *Selected Works of Mao Zedong*, 5 vols., hereafter *SW*, (Peking: Foreign Languages Press, 1965-77), III, p. 81.

2. Ch'u Chai and Winberg Chai, eds., *Li Chi* [The Book of Rites], tr. by James Legge [1872], (New Hyde Park, N.Y.: University Books, 1967), vol. II, p. 115. *The Book of Rites* (or Rituals) is one of the "Five Classics" of Confucian literature. Others cited in this chapter are *The Book of Odes* (or Songs) and *The Book of History* (or Documents). They were composed sometime before the second century B.C. The *Analects* (conversations) of Confucius, also cited here, is one of the "Four Books" of this canonic literature. See William McNaughton, *The Confucian Vision* (Ann Arbor: The University of Michigan Press, 1974).

3. *SW*, III, p. 185.

4. "The Treaty of Indestructible Friendship" with the USSR was written into the Constitution. Winberg Chai, *Essential Works of Chinese Communism*, revised edition. (New York: Bantam Books, 1972), pp. 250, 304.

5. Ralph C. Crozier, ed., *China's Cultural Legacy and Communism* (New York: Praeger Publishers, 1970), pp. 19-29.

6. Tr. by C.C. Huang, (Honolulu: University of Hawaii Press, 1972); and see James R. Pusey, *Wu Han: Attacking the Present through the Past* (Cambridge, Mass.: Harvard University Press, 1969).

7. *SW*, IV, pp. 412-13.

8. An article, "A Study of Physical Education," which appeared in a liberal Peking magazine, *La Jeunesse*. His earliest writing to appear in *SW* is "Analysis of the Various Classes of the Chinese Peasantry and Their Attitude towards Revolution," vol. I, pp. 13-21 (1926). A chronology appears in Jerome Ch'en, *Mao Papers* (New York: Oxford University Press, 1970), pp. 163 and 166 respectively for these citations.

9. Marx, "Great Asia's Potential," in the New York *Daily Tribune*, one of a series of articles he wrote 1853-1860 published in *Marx on China* (London: Lawrence and Wishart, 1951), pp. 1-2. V. I. Lenin, "The Awakening of Asia" (1913), *Collected Works* (hereafter *CW*). (Moscow: Progress Publishers, 1963), vol. XIX, pp. 85-86; "Backward Europe and Advanced Asia" (1913), ibid., pp. 99-100; "Better Fewer, But Better" (1923), ibid., XXXIII, pp. 487-88.

10. Mao, *SW* II, pp. 339-84, and see notes 2-7, 12, 16 and 23 therein for the references cited.

11. The first official English edition was *Nineteen Poems* in 1958 (Peking: Foreign Languages Press). Later official editions were published in

1966 (39 poems) and 1976 (36). Three posthumous poems made public in September 1978 are included in Nancy T. Lin, *Reverberations: A New Translation of Complete Poems of Mao Tse-tung* (Hong Kong: Joint Publishing Co., 1980). See notes 65 (Ch'en) and 69 (Barnstone) below.

12. *SW* II, p. 340.

13. Ibid., p. 372.

14. Ibid., pp. 380-81.

15. "On New Democracy," *SW* II, p. 382.

16. For a firsthand opinion by Mao's actress-wife who taught at the academy, see Roxane Witke, *Comrade Chiang Ch'ing* (Boston: Little, Brown, 1977), pp. 184-88. For another eyewitness account, by Liu Xuewei, see T. A. Hsia, "Twenty Years after the Yenan Forum," in *China Quarterly*, No. 13 (January-March 1963), pp. 226ff.

17. These quotations are from *SW* III (1967), pp. 69-98.

18. Ibid., pp. 71-72.

19. Ibid., p. 75.

20. Lenin, *CW* X, pp. 48-49.

21. Operas in the traditional style, that is, with prerevolutionary plots ("cleaned up"), historic costumes (usually of the Ming dynasty), and the stereotype melodies doggedly continue as a favorite amusement. In 1981 *Peking Opera and Mei Lanfang* (Beijing, New World Press), a book on the famous actor of women's roles, was published, written by Wu Zugang and others. A four-day festival of operas associated with Mei is described in Beijing Review (hereafter *BR*) September 14, 1981, pp. 28-29. A conspicuously successful Beijing troupe (1981-2), which boasts a repertoire of forty operas, is described in *BR*, April 4, 1983, pp. 25-28. Daily television schedules include traditional styles of opera. Foreign film viewers who were fortunate to see the five PRC films circulated in the West in 1981 and 1982 cannot have missed the preoccupation with traditional musical styles, despite the revolutionary messages of the plots and dialogue. These selected films were produced between 1959 and 1980. One was about Shanghai opera life in the twentieth century (*Two Stage Sisters*), another about a ninth-century folk singer and early revolutionist (*Third Sister Liu*), and one a biography of Abing, a famous blind musician who died in 1950.

22. *SW* III, p. 76.

23. Ibid., p. 81.

24. For example, Charles Sainte-Beuve: "The mission of art today is the human epic: to reflect and shine without interruption in a thousand hues the emotions of a progressive humanity. . . ." from "Premières Lundis," tr. and ed. by Frances Steegmuller and Norbert Guterman, in *Sainte-Beuve: Selected Essays* (Garden City, N. Y.: Doubleday & Co., 1963), p. 394.

25. *SW*, III, p. 81.

26. Ibid., p. 82.

27. Ibid., p. 84.

28. Ibid., p. 81.

29. Ibid., p. 89.

30. Ibid., p. 90.

31. Ibid., p. 94.

32. Anonymous, *Decision of the Central Committee of the Chinese Communist Party Concerning the Great Proletarian Cultural Revolution* (Peking: Foreign Languages Press, 1966), p. 13.

33. *Mao Zedong's "Talks at the Yan'an Conference on Literature and Art": A Translation of the 1943 Text with Commentary* (Ann Arbor, 1980), Michigan Papers in Chinese Studies, No. 39.

34. Ibid., pp. 19-20, 8, 11, and elsewhere. The *Talks* were dutifully commemorated in editorials in *The People's Daily*, the official organ of the Party, on each tenth anniversary, that is, May 23, 1952, 1962 and 1972; but also in 1967 and 1970, very likely because of the saturation program of Mao's writings during the Cultural Revolution. See Michel Oxsenberg and Gail Henderson, *Research Guide to People's Daily Editorials, 1949-1975* (Ann Arbor: Center for Chinese Studies, The University of Michigan, 1982), IX, and their index of Literature and Art (p. 148) for this day in these years. For recollections and reaffirmations on the fortieth anniversary, see *BR*, May 24, 1982, pp. 23-9; and May 31, 1982, pp. 5-6.

35. Edgar Snow, *Red Star over China* (New York: Grove Press, 1961), pp. 109-16; Ellen Judd, "New Yangge: The Case of 'A Worthy Sister-in-Law' " in *Chinoperl Papers* (Ithaca, New York: China-Japan Dept., Cornell University, 1981), No. 10 (1980-81), pp. 167-68.

36. *BR*, February 22, 1982, p. 20.

37. *SW*, IV, pp. 155-56.

38. Stuart Schram, *Chairman Mao Talks to the People, 1956-1971* (New York: Pantheon Books, 1974), p. 297.

39. *SW*, III, p. 186.

40. Ibid., p. 185.

41. *The Republic*, I, p. 289; see also p. 407.

42. *BR*, September 14, 1979, pp. 10-14. An earlier translation appeared in 1974 in Schram, *Chairman Mao Talks to the People*, pp. 84-90.

43. "The Role of the Chinese Communist Party in the National War" (1938), *SW*, II, p. 209. The obligation to shape Communism along the Soviet model was an ongoing problem in the Chinese Communist Party discussions. Mao's position was further justification of the later break between the two nations at the time of Khrushchev's de-Stalinization policies, which the Chinese Party viewed as revisionism, a retreat from socialist principles.

44. *BR*, ibid., p. 13. According to tradition Confucius's Six Arts (*Liu Yi*), which his students were to master, were rites, music, archery, horsemanship, writing and arithmetic.

45. "Spring Festival Day on Education," a talk published in *The People's Daily* (*Renmin Bao*), February 13, 1964; tr. in Ch'en, *Mao Papers*, pp. 93, 95.

46. *BR*, ibid., p. 14.

47. *BR*, March 30, 1979, pp. 9-16. In 1981, publication commenced in Beijing of the *Selected Works of Zhou Enlai* in an English edition.

48. An excerpt is in Crozier, *China's Cultural Legacy*, pp. 176-78.

49. The slogan used by Mao is the title of an address by Lu Ting-yi, Director of the Party Propaganda Department and Minister of Culture (English ed., Peking, 1964). A useful extract is in Crozier, pp. 20-21. Mao discusses the resulting controversy in his essay, "On the Correct Handling of Contradictions among the People" (1957), *SW*, V, Part 8, pp. 408-14.

50. English ed., Peking, 1961. Reprinted with comments in Chai, *Essential Works*, pp. 246-96.

51. English ed., Peking, 1965. This quotation is from Chai, *Essential Works*, p. 293. In *Communist Manifesto* and *Capital*, communism is termed "a higher type of society whose fundamental principle is the full and free development of every individual." Tr. in Baxandall and Morawski, *Karl Marx and Frederick Engels* (see Chapter 4), p. 39.

52 *BR*, December 27, 1982, p. 17.

53. For a brief historical survey, see *The New Grove Dictionary of Music and Musicians*, sixth edition (1980), vol. IV, pp. 250-53; and Alan Thrasher, "The Sociology of Chinese Music: An Introduction," in *Asian Music*, XII:2 (1981), pp. 17-53. Chinese history offers ample records of official music—for the court ceremonies, ritual songs and dances, and orchestra music, all for a multitude of calendar occasions. See Han Kuo-Huang, "The Modern Chinese Orchestra," in *Asian Music*, XI:1 (1979), pp. 1-8.

54. Thrasher, "Sociology of Chinese Music," p. 24 (tr. from the Chinese edition, Shanghai, 1934). For *yueh* (music) Thrasher uses the *pin yin* transliteration *yue*. For the Legge translation see Legge/Chai, *Li Chi*, II, p. 96.

55. Legge/Chai, *Li Chi*, I, pp. 232-34, 261, 266; II, pp. 274-76.

56. Michel Oxsenberg, *China: The Convulsive Society* (New York: Foreign Policy Association, 1970), p. 7.

57. Colin Mackerras, ed., *China: The Impact of Revolution, A Survey of Twentieth Century China* (New York: Longmans, 1976), p. 165.

58. See Harriet Mills, "Literature in Fetters," in Ross Terrill, *The China Difference* (New York: Harper & Row, 1979), p. 289.

59. Legge/Chai, *Li Chi* II, p. 118. *Shu Ching* (Book of History): "K'wei

said, 'Oh! When I strike the stone or tap the stone chime, all kinds of animals lead on one another to gambol, and all the chiefs of the officers become truly harmonious.'" At this the emperor himself made a song. Legge, *Shoo King,* II, iv, 3, paragraph 10. For a specific discussion see Siu-Chi Huang, "Musical Art in Early Confucian Philosophy," in *Philosophy East and West,* (XIII:1, April 1963, pp. 49-60 (Honolulu: University of Hawaii Press).

60. *BR,* December 7, 1981, p. 23. Another reference is *BR,* January 4, 1982, pp. 17-18. Of interest also are the remarks of the President of the Central Conservatory of Music (Beijing) on the dichotomy of influence by Western pop songs; that is, they offer folk song simplicity and impromptu performance experience, but at the same time, cheap sentimentality, occasional "mystic religious preaching", and disorder in the concert halls. "Zhao Feng on Pop Music," *BR,* July 20, 1981, pp. 28-29.

61. *BR,* December 7, 1981, p. 22. There were prerevolution propaganda songs too. See "Sino-Japanese War in Shanghai" by "Professor Chou," cited in Alexander Tcherepnine, "Music in Modern China" (Shanghai in 1931), in *The Musical Quarterly,* XXI:4 (October, 1935), p. 399. Chinese émigrés of my acquaintance can sing fervent songs against the invaders, recalled from that time.

62. Ibid., February 21, 1983, p. 7.

63. Kuo-Huang Han, "The Chinese Concept of Program Music," in *Asian Music,* X:1 (1978), pp. 17-38, and the same author's "The Modern Chinese Orchestra," see note 54 (there spelled Han Kuo-Huang).

64. From "forty-seven popular melodies" that were in existence from 206 B.C. to 704 A.D., according to the "Old T'ang Annual." David Ming-Yueh Liang, *The Chinese Ch'in: Its History and Music* (San Francisco: Chinese National Music Assn., San Francisco Conservatory of Music, 1972), p. 321.

65. Marcel Granet annotated a selection in *Festivals and Songs of Ancient China,* tr. E. D. Edwards (New York: E. P. Dutton, 1932), pp. 19ff.

Poems in classical style reveal a reliance on the form of ancient melodies. Mao, whose knowledge of Chinese poetic forms—like all his early education—was traditional, also followed the accustomed method of "filling the form." The subtitles of his poems show this; for example, "To the Melody of Shen Yuan Ch'un" for his poem, "Snow," or "To the Melody of Yu Chia Ao", for "The First Encirclement" (both tr. in Jerome Ch'en, *Mao and the Chinese Revolution* (New York: Oxford University Press, 1965). But this is not a literal meaning: the ancient melody prescribes the numbers of characters, the rhyme, and speech tones. (See Mao, *Poems,* 1976 edition, p. 53.) The actual melodies disappeared long ago. During the

Cultural Revolution one of the plethora of record albums issued in praise of Mao was "Poems of Chairman Mao Set to Music" (China Record Company, Beijing, No. WM-2165), which contained seven of his poems (including the two cited above), set to music and harmonized in Western style, and performed by a mixed chorus with the Central Philharmonic Orchestra of Beijing.

66. For example, Song VIII, *The River God*, and Song IX, *The Mountain Spirit*, in Arthur Waley, *The Nine Songs: A Study of Shamanism in Ancient China* (London: Allen and Unwin, 1955), pp. 47-58 (tr. and commentary). On "sacrifices to hills and rivers" see *Shu Ching* (Book of History), Legge, *Shoo King*, II, ch. I, par. 8.

67. Fredric Lieberman, "Texted Tunes in the Mai-An Ch'in P'u," *Asian Music*, VI:1,2 (1975), pp. 129-32. He notes that this instrumental repertoire did not disappear after the establishment of the PRC: "There was a renaissance of public interest in the ch'in" [and also its publications] (pp. 114-15). At this writing, the ch'in, among other pre-Cultural Revolution artistic activities, has been "rehabilitated." In Nanjing (Nanking) in the summer of 1984 I heard a recital that included six ch'in players whose ages ranged from about seventy to twenty. *BR*, August 24, 1981, published a full page article that discussed research societies which have been established in ten cities and a seminar that was held in Beijing to study the ch'in, and also reported that the famous ch'in piece, "Running Water," was recorded on a gilded copper record and sent into space aboard the American spacecraft *Voyager* in 1977 (p. 29). (In the phonetic transliteration used in the PRC, ch'in is spelled *qin*, or *guqin*, meaning ancient zither.)

68. Robert H. van Gulik, *The Lore of the Chinese Lute* (Rutland and Tokyo: Charles E. Tuttle, 1969), second edition. A recent study is Kenneth J. DeWoskin, *A Song for One or Two* (Ann Arbor: Michigan Papers in Chinese Studies No. 42. University of Michigan, 1982), Ch. VII.

69. A few of Mao's Classical references are: (1) "Order and Statement on the Southern Anhwei Incident," a historical military incident cited in the *Analects* of Confucius, Book XVI, Chapter I; (2) In *SW*, II, p. 456; "Stalin, Friend of the Chinese People" (on Stalin's sixtieth birthday), with a reference to the *Book of Odes*: "A bird sings out to draw a friend's response," *SW*, II, p. 335; (3) "Talk at an Enlarged Central Work Conference," tr. in Schram, *Chairman Mao Talks to the People*, Text 8, notes 2, 4, 5, and p. 321, in which Mao draws three analogies from the *Shu Ching* (Book of History), (The reference in Schram, note 5, is to a traditional Beijing style opera based on an historical incident.); (4) "The United Front in Cultural Work" (1944), where Mao quotes Confucius (*Analects*): "Haste brings no success" (Legge, tr., "Do not be desirous to

have things done quickly," Book XIII, chapter XVII); in *SW*, III, p. 186-87; (5) the poem "Swimming" (1956), Beijing ed., 1976, pp. 31-32, and Willis Barnstone, *The Poems of Mao Tse-Tung* (New York: Harper & Row, 1972), p. 85—an allusion to the *Analects*, Book IX, chapter XVI. (See Crozier, *China's Cultural Legacy*, pp. 52-53, 152 n.); (6) "Talk on Questions of Philosophy" (1964), in Schram, *Chairman Mao Talks*, pp. 213-15, 220; Mao comments on his own early study of the classics and make several judgments both positive and negative on such a literary foundation.

70. "On Contradiction," *SW*, I, p. 341.

71. Barnstone, *The Poems of Mao Tse-tung*, pp. 18-25.

72. Tr. in Stuart R. Schram, *The Political Thought of Mao Tse-tung* (New York: Praeger Publishers, 1969), p. 282.

73. For the plots of twenty traditional operas, see A.C. Scott, *An Introduction to the Chinese Theatre* (New York: Theatre Arts Books, 1959). For an analysis and chronicle of drama reform after the 1949 revolution, see David Shi-Peng Yang's unpublished dissertation, "The Traditional Theatre of China and Its Contemporary Setting" (University of Wisconsin, Madison, 1968), especially chapters II and III.

74. *Sonq Dynasty Music Sources and Their Interpretation* (Cambridge, Mass.: 1967), pp. 35 and 73-74, respectively. John Hazedel Levis, in *Chinese Musical Art* (New York: Paragon Book Reprint Corporation, 1963, second edition), quotes the Ch'ing musical authority, Hsu Ta-ch'un (1693-1771) on the seven points to observe in order to compose music, the third of which—nonmusical, it might seem—is: "You must observe the ceremonial connection, that is, for worship, for writing to friends, for military purposes, *etc.*" (p. 191).

75. See Lieberman, "Texted Tunes," pp. 114-46, on classical ch'in compositions which were constructed on poetic forms. Ch'in publications also offered a text underlying the tablature or accompanying it. In modern times the text is not sung, though the player may recite it silently as he plays (ibid., p. 114). Liang, in *The Chinese Ch'in*, p. 118, states that the practice of ch'in and voice style dwindled in the early Ch'ing dynasty (that is, about 1700).

76. Han, "Chinese . . . Program Music," pp. 26-29, 32-35.

77. In "The Meaning of the Meaning of Music," Jacques Barzun argues that ". . . all music is programmatic, explicitly or implicitly, and in more than one way." *The Musical Quarterly*, LXVI:I (January, 1980), p. 3.

78. *BR*, October 26, 1979, p. 31. See also the list of pieces played by a Chinese orchestra in July, 1979 (when visiting England) in "A Discussion on Chinese National Musical Tradition) by Fang Kun, in *Asian Music*, XII:2 (1981), pp. 2, 5. For another program of new symphonic works see *BR*, May 25, 1981, p. 28.

79. Translations of the librettos are found in L.W. Snow, *China on Stage*, pp. 40-98, 256-303, respectively.

80. The story is told in Scott, *Chinese Theatre*, pp. 75-76 ("The Restoration of Peace in Heaven"). The tale was made into a full-length animated film in the 1950s. All versions of the story were suppressed during the Cultural Revolution; see *BR*, October 26, 1979, pp. 30-31.

81. Han, "Modern Chinese Orchestra," p. 12.

82. Han, "Chinese Program Music," p. 26.

83. Ibid., p. 19.

84. *Lenin on Culture and Cultural Revolution* (Moscow: Progress Publishers, 1966), p. 251.

85. *BR*, November 16, 1981, p. 30.

86. *China Daily* (Beijing), July 23, 1984, p. 5.

87. Witke, *Comrade Chiang Ch'ing*, pp. 405-37. Alain Peyrefitte, *The Chinese: Portrait of a People*. Tr. by Graham Webb (New York: Bobbs-Merrill Co., 1977), p. 196. At the height of the Cultural Revolution, lavishly illustrated English editions of these works, as well as recordings in the Chinese languages, were available for export. Today all are presumed out of print. See the catalogues of importers over several years, such as *China Books and Periodicals*, San Francisco, California.

88. Read the commentary in the score published in Beijing, 1978. See also Witke, *Comrade Chiang Ch'ing*, pp. 390, 459.

89. Crozier, *China's Cultural Legacy*, p. 286; Mills, in Terrill, *The China Difference*, p. 297; Ch'en, *Mao Papers*, p. 133; Pusey, *Wu Han*, p. 53.

90. Lin Mohan, Vice Minister of Culture and Vice Chairman of the Chinese Federation of Literature and the Arts, who led a delegation of music and arts educators to the United States. His remarks accompanied the showing of a film of youthful prodigies who are now studying in the reopened conservatories of the PRC, particularly in Beijing. (The showing occurred during the Music Educators National Conference in Miami Beach, Florida on April 10, 1980.) The film was titled, "Budding Blossoms in Spring"—the "budding blossoms" obviously an allusion to the young children, and "spring," to the rational and tolerant policy that appeared after the extremes of the Gang of Four. It was thus a recall of the 1956 slogan, "Let a Hundred Flowers Blossom." The very young performers of Chinese or Western instrumental music were indeed astonishing, but there were no older children among them—evidence of the loss of that part of a generation because of the ten year suspension of education.

91. See "On the Role of the Individual in History" in *BR*, August 11, 1980, pp. 17-21.

92. Witke, *Comrade Chiang Ch'ing*, pp. 457-59; *U.S. News and World Report*, June 3, 1974, p. 58.

93. Ross Terrill, *800,000,000* (Boston: Little, Brown & Co., 1972), p. 50; *China! Inside the People's Republic* by the Committee of Concerned Asian Scholars (New York: Bantam Books, 1971), pp. 250-59, 264-65.

94. Chiang Ch'ing, *On the Revolution of Peking Opera* (Peking: Foreign Languages Press, 1968), especially pp. 38-43. For the refutation see Wan King, "How Our Revolutionary Operas Were Produced," in *Chinese Literature* vols. V-VI (1977), pp. 66-72. By the same author, "What Chiang Ch'ing Did to Culture" in *China Reconstructs*, XXVI:5 (Peking: May, 1977), pp. 2-6. In the same issue see also the article "How Premier Zhou Promoted Revolutionary Art and Literature" (anonymous), pp. 7-9. A revival of the earlier opera version of *The White Haired Girl* (1964) is cited in this same issue, p. i, and illustrated on the cover.

95. See Jürgen Domes, "China in 1977: Reversal of Verdicts," in *Asian Survey*, XVIII:1 (January, 1978), pp. 12-13. A succession of articles appears in *BR* at this time, continuing into the trial. See also Hsin Chi, *The Rise and Fall of the Gang of Four* (New York: Books New China, 1977).

96. *BR*, October 26, 1979, p. 31.

97. *Women of China*, November, 1981, pp. 12-15.

98. A conversation with Ying Ruocheng in St. Louis, November 15, 1982. Ying, a leading actor with the Beijing Art Theater, translated Arthur Miller's *Death of a Salesman*, which Miller was invited to direct in 1983.

99. Mao once warned against this extremism in the "Talks at the Yenan Forum." "To study Marxism means to apply the dialectical materialist and historical materialist viewpoint in our observation of the world of society and of literature and art; it does not mean writing philosophical lectures into works of literature and art." *SW*, III, p. 94.

100. *China Daily* (Beijing), July 21, 1984, p. 6.

101. *BR*, May 3, 1982, p. 3.

CHAPTER 6

Sacred or Profane: Music in Religion

Inasmuch as this kind of pleasure is thoroughly innate to our mind, and lest demons introducing lascivious songs should overthrow everything, God established the psalms, in order that singing might be both a pleasure and a help. From strange chants harm, ruin, and many grievous matters are brought in, for those things that are lascivious and vicious in all songs settle in parts of the mind, making it softer and weaker. . . .

St. John Chrysostom, (*ca.* 390)[1]

One of the things that still drugs the brain of youth is music. Music makes the brain inactive. . . . If you want your country to be independent, you must turn radio and television into educational institutions and eliminate music.

The Ayatollah Khomeini (1979).[2]

Music in public worship must also be viewed as art that is designed to persuade and control, in this case under the purview of the clergy, who must instruct and lead the faithful in the dogma and the rituals. It is easy to suggest examples, and many appear in the following discussion. One theme in the previous chapters continues: the conflict which may arise between the composer and the ruling authority on what is acceptable expression when music becomes propaganda.

This chapter, however, takes a different tack. Concepts of music in four world religions will be juxtaposed to expose the similarities, but more often, the striking differences, in the definitions of religious music. The four faiths are Judaism, Christianity, Islam and Hinduism. (Specialists in these four fields will be disappointed at the necessity of compressing so much information into a few pages.) A salutory result of observing this collage of religious musics, it seems to me, is that a second theme emerges: the insistence on stylistic change in Western music, and the impact it has had on the message, compared to the deliberate evolution of music in Asian religions, in which the reiteration of the past is similarly insistent.

Music in all worship is expected to heighten the desired emotional effect in the listener, to emphasize the ritual text, especially certain significant words, and to focus the worshipper's attention on the rite. But the danger of so sensuous a phenomenon as music is that it may be more seductive than the rite itself, and that the musicians may evoke more interest than the priests. If the music in the worship service is "entertaining," is the religious ambience destroyed? How can the worshipper's attention be shielded from wandering? In any one culture are there two kinds of musical expression, one identified as sacred, and the other as nonsacred and appropriate only for secular occasions? If the composer-musician is careless, clumsy, or impious, and mixes the two expressions, how will the religious leaders protect the faithful from this abuse of the worship service? If the religious message is confused, diluted, or (worst of all) replaced by an irreligious meaning, either explicit or implied in the sounds of the music, this propaganda has failed. Is it then wiser to allow only a liturgy with "dull" music? To the ambitious musician-composer, at least in the West, such a proscription would be a stifling and perpetual ban on artistic imagination.

At the simplest level, the music created for public worship is a word by word intoning of adorations and prayers. This is the ancient method for the nonliterate traditions of tribal religions (for example, in Polynesia), as well as for the written texts of high cultures, such as the Jewish, early Christian, Hindu, and Buddhist. The use of such music is everywhere proscribed by canonic regulations and performance traditions, which may change from era to era. Some of these regulations or customs govern the melodic range of the song, the setting of the words—syllabic or ornamented—and who shall sing the songs. Even in Islam, where by definition "music" is forbidden in the mosque, passages of the

Qur'ān are vocalized (*tartīl*) in a manner similar to Hebrew and Gregorian chant. The periodic public call to prayer from the minaret is a definable melody.

Is there a common ground? Six aspects, it seems to me, affect the music in all religious rites, and consequently the control of the message. Let me describe them briefly:

1. *The comprehension of the sacred words.* In liturgical practice, a primary objective of the spiritual leaders is to maintain the accuracy of the rites. This follows from several apparent requirements. In the most general terms: All the components of the rites are in themselves hallowed. They may not be altered through ignorance or willfulness on penalty of (a) offending the deity, (b) losing contact with the deity, and (c) failing to lead or instruct the faithful fully and correctly according to the doctrine. The improper utterance of the ritual words, as judged at a given time, by whatever means or intent, is a grave error. Therefore, we must weigh the effect on the meaning when music is added, including clarity, expressiveness, aesthetics, and suggestive interpretation.

When the words are sung (or chanted), this primary requirement—comprehension by the congregation—must be safeguarded: Intoning, "singing," must not destroy the clarity of the words. Alterations which are injurious may come from the rise and fall of musical pitches or the elongation or wrong accentuation of the words or of individual syllables.

2. *The preservation of traditional melody and performance practice.* Must the traditional melody fitted to the text be used in its customary form for all time, hallowed by its ancient (and very possibly forgotten) origin? Is such old music of equal sanctity, quality and authority as the old sacred words? If it is, clearly the music cannot be altered any more than the words. Contrariwise, are variants in the music permitted or encouraged by theological reforms or development or by aesthetic choices arising from artistic developments in the culture?

Beyond simple improvisations (a slight ornamentation, for example), are conspicuous changes acceptable through ornamentation, longer melodic phrases, instrumental accompaniments, free paraphrases, or (the ultimate change) a wholly new musical setting of the old text? Among the religious customs of the world there is an awesome conflict on what is acceptable: The musical practice of one religion may be both blasphemy and an artistic impossibility in another.

Whatever the styles employed, from the gambit of two, three or four pitches in the chants of Polynesia or the American Northwest Coast Indians to the panoply of solo and choral voices and orchestra demanded by eighteenth-century Christian Europe, music *per se* holds a high place in religion: It is intimately joined with the sacred words. With these words, and at some point with these sounds, the deity is invoked to bring about personal or community change, improvement and control.

Is musical tone itself divine? Or is it only the pious product of humankind, and thus on another level from the words, either because the words have divine attribution, or because they are explicit in meaning and musical tones are not? Thus, in the Old Testament God *spoke* to the prophets; He did not sing. In Judaism and Christianity, music is treated as the eloquent handmaiden of worship; it is a blessing from the Most High, but it is not itself the voice of God. Vocal music, to the Hebrews, was a divine gift, but it was also clear that instruments were the invention of man. The first Biblical reference is Genesis iv:21-22 on the descendants of Cain. Jubal "was the father of all those who play the lyre and pipe." His half brother, Tubal Cain, was the smith who made "all instruments of bronze and iron."[3] In the Roman pantheon, string, wind and percussion instruments were associated with Pan, Apollo, Mercury, Curetes, Dionysus and Triton. Awareness of these pagan traditions made the Jews and the early Christians cautious about the use of instruments and the people who played them.

In contrast are the origin and unblemished status of music in the mythology of Hindu India. In this culture music—all music—is recognized as a spiritual manifestation. In one of the ancient treatises, *Brhad Āranyaka Upaniṣad*, it is stated that all things emanate from the primordial soul (*ātman*),[4] including the four scriptural sources, the *Vedas*,[5] their verses, hymns, legends, and commentaries, and also food and drink, this world and the world beyond, and, of course, music. Within *ātman* is a "psychic sound [which ultimately] manifests itself as the audible pleasing sound . . . with the gross raw materials of tone, tune, rhythm, grace, etc."[6]

The physical sound, vibration, is termed *nāda*, and *nāda* is identified as a constituent of divine creation.[7]

In the Hindu ambience, music is at once and always a spiritual medium and an act of faith, in whatever setting it is performed, inside or outside the Vedic temple ritual; the study of music is thus all-embracing, its appearance in temple chant being but one use. One of the ancient (pre-Buddhist) "schools" was the *Gāndharva Veda*, which embraced "every use of musical sound, not only in different musical forms and systems but also in physics, medicine and magic."[8] Thus to study Indian musical analysis stripped of its firmly embedded religious substance is to arrive at an incomplete historical conclusion. Though some Western musicologists may feel uncomfortable at admitting metaphysical aspects to pitches, rhythms, melodies, et cetera, the broad cultural ambience of music, including the metaphysical, is not rejected. Further, Jewish and Christian writings provide examples of miraculous incidents in which music is the centerpiece, as cited here and there in this chapter. A contemporary Indian musicologist, Swāmī Prajñānān-anda, concludes a lengthy and theologically based chapter on "The Philosophy of Music" with these words:

India is the land of spirituality. Here philosophy of music is looked upon as a spiritual *sādhana* (meditation), which elevates and animates the level of man's consciousness, and kindles in the cave of his heart the perpetual light of the Divine knowledge, and makes him free from the den of delusion forever and ever. The intuitive authors of music of India are fully conscious of this secret, and have made music the best and purest means for attaining the God-realization.[9]

What spiritual authority is here! Music, without qualification, is a reference to the spiritual sphere, and a performance is an act of devotion. A Classical Indian recitalist—a dancer, a vocalist, an instrumentalist—characteristically commences with the Hindu (and Buddhist) gesture of offering (*anjali mudrā*), pressing the palms together as in the Christian attitude of prayer. The performance itself, even without verbal references, is a spiritual homage. Whatever the religious faith of a Western concert artist, he or she would likely think it inappropriate and *unnecessary* to begin a recital with such a dedication, so discrete are Western concepts of music for worship and entertainment. Admittedly, some Western performers and their audiences perceive a designated religious work in the concert hall (like Bach's B Minor Mass) as a spiritual experience; for some, it is a conscious act of devotion. A sacred concert in the church, extraliturgical, is sometimes presented as a service to the community. It may also hold a missionary value to attract new members or rekindle the enthusiasm of lapsed members. Music as propaganda!

Like Jewish and early Christian chant, the Hindu texts and melodies were an oral literature for many centuries. However, there were extraordinarily rigorous rules by which the repertoire was learned so that there remained no possibility either for error or for change. "It was in fact never necessary for [the priests] to report to the pen because of their superbly developed abilities for retaining orally transmitted information."[10] Where the liturgies are still vital today, the memorization and vocal techniques are awesome to behold.[11] The preservation of so much unwritten music is astounding when we learn even an inkling of the complexity of certain sacraments.

For example, a fragment of the instruction for a service to be sung (rather like the Roman Office of Prime) before dawn: ". . . before the sound of anything (a bird, etc.) is to be heard . . . [The priest] then squats down between the yokepieces of the two Soma-carts [on which the sacrifical soma plants have been brought to the temple], and begins his recitation with *Ṛg Veda* X, 30:12, 'Ye, O wealthy waters, verily possess good things; ye confer desirable energy and immortality; ye command riches with abundant offspring: may Sarasvati [the river] and [also] the goddess of Speech [learning] bestow on the bard that vital vigour!' . . . The prayer may consist of as many verses as can be recited between midnight and daybreak, but there should be at least one hymn in each of the seven metres to each of the three deities; nor should the recitation consist of less than a hundred verses. From the beginning of the recitation up to the end of the last hymn but one, *Ṛg Veda* I, 112, there is to be a gradual modulation of the voice so as to pass upward through the seven tones (*yama*) of the deep scale (*mandrasvāra*). . . ."[12]

The scrupulous care and the perfect recall of every element is imperative. Since the vibrations of sound (*nāda*) bear cosmic influence, it is understood that an error of tone or a misplaced syllable might upset the equilibrium of the universe. A famous story in the *Śatapatha-Brāhmana* (1.6.3.1.*ff.*) relates how the divine craftsman Tvaṣṭṛ attempted revenge against Indra, the king of heaven, by creating a son to slay the god. But during the incantation he made a slight error in accent. Instead of saying *Indraśatru* (slayer of Indra), he said *Índraśatru* (having Indra for his slayer), and his son was irrevocably killed by the god.[13] In addition to the cantillation, a repertoire of hand gestures (*mudrā*) is demanded.[14] The generations of Vedic "transmitters" did not consider themselves to be interpreters. Thus the Western preoccupation with progress in all matters, the persistent fascination for inventing and using a novel artistic vehicle or methodology, was absent in the Hindu priest-musician, who would have regarded it as frivolous, as well as blasphemous.

In later Hindu thought Brahmā, Viṣṇu and Siva were associated as a trinity, the latter two developing rich personalities. All three are associated with the creation of music, or rather *saṅgīta*, the Sanskrit term which includes song, dance, drama and playing instruments. The blend of these arts is also legendary.

To celebrate how the gods destroyed the demons, Brahmā produced a dramatic spectacle of *saṅgīta*. This celestial performance was deemed exemplary for humankind. Therefore the sage Bharata was directed to write down detailed instructions on reenacting the divine music drama. His one hundred sons were sent down to earth to teach and demonstrate this *Gesamtkunstwerk*. The compendium *Nātyaśāstra* (Laws of Dance-Drama), ascribed to Bharata-Muni (Bharata, the sage), includes chapters on music, both vocal and instrumental, melody, modes, rhythm, and the behavior of performers. The written form is variously dated between 200 B.C. and 200 A.D.[15] The Indian classical dance-dramas, as *Kathākali*, embrace all the performing arts and are ritual entertainments. The Lord Śiva, in his form as Naṭarāja, King of Dance, becomes the divine dancer. At dawn each day he shakes a small "hourglass" drum and reenacts the dance of life, by which the universe was shaped.[16] Thus the dance and the dancer in India are immediately a remembrance of God's promise. The dance dramas of Kathākali, and virtually all other dramatic spectacles of India, are based largely on the two epics *Mahābhārata* and *Rāmāyana*, in which Viṣṇu, in two of his incarnations, characteristically undertakes superhuman exploits against evil.

When we turn to the Jewish and Christian scriptures, we find that dance is rarely an occasion for divine intervention or an edifying subject matter. David's ecstatic behavior at the return of the Ark is a rare exception. The Roman church saw the vitality of social dancing as a persistent temptation in the middle ages. After all, John the Baptist had lost his holy head because Salome could dance so well! In the medieval Church the line between secular ebullience and ecclesiastical decorum was continually crossed to the distress of the bishops. At the Council of Avignon in 1209 preceding important festivals it was proclaimed: "There should not be, in the churches, any of this theatrical dancing, these immodest rejoicings, these meetings of singers with their worldly songs, which incite the souls of those who hear them to sin."[17] And in the same period the Council of Bayeux warned: "Priests will forbid gatherings for dancing and singing in churches and cemeteries, on pain of excommunication."[18] It was not amiss to use the metaphor of dance as heavenly locomotion. A nun's hymn from about 1440 reads:

> Let us all together go
> On the road to heaven.
> There, where joyous music rings,
> We shall with angels dance along,
> To the sweet heavenly strings.[19]

In Fra Angelico's painting, *The Last Judgment*, virgins and martyrs join in a heavenly dance, but they are safely beyond earthly temptations—and censure.

In Islam, the potential for ambiguity is of a different nature from that of the cultures just noted above. In Islamic thinking, there is no distinction between the sacred and the secular or the spiritual and the mundane; they are one domain. There is no priesthood and no church. The adherent is relatively free to act on his own. "The nature of an act, however secular in its import, becomes spiritual if inspired by the whole indivisible complexity of life."[20] This seems to mean that any tune, and any musical material, would be appropriate if piety desired it in the mosque. But this is certainly not the case.

First, music in Arabic by definition refers to entertainment, and the performance of it—with qualified exceptions—is of questionable propriety, if not actually profane. In Tehran in 1969, a time far less austere than the present, this standard still meant that music was absent from radio programs on religious holidays. Public concerts, and even rehearsals, were not scheduled, and the music department of the University of Tehran was closed, even though other departments held classes.[21] The term *mūsīqā* identifies only some genres of music. In order to use a term in Arabic which might signify what the West means by music, one American specialist in this field had to invent one! (*Handasah al sawt*, "the art or engineering of sound.")[22] Thus the chanting of the Qur'ān is not included in *mūsīqā*, for it is not within the meaning of "music." And the Ayatollah's ban did not refer to the chant. "Music" in worship would distract the devout from their concentration, and remind them of sensual pleasures. There seems little doubt, however, that the Qur'ān was in fact recited to definite pitches from the earliest times.[23] There is Qur'ānic authority, however terse, for doing so.[24]

The chant of the Qur'ān is a most important part of the service. Like much of the art music of this great cultural region, it is improvised from a traditional body of melodic formulas and is not written down. The performance tradition—chanting by a single voice—has been handed down with reverence by appointed reciters. A crisis arose when the faith was spread to non-Arabic peoples in the ninth century. The new adherents were unacquainted with the music culture which underlay the Arabic recitation; not surprisingly, they improvised their own melodies, in some cases, using current popular tunes. "It remained a concern for Islamic culture . . . to maintain that separation of [secular music and the traditional chant] throughout the centuries."[25] It was equally a concern in the administration of the Jewish and Christian liturgies, but with different results.

3. *The moral status of musical instruments.* How peculiar, how neurotic seem the anxious warnings of the medieval bishops beside

the all-embracing view of India. And there was also the moral ambiguity of European musical instruments. To the Western cleric, instruments served antagonistic purposes in their profane appearances in entertainment and the rare uses sanctioned in a house of worship. There is no such ambiguity in Hindu thinking.

The Lord Viṣṇu plays musical instruments such as the conch shell horn, as we see in many sculptural images.[26] It is also Viṣṇu who descended to earth in a series of evolutionary forms, the eighth avatar being Kṛṣṇa (Krishna). When young Kṛṣṇa is depicted as a cowherd, he carries a conch as a tool of his occupation. Before the legendary battles in the great Sanskrit epic, *Mahābhārata*, the divine heroes attempted to frighten their enemies with blasts on their battle conches. Each shell bore an exalted name, as we read in the famous episode, *Bhagavad gītā*, I:12-19. When Kṛṣṇa appears as the irresistible lover, he is a flutist of great charm. And more: "A man listening to the Lord Who holds the flute is freed from all his sins. For Krishna, as He is known, has become incarnate, Krishna, the supreme Brahman in the form of man."[27] Śiva is also shown in the Hindu iconology playing the *vīṇā*, the legendary precursor of South Asian plucked strings. Ancient philosophical references to the drum, conch and lute are found in the *Brhad Āraṇyaka Upaniṣad*, cited above.[28]

The illustrious performances by deities are replicated in *pūjā*, the worship service in the Hindu temple. A priest blows the conch, but this is considered a ritual act, not music. A shell is kept in every household, for it is the practice to blow the conch whenever an eclipse or an earthquake occurred. A blast would scare away the demon intent on devouring the moon or the sun or shaking the foundations of the world.[29]

Today, in a South Indian Tamil temple, a set of bells is rung during the service; this is the duty of an assistant. A priest punctuates his chant with finger cymbals. The long double reed, *nāgasvāram*, a double-headed drum, and cymbals form an ensemble to provide music for processions and circuits of the altars. In the North the equivalent ensemble is heard occasionally, as in Banaras.[30] Such an open acceptance of (traditional) music was demonstrated to me during visits to the Hindu Chettiar Temple in Singapore in 1975 and 1976. It was not unusual to find one or two drummers (with *mṛdanga* or *tablā*—both northern and southern drum types at once!) who had come to play informally in the temple when no service is in progress and without expecting an audience. In a Western synagogue or church it would be deemed improper—and as a devotional act, inexplicable—for a drummer to carry his drum and trap set into a sanctuary for a casual performance. The medieval tale of the humble "Juggler of Our Lady" is long forgotten!

Perhaps it is a function of the vivid Hindu personalization and humanizing of Viṣṇu, Śiva, and the goddess Sarasvatī that all their instruments, certainly the vīṇā, the flute and drums, are freely played by their human devotees. In the Hindu and Buddhist traditions, the Guardians or Kings of the Four Directions include *Dhṛtarāṣṭra*, Guardian of the East, who is often depicted playing a lute. In the Tantric explanation he uses the sound of music, rather than a sword as his weapon against evil.[31] Views on sanctified instruments and who may play them also distinguish the religions under discussion from one another. True, Jews and Christians play trumpets, as did their Biblical antecedents. But Jehovah did not sound the trumpet; it was played by the angels.

To perceive the gulf between these performance traditions more deeply, we need only try to visualize Christ, Muhammed, or Abraham or Moses, playing a drum or a lute or executing the vigorous ritual dance of Natarāja. Scriptural references to Christ or the apostles playing any instrument are nowhere to be found; rather, the suggestion of instrumental music, typically associated with secular entertainments, is distinctly avoided. The use of the bull roarer in some tribal societies to represent—to *be* the voice of the deity would be an unthinkable ritual action in Judaism, Christianity and Islam and would be regarded as blasphemy. Christian iconography depicts angels who sing and play instruments (for example, Van Eyck's Ghent Altarpiece, Grünewald's Angelic Concert in the Isenheim altar series, Sano di Pietro's "Virgin and Child"). But St. Cecilia is the only saint who is a musician, raised after death to the status of divine performer. Her iconography varies, however, and the depiction of her solo instrument changes through the centuries: an organ, a clavichord, or a harp![32] This mirrors, of course, the changing styles in European music.

Because of the popular and traditional use of instruments to support dance and folk singing, their acceptance in the Judaeo-

Christian rites has been severely limited: Instruments were prompt reminders of the sensuous delights and frivolities going on outside the house of worship. But there were solemn uses for certain instruments in history. Joshua's instructions on how to bring down the walls of Jericho included repeated processions by priests playing trumpets (Joshua vi:1-7, 15-21). There are frequent references in the Psalms to the custom of *singing* praise, accompanied by instruments which everyone knew: the tambourine, the lyre, harp, drums and flute (for example, Ps. 33, 81, 92, 108, 144, 149, and 150). There are also references outside the Psalms, as in the Song of Moses, Exodus xv:1-2, 20-21, Isaiah xii:5-6, the Song of Deborah, Judges v. But a uniform use of these instruments in all periods cannot be verified.[33]

David is credited with the invention of instruments appropriate for the great temple. But woe to those who likewise invent instruments for hedonistic pursuits (Amos vi:5), or play them (Isaiah v:12). In 1 Chronicles xxiii:5, for the edifice which is to be built, David assigns four thousand Levites (the clan of professional musicians) to "offer praises to the Lord with the instruments which I have made for praise."[34] In Solomon's Temple the musical practice, as distinguished from the purely vocal music in the synagogues (which commenced later), included an organ and brass ensembles. It is told that a hundred and twenty priests were trumpeters (2 Chronicles v:12). After the Romans destroyed Jerusalem and the Second Temple in 70 A.D., great numbers of Jewish people were dispersed, and the use of instruments in worship all but disappeared. Instruments like the organ could neither be constructed nor transported easily. Further, the Pharisees, who controlled the synagogues, discouraged the appearance of instruments except for the shofar, which was viewed not as a musical instrument but a ritual object, as in Hinduism.[35] The ban also became a mark of mourning for the loss of the Temple. Ritual music became purely vocal: *Not* playing instruments became a doctrinal statement. In the Jewish Emancipation in the nineteenth century, instruments were returned to use in the "liberal" synagogues.[36] The first Christians—Jews— continued the traditional contemporary practice of worship, including psalmody, among other customs. They also eschewed musical instruments, but for the pragmatic reason that they were members of an unauthorized religion and loud sounds from their clandestine meetings would draw the attention of the Roman guard.

In the Eastern Orthodox church unaccompanied chant also became the rule. In the presence of the emperor, Christ's viceregent, wind and percussion instruments were played, accompanied by the Acclamations sung to the emperor, especially during major feasts. A portative organ was carried in processions, but it had to be left outside the church.[37] There is a parallel in some African Islamic communities today: When the Emir rides to the mosque for the Friday noon service, he is accompanied by trumpets and drums up to the door. Elsewhere in Islam from the tenth to the nineteenth centuries military bands took part in the Call to Prayer in public performances three to five times daily. The instruments were not carried into the mosque.[38]

In the West the organ became acceptable in the church by the twelfth century, but other instruments were rejected because of their association with the ubiquitous and bawdy *jongleurs*.[39] A familiar fifteenth-century miniature from *Le Champion des Dames* uses the organ as a symbol for church music and depicts two celebrated composers of the sacred and the secular: Guillaume Dufay stands by a portative organ and faces Gilles Binchois, who rests one hand on a troubadour's harp.[40]

In the Islamic world there was no body of musicians, composers, or choirmasters to propose "enrichments." The Muslim liturgy has remained the prerogative and responsibility of one person, and he is a "reciter," not a "musician." "Performance practice, relying on the human voice, has avoided the secular associations which instruments might bring, as well as the chordal harmonies which could be suggestive of emotional or dramatic effects."[41]

In the society of Islam there may be the appearance of paradox when a secular setting and religious music or quasi-music are mingled indiscriminately, but this is neither a discrepancy nor a confusion of values. There is no clear separation between religious and secular conduct. A Muslim, for example, draws the Qur'ān and Islamic tenets into daily situations which the non-Muslim Westerner would likely think irrelevant or improper. As an illustration I will transpose a Muslim usage into a Christian culture: Imagine gymnastics executed to a rhythmic recitation of the four

Gospels, or Biblical texts sung by a coffeehouse entertainer. In Iran (ca. 1969), Bruno Nettl described men's physical exercise clubs (*zurkaneh*), whose vigorous routines are directed by a singer who accompanies himself on a drum. Since quotations from the Qur'ān are sung, the men feel that they are fulfilling a Muslim obligation by their workouts.[42] Nettl also noted that religious singing and instrumental music took place in coffeehouses, on the street, and in homes.[43] But musicians did not perform music at or near shrines or mosques in Iran.

From Muslim North Africa to Southeast Asia, one may hear accompanied religious songs on "secular" occasions. In Malaysia, during the extended marriage rituals of Muslims, the groom's friends march to the bride's home singing *ḥaḍrah*, songs in praise of Muhammad, with accompaniments of contrapuntal patterns of frame drums. This group activity is seen as an act of piety, but it would never be performed in the mosque. Another example is the central importance of music in the mystical societies of dervishes among Sufi Muslims, when men may perform group dances. Here there is unison singing of Qur'ānic and other texts, and Arabic instruments are played: a flute, violin, lute, vase drum, and cymbals. The location is generally the organization's headquarters. In their prayer services in the mosque, however, the Sufis have not departed from the mainstream: they restrict themselves to Qur'ānic chant.[44]

The use of popular or folk instruments, such as guitars and percussion, has been outside the practice of mainstream American Christian services, and their recent introduction seemed an affront to older worshippers. The appearance of pop and jazz styles, with the instruments necessary to those styles, was unprecedented, except in some Black churches in which jazz rhythms and instruments have long been part of the musical tradition. Religious dance, an integral part of eighteenth-century Negro spirituals, has also been a vital element of the Afro-American church.[45] The new sounds in some other churches were stimulated by social change which altered church practice, to wit, Vatican II, and, secondly, the impact of popular music in social protest movements.

The use of percussion instruments is indispensable in religious rites in non-Western cultures: Africa, Oceania, American Indian, Hindu and Buddhist. In Judaism and in Christianity, with rare exceptions (such as the Jewish Falashas, and the Coptic priests, in Ethiopia), playing drums has traditionally been considered a recollection of secular settings, dancing, merrymaking and the theater, or war. In Hindu culture the origin of drums is attributed to a direct inspiration of the great god, Indra, when he created resonant sounds by the rain falling on broad lotus leaves. The *Nāṭyaśāstra* gives a description of this occasion, along with detailed instructions on how to make drums and what to play.[46]

4. *Music in worship has an efficacy in itself.* The goal of the early Christian leaders was to provide instruction in the new faith, and, concomitantly, to insure the continued zeal and single-minded attention of the adherents. Congregational participation, such as singing, was a way of eliciting interest and visibly demonstrating continuing enthusiasm. Paul's vigorous and didactic letters to the several congregations shaped much of the new worship, and he urged singing in the service. (His were the first such statements to be written down; Christianity was an oral religion; its founder wrote nothing.) In Colossians iii:16 Paul wrote: "Let the word of Christ dwell in you richly, as you teach and admonish one another in all wisdom, and as you sing psalms and hymns and spiritual songs with thankfulness in your hearts to God." (See also Ephesians v:18-19.) As recorded in Acts xvi:25-26, impassioned singing may bring about divine intervention in grave circumstances: While imprisoned in Philippi, Macedonia, Paul and Silas prayed and sang hymns to God, and an earthquake shook the jail. The doors flew open and every prisoner's shackles fell off. This deliverance by music reinforced the miracle of Jericho in the playing of trumpets, and is a part of the apologia for the use of music in the Christian ritual.[47]

The expostulations on the use of proper music by the Patristics began in the second and third centuries. The erudition of some writers provided rich allusions from Hellenic mythology and thought, as well as historical and ritual knowledge of the Jewish antecedents. Clement of Alexandria, for example, interlaced his discussions with references to Orpheus, Amphion and Arion, as well as the Old Testament. In his *Exhortation to the Greeks* he employed Greek mythology as a polemical structure: The pagans were influenced by evil spirits to deceive mankind. Clement then declared that Jesus now replaced Orpheus, come to free all from demons. Christ was the new minstrel and his teaching was "The New Song."[48] Clement reminded his followers that King David the harpist also put to flight the demons with a "true music; and when Saul was possessed, David healed him merely by playing the harp.[49]

Implied here is the ethos doctrine of music, a conviction rooted in all ancient religions: Each mode or melody has the capacity to create and to express specific emotions, and the listener will respond to it in an expected manner. Tribal traditions and Confucian and Hellenic writings abound with such applications, and they are not absent in the religions discussed here. Further, intonation itself brings its own power. Thus the rabbinic literature admonishes the reader to chant, not simply read, scriptures in public worship.[50] The use of musical sounds to drive away evil spirits illustrates a belief in the atropaic power of music. Exodus xviii:35 describes the golden bells sewn in the hem of the priest's robe, which tinkle as he enters or departs the inner sanctum, "lest he die."[51] *Darhiel Cooke modern belief in*

In Hinduism, the *Nāṭyaśāstra* states: *modes*.

When auspicious words uttered with proper intonation in accompaniment of songs and playing instruments resound in a region, all evils will disappear, and prosperity will ensure there. . . . On hearing the sound of *Nāndī* [the chant] . . . ferocious spirits will make themselves scarce. And this sound will be equal to the exposition [of] Vedic Mantras. . . . Music, vocal as well as instrumental, is in fact a thousand times superior to a bath in the holy waters.[52] . . . The tones and tunes or melodies (*svāras* and *rāgas*) have also been depicted as living forces and deified as gods and goddesses.[53]

The Hindu-educated musician must avoid the misuse of music, for this will result in punishment. The performance of a *rāga* (in the North Indian ethos), if heard during an hour or season other than the proper time, may cause innocent persons to suffer, and they need not be among the listeners: The effect is unleashed into the world. Viṣṇu demonstrated this to teach a lesson to the brilliant but egotistical musician Nārada: The God took him to the cave where there lived people who had been horribly maimed and disfigured by the destructive effects of Nārada's willful selection of *rāgas*. He had misused the forces of sound.[54]

These references are outside the boundaries of temple music, but they illustrate the Indian belief in an inevitable metaphysical force innate in musical sound. More specifically, the *Chāndogya Upaniṣad* (I, xi, 4) warns that the priest must know the phenomena to which the vedic hymns refer or his head will fall off during the chant![55] The similar warnings in the West seem less dire, or perhaps only less graphic.

St. John Chrysostom became Bishop of Constantinople in 397, and was renowned as a preacher (*Chrysostom* means "golden-mouthed"). He offered examples of the beguiling power of music to comfort the weary or distressed: infants, travelers, peasants treading grapes, sailors pulling oars and women weaving.[56] Chrysostom noted that this pleasure in music "is thoroughly innate" and that demons can tempt the faithful with lascivious songs and "overthrow everything." Hence, "God established the psalms in order that singing might be both a pleasure and a help."[57] So highly beneficial did he consider the practice of psalmody that John urged everyone to sing psalms, even if their education was so modest that they did not fully understand the meaning of the words. St. Jerome (born 340), translator of the authorized Latin bible, the Vulgate, supported this view, emphasizing that the act of doing—reiterating the scriptures—was all-important: "Sing to God not with the voice, but with the heart; not, after the fashion of tragedians, in smearing the throat with a sweet drug, so that theatrical melodies and songs are heard in the church, but in fear, in work, and in knowledge of the Scriptures. And though a man be *kakophonos* [harsh voiced], to use a common expression, if he have good works, he is a sweet singer before God."[58] But cannot singing remind the worshippers of songs heard in the profane world?

5. *Music in worship may effect the wrong result.* There is a danger that the pleasure of melody may divert the mind from the lesson and that the seductive tune may "swallow" the holy words. The warnings of Basil, John Chrysostom, and Jerome resound in a most eloquent discussion in the *Confessions* of St. Augustine, who became Bishop of Hippo (now in Algeria) in 395. Augustine apparently regarded his flock as part of the cultural world of Rome, just as it was in fact part of its political world. The people were thus "more or less typical of Christians generally, who all had to resist

the attractions of the circus games and gladiatorial contests, astrology, the alluring eroticism of the theater, the remnants of paganism, and the snares of ancient letters."[59] Augustine perceived that the attention of the faithful, and he included himself, was inspired to devotion when the sacred words were accompanied by melody far more than when they were spoken. He admitted that his own senses, rather than "following patiently behind [his] reason, strive even to run before and be her leader. Thus in these things I sometimes sin at unawares, but afterwards am aware of it."[60] So indignant was he at his sensuous digressions that he considered that all music to which the psalms were chanted should be banished from the church. He recalled that Athanasius, Bishop of Alexandria (292–373), had instructed a lector to sing with "so little warbling [inflection] of the voice, as that it was nearer to speaking, than to singing."[61] Augustine continued:

Notwithstanding, so often as I call to mind the tears I shed at the hearing of thy church songs, in the beginning of my recovered faith, yea, and at this very time, when as I am moved not with the singing, but with the thing sung (when namely they are set off with a clear voice and suitable modulation), I then acknowledge the great good use of this institution. Thus float I between peril of pleasure, and an approved profitable custom: inclined the more (though herein I pronounce no irrevocable opinion) to allow of the old usage of singing in the Church; that so by the delight taken in at the ears, the weaker minds be roused up into some feeling of devotion. And yet again, so oft as it befalls me to be more moved with the voice than with the ditty [the prayer], I confess myself to have grievously offended: at which time I wish rather not to have heard the music. See now in what a state I am![62]

In Islam, the rare scriptural statements used to justify chanting in the mosque specifically entreat a beautiful voice and sensitive declamation. "Recite deliberately and pleasantly what is revealed to you of the Book." (Qur'ān 29:45.) Among sayings of the Prophet one finds: "Decorate the Qur'ān with your voices." "Allah never permitted anything as much [so strongly] as he permitted to the Prophet the beautification of the voice. . . ." "For everything there is a hulyah [ornament, decoration], and the hulyah of the Qur'ān is the good voice." "God never sent a prophet except with a beautiful voice." "The Prophet himself is remembered as being a reader who moved his hearers by his beautiful voice."[63] These historical references are regenerated today: A particularly expressive recitation elicits spontaneous exclamations of pleasure from the worshippers.[64]

The fear of the European church leaders of the misuse of music was vastly heightened with the development of polyphony. Ornamentation and highly melismatic settings, with precedents from Hebrew and Oriental chant, had long threatened the clarity of the words. But the collisions of different phrases or word fragments and the musical cross-rhythms of Notre Dame polyphony were a further attack on verbal clarity. The mixed textures of monophonic chant and polyphonic organum in a piece by Perotin was likely bewildering (and fascinating to some hearers), dislodging the attention of worshippers from the routine of long attendance at the rite. Ecclesiastical decorum was confronted by sounds which excited the senses. We may guess that the listener (like St. Augustine) was surely "more moved with the singing than with the thing sung." European vocal music now developed melodies of great rhythmic variety, some with extravagant runs of rapid notes.

In the middle of the twelfth century John of Salisbury, Bishop of Chartres, wrote:

Could you but hear one of these enervating performances executed with all the devices of the art you might think it a chorus of Sirens, but not of men, and you would be astonished at the singers' facility, with which indeed neither that of the nightingale or parrot, nor of whatever else there may be that is more remarkable in this kind, can compare. For this facility is displayed in long ascents and descents, in the dividing or in the redoubling of notes, in the repetition of phrases, and the clashing of the voices, while, in all this, the high or even the highest notes of the scale are so mingled with the lower and lowest, that the ears are almost deprived of their power to distinguish.[65]

Had the composer become the adversary of the Church?

6. *The rivalry of art and theology.* The several foregoing concerns come together under this topic: the performer-composer's desire to decorate the chant melody, to discard a too familiar rhythmic pattern, and certainly to experiment with the novel sonorities and forms of music which aroused admiration outside the Church, in the courts, where the musician might also display

his skills. Invention, experimentation and daring are demands of the composer's calling.

Perhaps the preeminent explanation for the historic conflicts between European music and theology is that we indeed speak of the composer, a personality, in a genre which is everywhere else in the world a collective and usually anonymous effort. Perhaps this ego manifestation in European sacred music is peculiarly Western. The rise of the professional musician alongside the professional clergy initiated a conflict, or at least a contest, not irreverent we may assume, and without indifference to the requisites of the liturgy. The admonitions of the scriptural authors show their concern about misapplications of the liturgical elements. The theologians did not dare lose control of the liturgy or the minds of the faithful. The Jewish and Christian clergy who recited chant did not see themselves as "composers." (Neither did the Brahmans who so flawlessly replicated Vedic chant.) But a musical ego appeared in the Christian practice, anonymous, invisible in a sense, and of growing influence in the execution of the liturgy. Music historians can scarcely curb their excitement at the record of the first identified composer, Leonin, in the twelfth-century collection, *Magnus liber organi*. Later celebrated names—who were in clerical orders—Machaut, Binchois, de Vitry and Landini, are admired by virtue of their music, not their religious devotion.[66]

In the Renaissance period humanism, a new concept of knowledge arose, and music became a means of consciously depicting the emotions of the individual soul. The establishment of choirs chosen for the quality of the voices was support for the composer's craft and its artistic value. Contemporary praise for the Burgundian chapel of Philip the Good declared that its choir was "the finest, the best in blend and numbers that could be found anywhere." A handful of singers is shown in a miniature of the period.[67] The choir, more or less trained, brought new luster to the service; it did not bring a new theology. In the Baroque period, the virtuoso organist became still another rival for the primary attention of the worshipper. Musical roles outside the church (and, in the modern era, the liberal Jewish temple) introduced a secular standard to be imitated: the voice of the popular opera soloist. The contest has scarcely disappeared today, when some worshippers will say that they "came to hear the music."

I do not imply that ego has not also existed in the performance of the clergy, either in the West or elsewhere. The ingredients of the several rites discussed here—physical movement, minute timings, expressive language and emotional range—are also art, and the sensitive liturgist is tempted to "perform." But his or her charge is the ritual. The artist and theologian need not be antagonists. They may, in fact, serve each other's objectives.

Still, the exploratory nature of the Western composer challenged almost every basic element—words, music, forms, praxis—in the development of European sacred music. In the growth of polyphonic composition in the twelfth and thirteenth centuries, both the complexity of the texture and the length of the new music, where performed, vastly affected the sound and clarity of the liturgy. There were repeated ecclesiastical pronouncements against this. In 1274, the second Council of Lyons issued several rules to curb the new music. Fifty years later, in 1324, Pope John XXII in residence at Avignon issued a decree vigorously denouncing this pernicious artistic trend:

Some followers of the new school, infatuated with the subdivision of tempora, devise new notes and prefer to sing these instead of the old ones, so that church music is now being sung in semibreves and minims and is infested [percutiuntur] with short notes. These people break up the melodies with hockets, debase them with discants, and load them with moteti and tripla in the vulgar style. Thus they lose sight of the foundation of the Antiphonale and Graduale and do not know what they are building on. They are ignorant of the modes, which they cannot distinguish; they even confound these one with another, as the moderate rise and fall of plainchant (by which the modes are discerned) is all distorted by the multitude of their notes, which run about incessantly and never come to rest, intoxicating rather than soothing the ears, while the singers imitate with their gestures the sentiments they utter; by all which things devotion (which should be pursued) is brought into contempt, and wantonness (which should be avoided) is increased.[68]

Traditionalists, not suprisingly, also looked with dismay at the growing search for sensual effect by the progressive composers. Jacob of Liège, in his encyclopedic *Speculum musicae*, written a few years after the papal decree, used quite similar expressions in his assessment:

Not content with simple, duplex, and triplex longs and with breves, and some not content even with semibreves, the practitioners of this art are still inventing new ways of corrupting what is perfect with many inperfections. . . . They have abandoned many other sorts of music, which they do not use in their proper form as the ancients did; for example, measured organa, organana not measured throughout. . . . Music was originally discreet, seemly, simple, masculine, and of good morals; have not the moderns rendered it lascivious beyond measure?[69]

In passing, it might be noted that a heretic, the Bohemian reformer Jan Huss (1375-1415), led a movement which banished polyphonic music and instruments in its churches until the middle of the sixteenth century. The Hussites were here more successful than the pope! They sang simple hymns, rather like folk songs, and usually monophonic.

A different aspect of the ambiguity of a supposed sacred style was the long-lived and varied use of *contrafactum*: the exchanging of a secular text with a sacred one, or fitting a sacred text to a popular melody. In the Renaissance the selection of a secular melody as *cantus firmus* for a mass or motet was acceptable raw material, the conventions of the polyphonic church style presumably concealing any evidence of impropriety. This contradiction did not escape scrutiny during the Council of Trent, when Catholic prelates met to correct abuses and laxities in the Church. When final pronouncements were made, however, the appealing practice was not specifically forbidden to composers. Twenty-five years after the labors of the Council of Trent in 1577, Pope Gregory XIII commissioned his chapel musicians Palestrina and Zoilo (Romano) to prepare new publications of the Antiphoners, Graduals and Psalters "to purge, correct and reform" them of the current excesses of "barbarisms, obscurities, contrarities, and superfluities as a result of the clumsiness or negligence or even wickedness of the composers, scribes, and printers, . . . so that through their agency [the music books] God's name may be reverently, distinctly, and devoutly praised. . . ."[70]

Many of the new hymns of the reformed faiths also utilized pre-existing melodies. One striking paradox is the evolution of the *Minnelied, Mein Gmüth ist mir* (My head is all confusion from a tender maiden's charms), published in a book of part songs by Hans Leo Hassler in 1601. In but a dozen years it served as a chorale tune, *Herzlich tut mich verlangen*. With Paul Gerhardt's text of 1656, *O Haupt voll Blut und Wunden*, based on a fourteenth-century Latin hymn, it became a moving chorale on the Crucifixion. An English version is *O Sacred Head Now Wounded*.[71] It was a beguiling tune, too beguiling to be overlooked in the earnest effort to find persuasive melodies for the new Reformed church repertory. A remark attributed to Martin Luther is, "Let us not leave all the good tunes to the devil!"

The busy Baroque composer commonly recycled music composed for one topical occasion for another quite different one. Bach's *Christmas Oratorio* of 1734 is largely a pastiche of the secular cantatas he had written earlier. The alto lullaby, *Schlafe, mein Liebster* (No. 19), was originally from a birthday cantata, *Lasst uns sorgen, lasst uns wachen* (BWV 213), a *dramma per musica*, in which Lust tries to tempt young Hercules. In that setting, it had been a soprano aria (No. 3) with the same title(!) but heard in g minor. Bach presumably "purified" the melody of sensuousness by transposing it to G major for Nativity music. Is the relocated melody now "religious"? Or is it simply *suitable* and its unquestioned charm also effective for the infant subject who must be persuaded to go to sleep?

There are similar contrafacta in the history of Jewish liturgical music. During the vast dispersal of the Jews outside Israel, the emigrants absorbed local cultural elements in religious and folk music wherever they settled. Some who were forced by law to renounce their faith (crypto-Jews) secretly observed the traditional practice. In their synagogal meetings they prudently sang well-known non-Jewish tunes, so that at least their singing would not betray them to hostile authorities.[72]

Another example of a contemporary style in conflict with tradition was the commission to the Italian composer, Salomone Rossi (b.c. 1570), to provide choral settings of thirty-three items in the Jewish prayer book, a liturgy which had ever been performed by a soloist with the congregation singing in unison. His collection of songs for three to eight voices in the contemporary fashion was published in Venice in 1623. In Christian music, western Europe had witnessed the gradual development from two-part parallel organum to polyphonic masses and motets requiring four to eight parts or more. In Rossi's one stroke, eight hundred years of this musical change was to be imposed on a monophonic tradition. The extraordinary idea required justification, and in a long introduction the chief rabbi of Venice declared, "There is nothing in the Talmud which can be cited against the introduction of choir-singing in our Temples. . . ."[73] Aron Marko Rothmüller deduced that there was in Italy a group of Jews, professionals or amateurs in music, who wanted to raise synagogue music to the level of art music. Rossi had preserved no musical relationship to the past; his melodies were original. (He was, after all, one of the pioneers of his time: His second book of madrigals, published in 1602, was apparently the first to show a *basso continuo*.) Rossi wrote, "I have subjected a large number of the Psalms of David to the laws of music, in order to make them more attractive." His *nuove musiche ebrea* must have been incoherent to the average members of the congregations, and the style was rejected at that time.[74]

The minimal service music espoused by the Protestant reformers Zwingli and Calvin—psalmody—in time also succumbed to the eloquent "competition" from the German and Anglican choral styles. The Pilgrims brought the unison singing of the psalters with them to the New World, but in the early eighteenth century this, too, changed as some Protestant churches initiated choral singing. The intimations of secular entertainments and, indeed, of "popish" grandeur so offended some members that they left the church. It was the congregation, not the church officers, who rejected the new music: It violated the accepted and desired message. A century later, independent Black denominations in America passed through the same bitter controversy. "You have brought the devil into the Church, and therefore we will go out," declared some members of the Philadelphia Bethel Church. The two-thousand-year-old anxiety over instrumental music was voiced again as the black minister Elisha Weaver was impeached in 1857 by his Chicago congregation for introducing choral and instrumental music into the service.[75]

Pope John's warning in 1324 had been astute and prophetic. The history of church music from that time on records an ever increasing complexity of textures, the evolution of the modal system into the harmonic and tonal, and the mingling of the same expressive devices and overall sonority of secular and sacred music. By the eighteenth century, Haydn and Mozart could write vocal music which, but for its Latin text, might be supposed to be operatic and

secular in spirit and purpose. Such an amb
arisen because the composer had but a sir
practice" of the past was scarcely preferred. Tl
contemporary style. The dilemma was exace
the equal artistic status of sacred and se
beginning perhaps with the period of Machaut,
genres was admired. It may also be from Macl
the first statement that beautiful sound is one of the composer's
criteria. In his letter of November 3, 1363 sent with two four-voice
ballades to a young friend, he wrote that he had "heard them
several times and like[d] them very much."[76]

When the secular musical "language" became virtually the same
as the sacred, the composer could introduce an emphasis where no
such emphasis was expected or conventional in liturgical usage, or
the reverse, to shift the expected emotional or textual emphasis or
to alter overall proportions to suit a secular form or applauded
effect. In his *Pange lingua* Mass, Josquin pressed the listener's
attention to the phrase, *Et incarnatus est . . . et homo factus est*
(And was incarnated . . . and made a man) by choosing long notes
in a chordal texture. It was theologically "right" to focus attention
on this phrase, as well as an artistically desirable contrast to the
plethora of short notes in the wordy *Credo*. With this action it was
the musician who was the preacher, emphasizing the message with
his nonverbal medium in a highly expressive and pious manner. He
seems to have continued—or begun—an admired tradition, and
other composers imitated this phrase. (For examples, compare this
passage in mass settings by Palestrina and Lassus, and, among later
composers, Haydn, Mozart, and Beethoven.)[77]

In the Lutheran Church, Johann Sebastian Bach became a great
preacher in music. In the eighteenth-century Sunday service, a
"core-hymn," the *Hauptlied*, contained the lesson for the day. The
familiar words and tune were customarily embedded in one or
more vocal and instrumental compositions. Bach's cantata, *Nun
komm, der Heiden Heiland* (Come, saviour of the heathen) (BWV
61), is an emphatic example. Indeed, it illustrates music as propaganda in the Christian tradition extending over thirteen hundred
years. The text (translated by Martin Luther) had been written in
the fourth century by St. Ambrose as *Veni redemptor gentium* and
had been Ambrose's weapon against the Arian heresy which denied

incarnation of Christ. In Bach's time, the prevailing controversy was that between Orthodoxy and Pietism and in various ways both the words and Bach's musical setting argued the case for Orthodoxy. The tenor aria carried "buzz words" (in German, of course), such as "in the honor of God's name," "pure" (referring to doctrine), "worship in Word [the pulpit] and Sacrament" [the altar]. The choir's first entries began with the highest voices and descended to the lowest, and symbolized the dogma of the incarnation to the listeners. For the closing chorale Bach inserted (unexpectedly) the last verse of Nicolai's Epiphany hymn, *Wir schön leuchtet* (How brightly shines the morning star), and bound together the three themes of Advent: Christ's coming at Bethlehem (the past), his coming in "Word and Sacrament" (the present), and his coming on the Last Day (the future). It was a sermon in music. (After which the congregation heard an hour's sermon in words without music!)[78]

But a composer's idiosyncratic solution to text-setting may get in the way of comprehension. His eloquent strokes may mar the demeanor, even the very execution, of the rite. To a later generation or epoch a musical setting may prove even less acceptable: Since liturgical change occurs slowly, if at all, and artistic change is rapid (in Western culture), the given work may be ritually still workable but aesthetically disdained, and the composition judged old-fashioned and trite. But the opposite has also occurred, and an earlier composition been admired aesthetically but seldom or never rendered as liturgy. Compare the settings of the *Dies irae* in the requiem masses of Mozart, Berlioz and Fauré for three dissimilar, but stylistically logical, (and certainly *au courant*) compositions of their day. Mozart and Berlioz wrote their masses for immediate liturgical use. Fauré's *Requiem* was a personal, and also contemporary, expression, but one rendered liturgically improper by his reordering of the text. Today all three are thought of as secular concert works and are so heard by the public.[79]

But are such compositions as Fauré's *Requiem*, or Bach's too-long B Minor Mass, imperfect by liturgical standards, also spiritual failures? The devout might willingly embrace the spiritual values of such eloquent, if unconventional, "sacred compositions." Artistic superiority succeeds in bringing the traditional objective to the listener, if not to the practicing clergy. Gerardus van der Leeuw found such art works sufficiently exalting to classify them as religious music: "Bach and Beethoven wrote Masses which were useless for worship, and just because at the same time they created truly religious music, the hybrid nature of that form is all the more clear to us: outwardly sacred, inwardly, already fully autonomous."[80] (That is, it is religious art which is valid without the liturgical setting.)

The preference by nineteenth-century composers, worshippers and many churchmen for the contemporary Romantic style resulted in liturgical compositions which, to the Catholic Church, maintained no distinct spiritual statement. If the contemporary liturgical piece reminded the listeners of secular music, then it was profane. And again, as propaganda it was ineffective: There was no message, or it was the wrong message. The vigor of the encroachments now seems almost unbelievable. In 1884 Pope Leo XIII found it necessary to issue these words:

It is absolutely forbidden that any music should be performed in Church, however brief it may be, which draws themes from theatrical works, from dance music of whatever type, whether polkas, waltzes, mazurkas, varsoviennes, quadrilles, galops, *contre danses, lithuaniennes,* etc., or profane pieces such as national hymns, popular songs, love songs, funny songs, romanzas, etc.[81]

In 1903 Pope Pius X, in the first year of his reign, issued an extended statement, *Motu Proprio*[82] (in the tradition of John XXII, and also Alexander VII, Innocent XII, Benedict XIV, Leo XII and Leo XIII!)[83], in which he defined appropriate musical styles for the modern Roman Catholic church. The historic concern over the clarity of text and a suitable decorum were enunciated yet again:

Sacred music, being a complementary part of the solemn liturgy, participates in the general scope of the liturgy, which is the glory of God and the sanctification and edification of the faithful. . . . its principal office is to clothe with suitable melody the liturgical text . . . that through it the faithful may be the more easily moved to devotion and better disposed for the reception of the fruits of grace belonging to the celebration of the most holy mysteries (Par. 1).

He declared that the use of but one section of the liturgy, as the *Kyrie* or *Gloria*, to form a complete composition in itself, was wrong. The traditional form must be preserved, and clearly transmitted to the participant. "It is not lawful, therefore, to compose, for instance a *Tantum ergo* in such wise that the first strophe presents a romanza, a cavatina, an adagio, and the *Genitori* an allegro" (Par. 11). Exaggerated proportions were also scrutinized: "It is not lawful to keep the priest at the altar waiting on account of the chant or the music for a length of time not allowed by the liturgy" (Par. 22). The anxiety of Augustine and others on the threat of this sensuous medium to override the sacred was voiced again. "In general it must be considered a very grave abuse when the liturgy in ecclesiastical functions is made to appear secondary to and in a manner at the service of the music, for the music is merely a part of the liturgy and its humble handmaid" (Par. 23).

The model for polyphonic music was recognized as the sixteenth-century style of Palestrina. Another effort to reach back to the relative simplicity of the past was to prohibit the use of instrumental music except for special occasions, to reduce organ playing to a modest role—and never to use the piano. (Par. 15-19). The ubiquitous piano surely reminded the worshipper of the concert stage and the parlor. (Van der Leeuw remembered a district judge in Holland who "determined that a piano is profane, but an organ edifying. It is, or course, suspicious that moving-picture theatres also acquire organs [c. 1930]."[84])

The *Motu Proprio* also instructed local Sees to examine their music by official committees. In the United States, the Convention of the Society of St. Gregory of America nineteen years later (1922) completed a list of music judged in violation of the Vatican standard ("The Black List"). Twenty-two hymn and choir books in common use were banned, together with a long list of masses by workaday composers from Ashmall and Battmann to Marzo and Wiegand. A blanket disapproval of the works of Mozart, Haydn, Schubert and Rossini was given, not questioning their musical value specifically, but "their liturgical unfitness according to the principles of the *Motu Proprio*" (Par. 72-74). A few pieces were singled out: the *Ave Marias* of Verdi, Bach-Gounod and Mascagni; arrangements of operatic melodies such as the Sextet from *Lucia di*

Lammermoor, the Quartet from *Rigoletto,* arias from *Tannhäuser,* *Lohengrin,* and *Otello,* the wedding marches of Wagner and Mendelssohn, and all songs in English (the pope had emphasized the exclusive use of Latin in the liturgy), including *The End of a Perfect Day, Beautiful Isle of Somewhere, O Promise Me,* and *I Love You Truly!* The Black List censured the unethical behavior of publishers who arranged popular songs "revised in accordance with the *Motu Proprio."* A flagrant example of such contrafacta was the affixing of the text of *Ave Maris Stella* to the sentimental melody of *Silver Threads Among the Gold.*[85] Church musicians were not bereft of suitable works, however, and "The White List" offered a very long list of acceptable publications.[86]

The historical conflict over changing styles in Christian liturgical music may be predominantly, if not exclusively, a Western cultural problem. As we have noted, it was aggravated by the fascination with newness in seeking a contrast with the past generations. This is a different outlook from that of most non-Western societies. In the high cultures of the East, tradition and the past are enormously respected. In Asia, stylistic changes in art have occurred so slowly and conservatively that they seem imperceptible to the alien observer who attempts a historical survey. I do not allege that there was *no* change in the history of Islamic or Hindu (or Buddhist) music. The degree of change in Western liturgical music from the first centuries to the nineteenth, however, is unparalleled in the East. The continuous, sometimes contradictory changes in the accepted liturgical style from epoch to epoch produced a history of music peculiar to the West.

In the East, the Hindu and Buddhist clergy did not recast the *sutras* in the secular vocal and instrumental styles, textures, rhythms and timbres of, say, *Kathākali,* the *Khon* dance-drama, or Chinese Opera. The inspirations for these Asian (music) dramas were religious, but they developed independently; the ear does not confuse them with temple rites, or vice versa. The liturgical chant of India and Islam was not reshaped by the eager experiments which agitated European composers. Is further evidence needed? Where are equivalent stylistic changes in the non-West of *organa,* imitative polyphony, *basso continuo* texture, or the accompanied homophonic style? Such cataclysms of aesthetics did not arise.

The religious traditions of India were established long before the advent of Christianity, if not Judaism. Indians displayed only occasional interest in Europe's religious beliefs, and small demand for its musical methodology, until the twentieth century. The introduction of "new music" in nineteenth-century India as hymns for the Hindu service does not, in my judgment, detract from the evidence of this divergence in the histories of liturgical music of East and West. Quite unlike Christian monophony in the West, Hindu chant has not receded to a position of secondary favor by virtue of six centuries of polyphonic development. In India today, the fragile status of Vedic music is attributable to a waning interest in the practice of Hinduism and the formidable obligation to memorize the rituals, to political and social shifts that include rejection of the Brahman social system, and to the acceptance of Western attitudes and education.[87] But the Indian mythology of music—a religious doctrine—among some Indian scholars remains unshaken: God created music; the ancient sages explained its purpose and left sublime models of the art, and no one today can possibly equal them; and for Western analysts (beginning with Freud) to argue that heredity and environment are the causes of musical creativity is both pointless and mundane.[88]

In Western music we teach a history of styles, and the immediate stylistic sequence often exhibits polar opposites in aesthetic criteria; for example, Palestrina vis à vis (young) Schutz, and Haydn followed by Liszt. A transitional period records radical directions, often in the career of one artist, such as Monteverdi, Beethoven or Schoenberg. Each generation, even within a lengthy period (like the Baroque) looked back with small interest, even disdain, on the oeuvres of thirty or forty years before. Until the awareness of music history (and of history) in the early nineteenth century, no European audience wanted to hear "last year's opera," or what was supposed to be the symphonies of an epoch long past. In music the church hierarchy, a conservative force in itself, controlled the liturgy and preserved a body of the founding generation's musical art: plainchant. But there was no artistic hierarchy to control the minds of composers. New sacred styles appeared persistently and were fitted to the liturgy with enthusiasm or disapproval, according to local attitudes.

The causes for the conflicts and the rivalry discussed here are not explained solely by the aesthetic or intellectual vitality (or arrogance?) of the composers. Sometimes a musical change was directed by the theologians, particularly during a vigorous religious movement. The Protestant Reformations in Germany, France and England illustrate such an impetus, and some have been cited here.

There is another in modern Judaism. Political enlightenment in Europe toward the end of the eighteenth century brought powerful changes to the Jews, who had often lived in physical, as well as cultural, isolation, and were now given emancipation. Freedom to live outside the ghettos was particularly significant. Progressive and wealthy Jews began to enjoy a closer social relationship with the Christian mainstream. In Germany acculturation proceeded rapidly, and in some ways it altered Judaism. The Reform Movement introduced non-Jewish sacred and secular songs, the German language, and four-part choral writing (as the preferred style) into synagogal music. Progressive and influential composers for the synagogue, such as Sulzer, Lewandowski and Naumbourg, wrote in the prevailing Romantic style. Local rabbis found that the pleasing sound of choral singing with organ accompaniment was attractive to the youth.[89] It was scarcely the last time a pastor employed a current fashion to hold on to teenagers!

If we are to understand the adoption of homophonic accompanied music—a sound which is anathema in the ancient tradition—by the Jewish reform synagogues in the nineteenth century, it is impossible to disregard the ambient European aesthetic criteria as immediate and secular influences. Was this not an example of a double meaning embedded in the liturgical music? To the conservatives, the alien musical style bespoke a contradiction.

The Eastern Christian or Byzantine rite, however, remained overwhelmingly unison chant, the occasional use of an unwritten drone by the antiphonal choir notwithstanding.[90] In the Russian Church, whose liturgy derives from the Byzantine, attempts at polyphony (*strochny* chant) began in the late 1600s. Homophonic choral writing was admitted in the eighteenth century, a corruption, like that among the Reform Jews, carried by the growing fascination with European models of culture, including the import of Italian opera. The distinctive *Cherubic Hymn* of the Eastern rite, sung at the Great Entrance (comparable in location to the Offertory in the Roman rite), became an opportunity for eloquent choral settings (for example, those by Bortniansky, Tchaikovsky, and

Rachmaninov). But such temptations were not admitted into the Byzantine (Greek) service. The Great Schism had cut off the Eastern Christians from the artistic experimentation of Europe; further, after 1453 the territory of ancient Byzantium was guarded even more stiffly by the Ottoman Empire. Even today, the sounds of four-part choirs heard in American Greek Orthodox churches would be regarded as absurd in Greece.

Music in the mosque has also remained virtually unchanged. A single style, monophony, endures, shielded by the view that music is improper in a prayer service and the chant used is not music. The Qur'ān remains the only literary text used in the prayerservice, and it is believed that the cantillation has changed but little over the centuries.[91] The free use of other forms of devotional music outside the mosque has perhaps served the artist's creative aspirations. This choice may be as relevant to some composers and performers in Islam as it has been elsewhere.

An Asian philosopher, during a conference on East and West culture in 1959, offered this observation:

If you were to ask a Burmese or an Indonesian or an Arab, one of his very first reactions would be to say that the West is a world of movement. This inquisitiveness, this questioning of established values, this creative anxiety . . . this recklessness—this is the rhythm and the tempo of Western civilization which some of us are afraid of, which others, more and more numerous, are eager to imitate. . . . If this free creation of problems and questionings is taken away from Western civilization, it droops; but let the unexpected come back again as a challenge, and Western civilization is re-animated.[92]

We have seen that music is not "a universal language," if "universal" is to mean that all peoples and all cultures find the same musical expression (or styles) meaningful. It is known that the world sustains many musics and many definitions of music. But ritual song, as we noted at the beginning of this chapter, is a universal element in religious worship. The cultures of the world have fashioned music in many ways to carry their sacred messages. The West generated a vast stream of sacred composers, many of whose aesthetics reveal diametrically opposed criteria from each other. In retrospect, we may grant them all devout hearts as well as imaginative ears, and suppose that their efforts were no worse than those of reckless liturgics and, at best inspired declarations of faith which added conviction and vivacity to the ritual message.[93] But no other genre of Western music documents such a long and strenuous contest between artist and "ruler" for the attention of their audience.

NOTES

1. Oliver Strunk, *Source Readings in Music History* (New York: W. W. Norton & Co., 1950), p. 68.

2. As reported by Reuters and The Associated Press from Tehran on July 26, 1979. The Islamic leader's view was that the former Shah's regime and "monarchies everywhere were intent on corrupting the younger generation so that they would not revolt." Islamic attitudes on music are discussed further in this chapter.

3. Eric Werner sees these figures as the counterparts of Roman mythology. *NG*, IX, p. 616.

4. Franklin Edgerton, *The Beginnings of Indian Philosophy* (Cambridge: Harvard University Press, 1965), see p. 167 (IV.5:11), also R. C. Zaehner, ed. and tr., *Hindu Scriptures* (London: J. M. Dent & Sons, 1966), p. 17.

5. The most ancient sources of Hindu music are the four *Vedas* (literally, "knowledge"). Each is a compendium of hymns, ritual formulas, and detailed instruction on the rites. The verses vary from the aristocratic forms of the *Ṛg Veda* to the simpler ceremonies for the mass of the people in the *Atharva Veda*. (Edgerton, *Indian Philosophy*, pp. 17-18.) A fourth collection is the *Sāma Veda*, which contains the texts for the most solemn ritual, the soma sacrifice, in which an intoxicating juice was ritually pressed from the soma plant and presented to the deity. The musical material of these hymns in turn varies from syllabic chant in a narrow range of a few pitches, to wide-ranged, melismatic melodies, the latter often in the challenging and eloquent chants of the *Sāma Veda*.

6. Swāmī Prajñānānanda,*A Historical Study of Indian Music* (Calcutta: Anandadhara, Prakashan 1965), pp. 407, 417.

7. To be more precise: There are two kinds of *nāda*, or sound. One is a"vibration of ether," and cannot be perceived by the physical sense. It is theprinciple of manifestation, what the neo-Pythagoreans termed the "music of the spheres." The other kind of sound is caused by physical shock (friction, etc.), and is audible sound. The former is called *anāhata*, "unstruck" sound, "in which the Gods delight." The physical sound is *āhata* or "struck" sound, and it yields (material) pleasure. The yoga masters project their minds into the unstruck sound and reach liberation. From

Alain Daniélou, *Northern Indian Music* (New York: Frederick A. Praeger, 1969), p. 21, based on his readings of Sanskrit authors. The syllable "nā" means breath, and "da," fire (of intellect) (Ibid., p. 22). *Nāda* is perceived by the Divine Mind without any medium (physical vibration) or receiver (the ear): "It is the primordial causal stress, the creative energy of all manifestation. By condensation of *Nāda*, energy becomes nuclear, and that gives rise to shapes and forms." (Jaidev Singh, "Nāda in Indian Tradition," in *Journal of the Indian Musicological Society*, vol. XI:1, 2 (March, June, 1980), p. 38). Sound as an element of first creation is not inimical to Biblical thought, either: In the first chapter of Genesis action commences with each repeated phrase, "And God said. . . ."

8. Daniélou, *Northern Indian Music*, p. 3.

9. Prajñānānda, *Historical Study*, p. 419.

10. Wayne Howard, *Sāmavedic Chant* (New Haven: Yale University Press, 1977), p. 3.

11. Ibid., p. 4.

12. *Sacred Books of the East*, F. Max Müller, ed. (Delhi: Motila Banarsidass, 1963. Reprint of 1885 edition), vol. XXVI (tr. by Julius Eggeling), pp. 229-30.

13. Ibid., vol. XII, pp. 164 ff.

14. Howard, *Sāmavedic Chant*, pp. 18-24, 78-91, 220-48.

15. *The Nāṭyaśāstra*, attributed to Bharatamuni, Manomohan Ghosh, tr. and commentary (Calcutta: The Asiatic Society, 1961), vol. II, Preface. See also Daniélou, *Northern Indian Music*, pp. 9-10.

16. Alain Daniélou, *Hindu Polytheism* (New York: Pantheon Books, 1964), pp. 200, 354.

The ancient knowledge also includes a "Śiva School of Music." This is conspicuous in Tantric Hinduism, whose sources (distinct from the Vedic literature) are the *Tantra*, and emphasize magic rites. From Śiva comes all the elements of music, and he is an embodiment of *Nāda*. See Sures Chandra Banerji, "Influence of Tantra on Indian Music and Dance," *Journal of the Indian Musicological Society*, X:3, 4 (September, December 1979), p. 22; see also Daniélou, *Northern Indian Music*, p. 3. *Nāda* is the union of Śiva and his consort Śakti, "passing from the state of mere potency into that of the first ideating movement from which the whole universe is evolved." Singh, "Nada in Indian Tradition," p. 38.

17. Romain Goldron [A. Louis Burkhalter], *Minstrels and Masters: The Triumph of Polyphony* (New York: H. S. Stuttman Co./Doubleday & Co., 1960), p. 18. For a specialized study see E. L. Backman, *Religious Dances in the Christian Church and in Popular Medicine*, tr. by E. Classen (New York: Macmillan, 1952).

18. Goldron, *Minstrels and Masters*, p. 19.

19. Gerardus van der Leeuw, *Sacred and Profane Beauty: The Holy in Art* (New York: Holt, Rinehart and Winston, 1963), p. 70.

20. M. M. Sharif, "Islam and Spiritual Values," in Charles A. Moore, ed., *Philosophy and Culture East and West: East-West Philosophy in Practical Perspective* (Honolulu: University of Hawaii Press, 1962), p. 293.

21. Bruno Nettl, "Attitudes Toward Persian Music, Tehran, 1969," in *The Musical Quarterly*, LVI:2 (April 1970), p. 186, n.5.

22. Lois Ibsen al Faruqi, "Factors of Continuity in the Musical Cultures of the Muslim World." Paper read at the Annual Meeting of the Society for Ethnomusicology, College Park, Maryland (October, 1982), p. 2. See also *An Annotated Glossary of Arabic Musical Terms*, compiled by al Faruqi (Westport, Ct.: Greenwood Press, 1981), for other terms with discrete meanings and, conversely, multiple meanings for the same term. The place to begin in this extraordinary compendium is the Index of English Terms, pp. 417ff.

23. [Lois] Lamya' [Ibsen] al Faruqi, "Tartīl al-Qur'ān al-Karīm," in *Islamic Perspectives: Studies in Honour of Sayyid Abul A'la Mawdudi* (Leicester, U. K.: The Islamic Foundation, 1979), pp. 109-11.

24. Ibid., pp. 105-7.

25. al Faruqi, "Tartīl al-Qur'ān," pp. 111-12.

26. For example, Pratapaditya Pal, *The Ideal Image* (New York: The Asia Society, 1978), plates 3, 28, 92, and 22 with the vīṇā (lute). See also Prajñānānanda, *Historical Study*, Chapters VI and XIV.

27. José Pereira, ed., *Hindu Theology: A Reader* (New York: Image Books/Doubleday & Co., 1976), p. 345.

28. Edgerton, *Beginnings of Indian Philosophy*, p. 167, (iv:8-10); Zaehner, *Hindu Scriptures*, p. 46, (iv:7-9).

29. James Hornell, *The Indian Conch and Its Relation to Hindu Life and Religion* (London: William & Norgate, 1915), p. 11.

30. *NG*, IX, p. 74.

31. See Arnold Perris, "Padmasaṃbhava's Paradise," in *Imago Musicae: The Yearbook of Musical Iconography* (Kassel: Barenreiter Verlag, 1984, vol. I, p. 182 and Fig. 5, p. 180. The subject is a Tibetan ritual painting (*thanka*). Dhṛtarāṣṭra is one of thirty figures with musical instruments.

32. See Emanuel Winternitz, *Musical Instruments and Their Symbolism in Western Art* (New York: W. W. Norton & Co., 1967), pp. 37, 40, 47.

33. In fact, the accounts of such instruments were written generations, even centuries, after the persons and events they describe. In many ancient and medieval sources—from Greek and Latin to modern languages and cultures—the identification of Biblical instruments is confounded from one era to another. Compare the reference to Jubal in the Revised Standard Version (1951), "lyre and pipe," with the King James's Version (1611):

"harp and organ"! See *NG*, IX, p. 618; also Joan Rimmer, *Ancient Musical Instruments of Western Asia in the British Museum* (London: British Museum, 1969), Appendix.

34. Some of the Levites were responsible for playing instruments in the sanctuary, though not to accompany the chant. *The Code of Maimonides*, one of the later commentaries (twelfth century) on the *Torah*, spelled out in detail what instruments were used, how many, and on what occasions they were to be heard. (His remarks spring from the reminiscences of post-biblical writers, and are not based on historical evidence.)

Never less than two lyres nor more than six; never less than two flutes, nor more than twelve; never less than two trumpets nor more than one hundred and twenty; never less than nine harps, but their number could be increased without limit. There was only one cymbal. . . . On all Festival Days and the New Moon Days the priests would blow on the trumpets at the time of the offering, and the Levites would chant.

Code of Maimonides, Book 8, *The Book of the Temple*, tr. Mendell Lewittes (New Haven: Yale University Press, 1957), p. 51. See also Numbers x:10.

35. Eric Werner, *The Sacred Bridge: The Interdependence of Liturgy and Music in Synagogue and Church during the First Milennium* (New York: Columbia University Press, 1966), p. 15, n.37. The use of the shofar was (and still is) very specific. In the liturgy, after the reading of the lesson for the holy day, the sound of the shofar was heard. It was sounded to proclaim the Jubilee Year and "freedom throughout the land." When used in the temple, it was usually supported by the trumpet. See *Encyclopaedia Judaica* (New York: Macmillan, 1971), vol. XIV, p. 1443. This source counts sixty-nine references to the shofar in the Bible; the first is Exodus xix:16. In Hinduism, however, the conch shell horn is not so proscribed an article. Ghosh, *Nātyaśāstra*, II, p. 50, n.1. See also Ch. XXXIII, p. 17.

36. *NG*, VI, p. 618.

37. *Cambridge Medieval History*, vol. IV: *The Byzantine Empire*, part 2, *Government, Church and Civilisation*, J. M. Hussey, ed. (London: Cambridge University Press, 1967), pp. 136-37; Egon Wellesz, *A History of Byzantine Music and Hymnography*, (London: Oxford University Press, 1961), second edition, pp. 32, 105-8.

38. *NG*, IX, p. 342.

39. Martin Gerbert, ed., *Scriptores ecclesiastici de musica sacra.* (Hildesheim: Georg Olms, 1963. Reprint of 1784 ed.) vol. II, p. 388.

40. Reproduced in Donald Grout, *A History of Western Music* (New York: W. W. Norton & Co., 1973), revised edition, p. 161; also Paul Lang and Otto Bettmann, *A Pictorial History of Music* (New York: W. W. Norton & Co., 1960), p. 12.

41. Lois Ibsen al Faruqi, "What Makes 'Religious Music' Religious?" in Joyce Irwin, ed., *Sacred Sound: Music in Religious Thought and Practice, Journal of the American Academy of Religion Thematic Studies* (Chico, Ca.: Scholars Press, 1983), L:1, p. 28.

42. Charles Hamm, Bruno Nettl, and Ronald Byrnside, *Contemporary Music and Music Cultures* (Englewood Cliffs, N. J.: Prentice-Hall, 1975), p. 76.

43. Ibid., pp. 90-91.

44. al Faruqi, "What Makes 'Religious Music' Religious?" p. 31. Jafran Jones investigated the public performance of religious music by the *'Isāwīya*, Sufi brotherhoods in Tunisia. The purpose of the ceremonies (*dhikr*) is to bring devotion to a point of ecstasy. She also pointed out the contradiction of the term "religious music" in Islamic culture: "Tunisian terms for musical genres are scarce." "The 'Isāwīya of Tunisia and Their Music" Unpublished Ph.D. diss., University of Washington, 1978, p. vii.

45. See Dena Epstein, *Sinful Tunes and Spirituals* (Chicago: University of Illinois, 1977), chapters XI and XII. See also Albert J. Raboteau, *Slave Religion*. (New York: Oxford University Press, 1978), passim, and Mellonee Burnim, "The Black Gospel Music Tradition: Symbol of Ethnicity." Unpublished Ph.D. diss. Indiana University, 1980.

46. Bharatamuni, *Nāṭyaśāstra*, chapter XXXIII, pp. 5-13, 242-59.

47. For a tenth-century reaffirmation of this dogma, see the illustration from the "Roll of Joshua" in *NG*, IX, p. 617.

48. Strunk, *Source Readings*, p. 61.

49. Ibid., p. 63.

50. Eric Werner, *The Sacred Bridge*, p. 103.

51. See ibid., pp. 332-33. Bells, in particular, are believed to frighten off bad spirits in many cultures and situations. See James George Frazer, *Folklore in the Old Testament* (London: Macmillan, 1919), vol. III, Chapter VII, "The Golden Bells," pp. 446-80.

52. Bharatamuni, *Nāṭyaśāstra*, chapter XXXVI, pp. 23, 25-27.

53. Prajñānānanda, *Historical Study*, p. 370.

54. B. Chaitanya Deva, *An Introduction to Indian Music* (New Delhi: Publications Division, Ministry of Information and Broadcasting, 1973), pp. 71-72. A recent psychological test of 228 persons in India reported a "staggeringly complete" recognition of traditional moods, time of day, season and color for ragas by the respondents, only some of whom were trained in Indian classical music. The authors' explanation of the accuracy was the possibility of a "racial memory," existent over the last three hundred years, during whic h the ragas' "definable emotional state" has remained fairly constant. B. C. Deva and K. G. Virmani, "A Study in the Psychological Response to Ragas" (abstract) in *Journal of the Indian Musicological Society* XI: 1, 2 (March/June, 1980), pp. 33-36.

55. Translated in Zaehner, *Hindu Scriptures*, p. 84.

56. Strunk, *Source Readings*, pp. 67-68.

57. Ibid., p. 68.

58. Ibid., 72. In Werner, *The Sacred Bridge*, pp. 313-26, a chapter is devoted to "The Aesthetic and Ethical Evaluation of Music in Synagogue and Church." He remarked:

To biblical literature the idea that music is beautiful is evidently alien; music had its place in the ritual of the Temple, or it served as a spontaneous expression of an individual or a group, but it did not have any direct connection with the aesthetically beautiful. That conception is linked to visual sensations only, as the Song of Songs and similar poems seem to indicate. Even so late a book as Ecclesiasticus, [The Apochryphal Ecclesiasticus: 48-50] which described in the most glowing terms the cult of the Temple, used the word beautiful only where a visual sensation was involved.

59. Robert J. O'Connell, *St. Augustine's Confessions: The Odyssey of Soul* (Cambridge: Harvard University Press, 1969), p. 22, summarizing Fredrick van der Meer's observations in *Augustine the Bishop*, (New York: Sheed and Ward, 1961), *passim*.

60. Augustine, *St. Augustine's Confessions*, tr. William Watts (1631) in the Loeb Classical Library (Cambridge: Harvard University Press, 1961), Vol. II, p. 167.

61. Ibid.

62. Ibid., pp. 167, 169.

63. al Faruqi, "Tartīl al-Qur'ān," pp. 109-10.

64. Ibid., p. 117.

65. *The Oxford History of Music*. (London: Oxford University Press, 1929), second edition, I, p. 209.

66. Gabriele and Walter Salmen believe that Landini (d. 1397) was the first musician judged worthy enough to be memorialized in marble, as bishops and princes were. "In this depiction [in the Church of San Lorenzo, Florence], Landini's occupation is clear: Rather than a sword or pen as attribute, he carries an organ." "Portraits of Musicians in the Course of Social History," paper delivered to the Ninth International Conference on Musical Iconography, summarized in *RIdIM Newsletter* (New York: City University of New York, Graduate School, 1983), VIII; 1, p. 5.

67. See François Lesure, *Music and Art in Society* (University Park: Pennsylvania State University Press, 1968), plate 84, and Goldron, *Minstrels and Masters*, pp. 68, 94. The miniature, said to be of Ockeghem in his chapel, shows nine singers. Our slender reading on the numbers of choir singers in the medieval Christian church is contrasted with the explicit

directions for the Hebrew temple, as recorded in the *Code of Maimonides*: "There must never be less than twelve Levites standing on the Platform every day to chant over the offering, but their number could be increased without limit." The Levites were the professional singers in the temple, and the clan had been "separated from the rest of the community (of Israel) so they would be ready to serve at all times in the sanctuary." (*Code*:51.)

68. Grout, *History of Western Music* (first edition 1960), p. 117. This quotation is not found in later editions.

69. Strunk, *Source Readings*, pp. 183, 185, 189-90.

70. Strunk, *Source Readings*, pp. 158-59. See *Papal Documents on Sacred Music* (New York: St. Gregory Society of America, 1939), third edition, pp. 3-4.

71. Hassler's original song is found in his *Lustgarten neuer teutscher Gesang* (New York: Broude Bros., 1966), p. 24. The later chorale versions are found in Luther Noss, *Christian Hymns* (Cleveland and New York: Meridian Books, 1963), Nos. 79i, 79ii.

72. Aron Marko Rothmüller, *The Music of the Jews: An Historical Appreciation*, new and revised edition, tr. by H. S. Stevens (South Brunswick, N. J. and London: Thomas Yoseloff, 1967), p. 112.

73. Ibid., p. 118.

74. Ibid., pp. 118-19.

75. Eileen Southern, *The Music of Black Americans* (New York: W.W. Norton & Co., 1971), pp. 132-34.

76. Piero Weiss, *Letters of Composers through Six Centuries* (Philadelphia: Chilton Book Co., 1967), p. 3.

77. See Palestrina, *Spem in alium, Primi Toni, Ave Maria, Brevis*, and *Papae Marcelli*. In *L'Homme armé*, the words received long notes, though the passage is not strictly homophonic. To be sure, there are other works in which this is not his chosen setting, such as *Sine nomine* and *De Beata Virgine*. (*Le Opera complete di Giovanni Pierluigi da Palestrina*. Rome: Instituto Italiano per la Storia della Musica, 1956-60.) See also Lassus, *Super confundantur superbi* (Mass No. 42), *Paschalis* (No. 48), *Le Berger et la bergère* (!) (No. 5), and (*Sämtliche Werke, neue Reihe*, vol. IX. Kassel: Barenreiter Verlag, 1969). In the Classical period this sentence commands attention often by a contrast of sonority, from full chorus to solo voice or solo quartet, and frequently, also, a change to a slow tempo. For example: Haydn, "Lord Nelson" Mass (No. 3); Mozart, K. 137, 194, 262, 258, 337 and 427; Beethoven, *Missa Solemnis*.

78. I am grateful to the Reverend J. Jeffrey Zetto, Th.D., of Bloomsburg, Pennsylvania, for his analysis. For a musical analysis, see W. Gillies Whittaker, *The Cantatas of Johann Sebastian Bach, Sacred and Secular* (London: Oxford University Press, 1959), vol. I, pp. 146-50. In

Bach's first job as organist in a church in Arnstadt, he led the congregation astray with his all-too-inventive ornamentations of the hymn, and received a reprimand from the Church officers. The record is found in Hans T. David and Arthur Mendel, *The Bach Reader* (New York: W. W. Norton & Co., 1966), revised edition, p. 52.

79. Whatever the ecclesiastical and historical judgment of Berlioz's *Grande Messe* in 1837, it was in fact used—once, in its premiere performance—for a solemn and national service, the memorial for General Damrémont, hero of the Algerian campaign, in the Church of St. Louis at the Invalides. See Jacques Barzun, *Berlioz and the Romantic Century* (New York: Columbia University Press, 1969), third edition, vol. I, pp. 279, 280.

80. *Sacred and Profane*, p. 223.

81. *Regulations for Sacred Music*, in *Papal Documents*, p. 6.

82. Ibid., pp. 7-11.

83. Ibid., pp. 4-6.

84. *Sacred and Profane*, p. 269.

85. *Papal Documents*, p. 11.

86. Ibid., pp. 32-71.

87. Howard, *Sāmavedic Chant*, pp. 76 *ff.*, 154-55; Shyamala Vanarase, "Modernity and Musical Taste: Some Psychological Considerations," in *Journal of the Indian Musicological Society*, X:1, 2 (March/June 1979), pp. 5-6.

88. See Somnath Bhattacharya, "Psychoanalysis and Creativity: With Special Reference to Musical Creativity," in *Journal of the Indian Musicological Society*, XI: 1, 2 (March/June, 1980), pp. 90-104.

89. Rothmüller, *Music of the Jews*, pp. 125-26.

90. See Dimitri Conomos, "Experimental Polyphony, 'According to the . . . Latins,' in Late Byzantine Psalmody," in *Early Music History*, II (1983), pp. 1-16.

91. al Faruqi, "What Makes 'Religious Music' Religious?", p. 25.

92. "The Islamic Cultural Tradition and the West" by N. Bammate, in *Philosophy and Culture East and West: East-West Philosophy in Practical Perspective*, Charles A. Moore, ed., p. 724.

93. "The artist who is firm in his faith and leads a life worthy of a Christian, who . . . expresses the piety he possesses so skilfully, beautifully and pleasingly in colors and lines or sounds and harmonies that this sacred labor of art is an act of worship and religion for him. It also effectively arouses and inspires people to profess the faith and cultivate piety. The Church has always honored and always will honor this kind of an artist. It opens wide the doors of its temples to them because what these people contribute through their art and industry is a welcome and important help to the Church in carrying out its apostolic ministry more effectively." Pius

XII, encyclical letter, *Musicae sacrae disciplina* ("On Sacred Music"), December 25, 1955 (Washington, D.C.: National Catholic Welfare Conference, 1956).

CHAPTER 7

The Hidden Rostrum of Opera and the Broadway Musical

Our time will come; we'll wait in silence,
One day a daring deed to do.
Take heart, no matter what comes;
Skill alone can undo this yoke.
Better to die on the ramparts of danger,
Than live in chains, outcasts and slaves!
Let us unite and throw out the strangers,
With one blow, save our country's freedom!

La Muette de Portici, act II

A French opera about a revolution so inflamed the Belgian public in 1830 that it led to their independence from Holland. The opera, *La Muette de Portici* or *Masaniello,* by Daniel Auber, had caused a theatrical sensation when given its premiere two years before in Paris. The story of a commoner's rebellion in seventeenth-century Naples found sympathy among the French. In 1828 they were on the eve of a middle-class revolution which exploded in July, 1830 and brought to the throne Louis Philippe, who called himself the Citizen King.

The libretto of *La Muette* (The mute girl), written by Eugène Scribe, told of the revolt in the Kingdom of Naples against the Spanish ruler in 1647. A fisherman called Masaniello for a time became the king. His sister, Fenella, was a go-between as he undertook his campaign. The hazards of her duty were intensified because she was mute. In opera this meant that she did not sing; the role was performed by a dancer and her pantomimed movements were spelled out in the libretto.

One month following the 1830 French Revolution Auber's stirring opera was sung in Brussels. There the story became more than a sympathetic theme; the successful rebellion depicted on stage was another spark which soon moved the populace to a real-life revolt. The tragic consequences to the operatic hero were no deterrent and this make-believe revolution moved past the stage footlights. The story depicted the people of a small country rising up against a foreign rule—and winning, at least for a time. In real life that year, the Belgians established an independent constitutional monarchy.

The music of *La Muette* also seemed electrifying in 1828. It was Auber's greatest triumph, and he never matched it again, in a long life highly esteemed by his nation and his public. *La Muette de Portici*, nevertheless, was the immediate forerunner of the spectacular style which became known as French Grand Opera. The century was filled with highly dramatic stage works by Meyerbeer, Halévy, Donizetti, Verdi, and others.[1] In *La Muette*, the eruption of Mt. Vesuvius in 1631 is "delayed" sixteen years to provide a hair-raising finale in which the pitiful Fenella is buried in the cataclysm.

And there was another opera at the same time and on the same theme: the overthrow of a foreign tyrant by a courageous man of the people. This was an opera which far exceeded Auber's effort in musical content and literary force. It was based on one of Friedrich Schiller's plays of political protest: the story of the Swiss patriot, William Tell. It was the longest, and the most serious, of the operas by the immensely popular Gioacchino Rossini. He labored over the work for several months—quite uncommon for him. (*The Barber of Seville* was written in ten days!) In its original form *William Tell*, staged at the prestigious Paris Opera, was a six-hour epic. In cut versions, it soon received many performances.

The famous overture is about all that we have to remember it by today. Yet Rossini reached for a more profound expression, and for psychological insights in this opera beyond all his previous efforts. It was a "political opera" on a perpetually dangerous theme: insurrection.

Rossini was not motivated by social concern, but he was an astute businessman. He was aware of the popularity of political causes in the 1820s. A fashionable topic in the arts was the Greek fight for independence from Turkey, on the subject of which poems by Byron and Shelley and paintings by Delacroix had appeared. The Italian composer had earlier provided a parallel in his *Siege of Corinth* in 1826, and the libretto had been based on Byron's poem. The story of William Tell came from Swiss legends about the founding of their republic in the thirteenth century. Schiller elevated the personal trials of a few villagers to the greater needs of the people, who were oppressed by an Austrian governor, Gessler. In the operatic version of Schiller's play, there is a romance between Arnold, son of the Swiss patriarch, Melcthal, and Mathilda, a princess from the hated royal family of Habsburgs. In some versions, she is made Gessler's daughter, to intensify a dilemma familiar in the theatre: young lovers who are born to antagonistic families, like the Montagues and the Capulets. Unlike Shakespeare's situation, the emotional aspect of patriotism is introduced: The plot resembles Verdi's opera of *Aida* and her Rhadames, in which the ultimate test is to choose country or love. The romantic conflict becomes a part of a larger canvas, depicting the trials of an entire people in a struggle for liberty.

Schiller's plays, like many by Shakespeare, were a rich source for opera composers in the nineteenth century. The reason was their literary quality, but it would be careless to overlook Schiller's persistent selection of historical crises about political, religious, or social oppression, either of a people or of an individual. Giuseppe Verdi, the greatest of Italian opera composers, was stimulated by four of Schiller's plays, and turned them into operas: *Don Carlo*, *Giovanna d'Arco*, *I Masnadieri* (Schiller's *Robbers*), and *Luisa Miller*.

Verdi's long career—he composed the last of his thirty-six operas at age eighty—was a determined search for significant dramatic subjects, and those subjects again and again revealed (or deliberately disguised) his passionate support of Italian independence from Austria. His opera plots expose tyrants and tyrannies over individuals and upon whole peoples, from the self-indulgence of the duke in *Rigoletto* to the despotism of Philip II of Spain over the Flemish (*Don Carlo*), and the enslavement of the Ethiopian war victims by the Pharoah in *Aida*.

In *A Hundred Years of Music* Gerald Abraham makes this summary:

But one *subsidiary motive is noticeable* in Verdi's choice of subjects, that of *patriotism*. In *Nabucco* the captivity of the Jews obviously symbolizes the captivity of the Italians; *I Lombardi alla Prima Crociato* (1843) similarly uses the First Crusade as a mere stalking-horse . . . in the minds of the listeners, not the Holy Places but the cities of Italy. The subject was meant to remind Italians in general, and the Lombard city, Milan, for which it was written in particular, of their ancient military glory. . . . *Attila* (1846) again deliberately played on patriotic, anti-Austrian feeling, and probably owed its success to that fact rather than to its not very remarkable musical value; the libretto contains, among other things, the famous line addressed to Attila by the Roman envoy, Ezio, "You shall have the universe, if I may have Italy." *La Battaglia di Legnano* was frankly inspired by the revolutionary movement of 1848 and produced in Rome in January, 1849, on the eve of the proclamation of the Roman Republic.[2]

Nabucodonosor, shortened to *Nabucco*, was Verdi's third opera. It is based on the biblical story of Nebuchadnezzar's defeat of the Hebrews, the destruction of their temple, and their enslavement. In the first year of the opera's appearance in 1842 it was performed at Milan's La Scala Theatre sixty-two times, an unprecedented record for that time. It was the first of his stream of fiery operas that were read by the Italians as metaphors for the revolution they wanted, intermittently attempted, and lost. The remote—and pious— setting of the Bible gave the opera a cachet of untouchability which apparently shielded it from the censorship laid on many of Verdi's later works, whose characters and situations were all too close to the political realities of Europe.

In act II, on the banks of the Euphrates, the Hebrews in chains are at forced labor. Verdi wrote a slow, poignant chorus of the homesick captives, which became a symbolic, if subdued, rallying cry for his countrymen. It made Verdi a national hero. The text of the chorus is a paraphrase of Psalm 137, "By the waters of Babylon we sat down and wept." They are exhorted by their prophet, Zeccharia, to raise their heads proudly. They will one day be free of their bonds, he promises, and Babylon will be reduced to dust. "Not a stone will be left to tell where proud Babylon once stood."

In the final scene, with the legendary Hanging Gardens for a backdrop, the tyrant, Nabucco (that is, Nebuchadnezzar), has been driven to a mental breakdown by the treachery of his adopted daughter, Abigail, who has uncrowned him and assumed the throne.

His true daughter, Fenena, has been condemned to death because she has accepted the faith of the Hebrew captives and her hero, Ishmael. The condemned Hebrews are marched in. The king bursts into the temple. He has recovered his mind, and, with new insight, commands the destruction of the golden image of Baal, and that the captives be freed to return to their homeland. Before anyone can attack the statue, it crashes to the floor. The Hebrews proclaim the supremacy of Jehovah. The message: A tyrant may receive enlightenment, become a true believer, and redeem his evil by granting liberty to his victims; but of still greater impact: A captive people may win freedom if they will endure years of tribulation. All this was a potent allegory—and hope—for Verdi's countrymen. It was not one they would see as a fact for many years.

Another contemporary playwright attracted Verdi's imagination: Victor Hugo. The young and radical Hugo aroused a furor in 1830 in Paris with the premiere of *Hernani*. The play was a deliberate literary attack on the French Classical style, and it became a milestone of French Romanticism. In 1844 Verdi based an opera on the play: *Ernani*. The libretto was resisted by the Austrian censors, since it depicted a conspiracy to murder Don Carlos of Spain, who became the illustrious Charles V of Austria.

A second Hugo play seized Verdi's attention when he read *Le Roi s'amuse* (The king amuses himself). This became *Rigoletto* (1851). The story is a personal tragedy on the surface: a father attempts to avenge the seduction of his daughter by his employer, a cynical aristocrat whose every selfish whim is always fulfilled.

Hugo had constructed a violent drama about the licentious King Francis I of France and his jester, Triboulet. Following the Paris premiere in 1832, the play was banned for fifty years. Verdi and his Italian librettist, Francesco Piave, were compelled by the Austrian censor to make many changes in order to avoid the appearance on stage of a supreme ruler whose amoral behavior placed his subjects in bondage to his desires. The character of the French king was "downgraded" to that of a provincial duke. The young lady carried off by the French king was also a historic figure, Diane de Poitiers. In the Italian libretto, the heroine became the daughter of the jester, hidden away from the sophisticated court in a suburban home.

Despite many suggestions and revisions, the military governor of Venice rejected the final text. Further, he rebuked both the poet and the (by now) illustrious composer for selecting a plot "of such repulsive immorality and obscene triviality."[3] Piave, an easygoing personality, was willing to change anything to save the opera, but Verdi, always with resolute intentions and standards, refused. Some things in the story could not be changed, he insisted. The prince, whether called a king or a duke, could not be made less a rake; the jester, made a hunchback, could not be deprived of his ugly handicap because to do so would contradict the bitter music Verdi provided for him. The opera, first termed *The Curse*, was saved by a characteristic Italian paradox. A censorship official suggested the way out: The action was transferred from France to Italy, the historical King of France became a fictitious Duke of Mantua, and the time was set safely back in the sixteenth century. Verdi endured a similar tussle in 1859 over *The Masked Ball*, in which a king is assassinated.[4]

The propaganda power of the musical stage has also been noted in other chapters in citing operas of Beethoven, Mozart, Smetana, Wagner and others. The familiar and often glamorous genre of opera began only at the end of the sixteenth century. The originators were a small group of cultivated Florentine amateurs, joined by a handful of professional writers and musicians; they called themselves the Camerata. Their ambition was to stage the stories of Greek myths in the style of Classical drama, as they supposed it was declaimed in antiquity. Their "revival" produced a new genre.

The theatricality of the new style was so attractive, so full of challenge to a composer's skill in depicting various emotions, that it quickly slipped from the care of the small elite. In the hands of Claudio Monteverdi opera became a dramatic play, especially a tragedy, told by means of solo singers, a chorus, dancers, and accompanied by the beginning of the modern orchestra. To this charm for the ears was added the visual appeal of the stage, costumes, and quite often extraordinary scenic effects. The confrontations of gods and men, the dilemmas over love or honor, self or kingdom, life or death, enthralled audiences in the 1600s and still do.

A historical marker that illustrates the close connection of opera with social history is *Il Pomo d'oro* (The golden apple) of Marc' Antonio Cesti. He was commissioned to compose an opera suitable for the marriage celebration of Infanta Margherita of Spain to

Emperor Leopold I of Austria. The festivities sealed the union of two ruling families and thoroughly preoccupied the Viennese court at the end of 1666.

To symbolize the opulence of the Emperor, and demonstrate that his artists could equal those of the admired court of Versailles, no limitation was admitted. The opera contained five acts, with sixty-six scenes and twenty-three different stage sets. Each act featured several ballet numbers. The astonishing stage designs by Burnacini are still a marvel as seen in engravings.[5] The sumptuous show was but one assignment for Cesti and the designers. Another was to supply elegant flattery in the libretto by Francesco Sbarra. In the translation from the mythological source, the scheming of the three goddesses became a satire on intrigues of the court, including the faulty method of administering justice. Allegorical persons in the Prologue represented the various territories of the Austrian and Spanish Habsburgs. In the epilogue, Jupiter's eagle plucked the apple and gave it to the new empress, as more worthy to receive it than the three goddesses (whose contention for it caused the Trojan War). The extravaganza was staged in an open-air theater before five thousand people, and was talked about for years because of its cost: one hundred thousand thalers. Such notoriety was a successful stroke of statecraft![6]

Opera continued to be an ornament to the royal courts. With this political authority over the composer, librettist, and audience, we should not expect to find operas uttering hints of revolution. Current literary fashions were typical themes, if savored by the monarch. Though public opera houses were opened (first in Venice) in the early seventeenth century, the closely held civil and economic power of the state bound the composer and librettist to the artistic taste of the ruler. It was this social system, however, that witnessed Mozart's audacious Figaro; and his morality drama, *Don Giovanni* (Don Juan), in which the profligate one is a person of the highest social status; and *The Magic Flute*, that extolled a noble brotherhood selected not by birth but by proven virtue and included symbols of Freemasonry, often outlawed by the crown.

The monarchical system began to crumble from the shocks of the French and American revolutions and the continuing polemics for democracy among some intellectuals. The literature, drama and theater of the time in turn reveal disguised critiques on the social and political status quo: Mozart's *Marriage* once again, and Beethoven's *Fidelio*, and Verdi, as we have observed. Another notable example is Donizetti's *Don Pasquale*, which struck a blow for social and sexual equality (1843). As 1800 passed, the attitudes, the plots, and indeed the sound of music changed forever. It was now the middle class who were to be flattered and reassured that their new wealth and civil importance were a worthy replacement to the aristocrats they supplanted. No longer did the composer write for an audience of one, a king or an emperor or a prince or a duke. True, Wagner's royal patron for many years was King Ludwig II of Bavaria. But Wagner bowed to no one about the content of his work.

The first obligation of any composer for the theater is to invent music which enhances the drama. That a social or political motivation, an extramusical objective, has been included is not to be presumed in all instances. Evidence is not available, for example, that Auber and Scribe were secret republicans who with *La Muette* implanted a virulent germ of revolt in the Parisians in 1828 and the Belgians in 1830. It is more plausible that they knew they had a good idea and succeeded in making an opera out of it. But it seems responsible to admit that a political or social statement, or other didacticism, is present when such concerns are in evidence. The "extramural" result of *La Muette*, whether it gratified Auber and Scribe or not, was an exceptional patriotic surge of emotion which fueled political action. The propaganda thrust, if not planned by the authors (or, presumably, the theater managers) was created by circumstances, more or less spontaneously. (It was always conceivable, if risky, to plan a demonstration and to hire a claque to shout "Down with the king!" at the likely flashpoint.)

Yet even the relentless patriot Verdi turned to non-nationalist subjects, as in *La Traviata*, the realist, contemporary romance of Alexandre Dumas *fils' La Dame aux camélias*. This was not a drama, like Schiller's *William Tell*, in which "the personal trials of a few villagers are elevated to the greater needs of a people." The story is of a private infatuation, pure sentiment and pure theatre. But a moral tale is told! Dumas and Verdi convince us to scorn middle-class snobbery. Verdi's musical persuasion is the more lasting: it is *Traviata* which is staged regularly today, not *The Lady of the Camellias*. Similarly, Gounod's saccharine slice of Goethe's great *Faust* confirmed the sanctimonious Romantics' views on virtue, Satan's wiles, and the efficacy of last minute prayer. *Faust* was a pretty and inspirational opera about middle-class values for the middle-class audience; it followed a safe direction, and pleased everyone—especially after a ballet was added.

The audience, even the individual royal patron, expected to go to the theater and receive entertainment from the performance of an opera, a farce, a sentimental operetta, or one of Wagner's somber epics. If the work also "pricked the conscience of the king" (and others), whether boldly or subtly, it was first and last a musical entertainment. It is essential to hold in mind that the musical element of a drama-with-music is never incidental or "optional": book and lyrics cannot be stated without it; otherwise it is not music drama. Even a libretto which is closely based on a previous play, like Shakespeare's *Othello* in Verdi's hands, or Molnar's *Liliom* rewritten by Rodgers and Hammerstein as the musical *Carousel*, "must be incomplete without music and lyrics."[7]

William S. Gilbert and Arthur Sullivan proved with witty and delightful satires that the music need not be profound to succeed as social criticism. The spoofs of the British aristocracy and government traditions were immensely successful in *The Mikado, Iolanthe, H.M.S. Pinafore, Trial by Jury*, and others. And their thrust was felt again and again with each repeated performance.

The genre of American operetta at the turn of this century copied the charm and stereotyped plots of our European forbears, "G and S," of course, but more often the Viennese style. No one expected profundity, much less an edifying subject, in *The Merry Widow* and *The Prince of Pilsen*. The most brilliant models, such as *Die Fledermaus* by Johann Strauss, Jr., "exposed" the foibles of the rich and mighty, but a comedy of manners was a long-standing literary excuse to entertain. In the United States *The Vagabond King* and *Rose Marie* (Rudolf Friml), *Naughty Marietta* (Victor Herbert), and *The Desert Song* and *The Student Prince* (Sigmund Romberg) equalled the standards of the Europeans, though without the grand opera ambience of the Viennese. Carefree comedies and good-natured satires in the 1930s also gave the American public generously what it wanted. *No, No, Nanette* (Vincent Youmans), *Girl Crazy* (George Gershwin), and *Roberta* (Jerome Kern) were great favorites.

The team of Ira and George Gershwin with George S. Kaufman attempted three "political" operettas, twentieth-century
replacements for Gilbert and Sullivan. The first was *Strike Up the
Band* in 1927, which shot barbs at war, big business, international
politics and the ego of the American millionaire. It was not a
success in the tryouts, but three years later the book was rewritten,
with the abrasive jabs softened, and the show proved successful.
The fantasy was no more nonsensical than *Pinafore* or *Mikado*.
The story was framed as a dream: An American chocolate manufacturer, Horace Fletcher, plots a war on the Swiss because of their
tariff on chocolate. He offers to pay for the war if it can be known
as the Horace J. Fletcher Memorial War. Perhaps it was the despair
of the Depression which attracted audiences to this energetic satire
on Big Business. The Gershwins wrote a second satire, *Of Thee I
Sing*, which made fun of the absurdities in a presidential election.
Here a candidate, unable to find a genuine issue, campaigns on the
platform of Love. "Love Is Sweeping the Country" was a hit song.
The show received a Pulitzer Prize in 1932, the first time the annual
drama award was given to a musical play.[8] The third musical, *Let
'Em Eat Cake*, was a sequel to *Of Thee I Sing*. President
Wintergreen returned with his Vice President, whose name nobody
can remember. To solve the woes of unemployment and dole, the
leaders turned to fascism and established an elite of "Blue Shirts."
This was not a subject for jokes in the time when Hitler's Brown
Shirts and Mussolini's Black Shirts intruded harshly on the daily
news. The show closed quickly, and the talented Gershwins turned
away from political subjects.

There was also a political musical which so boldly attacked the
sacred cows of American life that it provoked a ban before it
opened. This was *The Cradle Will Rock* in 1937, with words and
music by Marc Blitzstein.[9] The young American composer was supplied the artistic facilities of the Works Progress Administration, a
government agency set up to provide employment during the Depression. Blitzstein also enjoyed considerable assistance by other
artists: Orson Welles was the stage director and Lehman Engel was
the conductor.

Apparently no responsible person in the WPA paid serious attention to the content of their musical. How typical of the "practical"
world in the United States to see the artist's work as of little
consequence! The plot concerned a proposed strike against a steel

industry boss, Mr. Mister, whose power in the community was so crushing that he was able to intimidate the doctors, professors, ministers, artists, editors, gangsters—everyone except the factory workers themselves—to bring pressure against the employees' wish to strike. When the subject of this "leftist play" leaked out in the dress rehearsal, it brought cries of indignation upon the government sponsors. The next day, the premiere, the play was banned. The theater was padlocked and the cast, the orchestra, and the gathering audience left outside the building, angry and disappointed.

John Houseman, head of the WPA-Federal theater project, was adamant that the work should be heard right then. He rented the vacant Venice Theater nineteen blocks away for a makeshift premiere. But the cast and orchestra, by union regulations, were then not a licensed company! Alone, Blitzstein went up to the stage and played the score on an upright piano. The cast, scattered about the audience, informally stood up and rendered their lines on cue. The chorus sat in the front row with Engel. The audience relished the atmosphere of militant protest. After the commotion faded away *The Cradle Will Rock* officially opened in the Windsor Theater in concert style, without costumes and sets, and ran for fourteen weeks. In retrospect, it was a significant date in American protest music—both as subject matter (a factory union is organized) and in the determination to fight censorship. In retrospect also, it is a dated work, and is rarely staged today.[10]

Another musical which was unique in Broadway history was *Pins and Needles*, also a candid social comment for 1937, written for the International Ladies' Garment Workers' Union. Its unvarnished purpose was to propagandize for the trade union movement, and the roles were played entirely by union members. Young Harold Rome produced songs both joyous and thought provoking, and the revue developed a life of its own. It ran for 1108 performances and was taken on tour.

In 1940, Richard Rodgers and Lorenz Hart wrote *Pal Joey*, in which the hero is a heel. The despicable leading role repelled audiences and the show had a disappointing initial run. A dozen years later, a new concept of the musical was acceptable and, with a revival, *Pal Joey* was recognized as a classic.[11] In 1943 Rodgers, with Oscar Hammerstein II, presented *Oklahoma!* touched by emotions of bitterness, loneliness and violence. Both these shows set a mark for both musical score and story line in the Broadway musical that changed attitudes toward the musical stage.[12] The blithe theme of a sweet romantic tangle, interrupted on schedule by tunes, and unraveled neatly at the final curtain, was displaced by a synthesis of script and music, and a serious vein that past generations would not have accepted in this genre. The musical techniques for composers occasionally borrowed from the craft of the "serious" musician: more sophisticated modulations, as in Rodgers' songs here and there, Tony's songs in *Most Happy Fella*; a fugue in *Guys and Dolls*, freer song forms in *South Pacific* and *No Strings*, and extended quasi-arias in *Carousel* and *Most Happy Fella*. The integration of dance numbers by Agnes deMille made a precedent in *Oklahoma!* No tapping chorus line appeared in the middle of the box supper scene but rather, a "dream ballet" in which the heroine's imagination frightens her into accepting an invitation from the villain. Dance—ballet—became integrated with the plot.

It is not irrelevant to note that *Oklahoma!* appeared at the height of World War II. The historic centers for the traditional operetta—Vienna and Berlin—were now the sites of enemy ideology. The American folk setting was gratefully embraced by audiences. Indirectly it joined in the support for patriotic unity. Yet by a twist of merchandising, a revival of *The Merry Widow* opened across the street from *Oklahoma!* The New York critic, Louis Kronenberger, assured his readers in *PM* that Lehar (who still enjoyed a secure life in Austria with a Jewish wife) would not receive a penny of American royalties, which might give aid to the enemy![13]

The popular interest in psychology and the lascivious by-products of psychoanalysis have permeated twentieth-century literature in all its genres, including musical theater. The reader or spectator now feels compelled to examine virtually every work of art for the "real meaning." The troubled psyche is to be found in many musical shows, with the implication of some behavioral problem to be identified by the audience to elicit sympathy, or perhaps revulsion. A selection includes *Lady in the Dark*, *Most Happy Fella* (Sidney Howard's unhappy play, *They Knew What They Wanted*, with the addition of some hilarious characters not in the original drama), *Flower Drum Song* (Chinese-Americans), *Regina*

(Blitzstein's operatic expansion of Hellman's *Little Foxes*), *Street Scene* (Elmer Rice's urban tragedy, as set to music by Kurt Weill), and *Finian's Rainbow* (racism). Later examples were depicted in *Fiddler on the Roof*, based on Sholem Aleichen's tales of the disintegration and persecution of Russian Jewish culture; the melancholy and sometimes cruel *Man of La Mancha*, and in Stephen Sondheim's harsh and mordant *Sweeney Todd*, invincibly amoral till the very end.[14]

To be sure, troubling subjects had appeared on the musical stage before these. Jerome Kern's superlative score for *Showboat* presumably assuaged the spectator's distress at the raising of the "Negro problem." Edna Ferber's character, Joe, here broke the stereotypes of the operetta. And in *Ol' Man River* he crystallized the despair of the Black laborer and the futility of his status. *Showboat* was frequently unhappy in mood, but this largely old-fashioned operetta became a lasting success.

More ambitious musically were the operas that belong here because they were presented in Broadway runs and often revived, such as Gershwin's *Porgy and Bess* of 1935, which viewed American life totally from the position of the poor Southern Black. Others were Gian-Carlo Menotti's *The Consul* (in which a resistance fighter and his family seek escape through the Iron Curtain but are doomed to death by indifference from a Western bureaucrat's office), and *The Saint of Bleecker Street* (a collision of spirituality and atheism, familial love and incest).[15]

Amidst the native-American artists a refugee from Nazi Germany quickly joined the top ranked composers. Kurt Weill came to the United States in 1935 after brilliant collaborations with Bertolt Brecht in Germany. Their satire, *Der Dreigroschenoper* (*The Three Penny Opera*), was an immense success in Europe, but banned where Nazi authority ruled. Marc Blitzstein's later enthusiasm for *The Three Penny Opera* encouraged New York support for an American production, for which Blitzstein made an English translation. The enormous range of song styles now delighted the audiences of a second continent. The jarring sounds, audacious dissonance, and jazzy rhythms of the impudent little stage band again jolted the conventional theatergoers, and fixed attention on Brecht's scorn of a cynical, venal society of small capitalists, cutthroats, and officers of the law. (The historical period was the year of Queen Victoria's coronation.) *Mack the Knife* became a long lasting hit, though few of the millions who heard a recording of the haunting song saw the play from which it came.

Weill's private commitment to social justice was not diminished by America's remoteness—for a time—from the repression of Europe's dictatorships. Weill created sophisticated scores for two of Maxwell Anderson's plays. The first was *Knickerbocker Holiday* (1938), set in Dutch Colonial days in New York, in which the new leader, Peter Stuyvesant, is a tyrant who is opposed by the towns-people. There was enough "critical bewilderment" at the feisty opinions expressed about democracy that Anderson wrote "A Preface to the Politics of *Knickerbocker Holiday*" in the published playscript.[16] There he argued that the Founding Fathers had mistrusted the state and carefully limited the powers and the potential "selfish interest" of any branch of government. In the play, Stuyvesant sings one of the outstanding songs in American popular music, *September Song*, when he demands that a woman much younger than himself marry him, although she is already in love with another man.

Weill's setting of a second Anderson play was *Lost in the Stars*, based on Alan Paton's novel of apartheid in South Africa, *Cry the Beloved Country*. As in *Porgy and Bess*, the casting itself was a social statement on the American stage, now made in 1949. Black characters played blacks, whites played whites. In the big musical fashion was Weill's *Lady in the Dark*, and close to tragic opera style was *Street Scene*. The underlying theme of the latter two was the tension of modern urban life, and a compassionate plea for those who carried such burdens.

A survey of the Broadway musical reveals that a few other composers and writers were consistent in presenting a social message within the professional routine of the well made score, book and lyrics. Leonard Bernstein and Rodgers and Hammerstein were not satisfied with anything less than a serious conception at the base. *West Side Story* is a contemporary *Romeo and Juliet* in which two unsavory New York street gangs become the Montagues and Capulets, inflamed by ethnic hatred. Bernstein's *Candide* subtly preached the trenchant and cynical epigrams of Voltaire.

Rodgers and Hammerstein invariably enunciated a social state-ment. The viewer of the 1980s who sees *South Pacific* played by high school students or a summer stock company may scarcely believe that this was a message musical forty years ago. The subject was war, unquestionably a patriotic war, but one that controlled men and women of all social levels and ethical beliefs. Everyone who saw *South Pacific* then was altered in some manner by that war. One new experience was to bring face-to-face races which had not worked side by side before. The crises of the story, most poignantly carried in songs by Emile and Lieutenant Cable, arose from racial bigotry. How, asks Emile of Cable, do people learn hatred? The young American replies in the song, *You've Got to Be Taught*. The habit begins early; children learn to hate the people their parents hate.

Rodgers' and Hammerstein's *The King and I* (1951), a kaleidoscope of East-West sights and sounds, again projected the collision of moral codes, Western democracy, and Oriental despotism; at base, respect for the inviolability of dignity, the Asian "face." The dramatic climax is reached during the musical play invented by the English governess, Anna, and the Siamese Queen, "The Little House of Uncle Thomas," a barely concealed condemnation of slavery at the court. Their entertainment was courageously staged before the king and his foreign guests. In the same scene the king also faces the insult of a concubine who attempts to run away with her lover. His traditional punishment of the lawbreakers, which seemed inhuman to Anna, but appropriate to the king, destroyed the mutual respect of the monarch and the governess, the bridge between East and West.

Whether or not the American spectator accepts the social statements of *The King and I* on a personal level, Rodgers' incandescent music is a seductive instructor. It is impossible to divorce the melodies from the words or the bewitching orchestral color from the recurrent scenes of pathos, injustice and cruelty. These authors delivered a similar message in *The Sound of Music* (1959), in which the danger of Nazi brutality and tyranny is relearned in each performance witnessed, year after year. Of all the opportunities for musical propaganda, in the hands of a master, the musical stage may be the most persuasive and most advantageous for repeated hearings.

NOTES

1. See William L. Crosten, *French Grand Opera: An Art and a Business* (New York: King's Crown Press, 1948), and Arnold Perris, "Art as a Substitute for the Heroic Experience: French Music in the Reign of Louis-Philippe." Unpublished Ph.D. diss., Northwestern University, 1967.

2. Third edition (London: Methuen and Co., 1964), p. 82.

3. Julien Budden, *The Operas of Verdi*, vol. I: *From Oberto to Rigoletto* (New York: Praeger Publishers, 1973), pp. 744ff.

4. Ibid., vol. II: *From Il Trovatore to La Forza del Destino* (London: Cassell, 1978). See Chapter VIII, *Un ballo in maschera* (A masked ball), especially pp. 367-73.

5. *Denkmäler der Tonkunst in Öisterreich*, III, p. 2; IV, p. 2, following Adler's edition of the extant score (acts 1, 2, and 4); one engraving is also reproduced in the handbook to *The History of Music in Sound* (RCA Victor Co., 1961), frontispiece.

6. *History of Music in Sound*, pp. 27-28. Also Donald Jay Grout, *A Short History of Opera* (New York: Columbia University Press, 1947, one volume edition) p. 97.

7. Lehman Engel, *The American Musical Theatre: a Consideration* (New York: Macmillan 1967), p. 91.

8. The announcement of the Pulitzer judges included this statement: "This award may seem unusual, but the play is unusual. . . . Its effect on the stage promises to be very considerable, because musical plays are always popular, and by injecting genuine satire and point into them, a very large public is reached." Slonimsky, *Music Since 1900*, 4th ed., p. 550. Other musicals which won this accolade were *South Pacific, How to Succeed in Business without Really Trying,* and *Fiorello!* See John L. Toohey, *A History of the Pulitzer Prize Plays* (New York: The Citadel Press, 1967). A later winner was *A Chorus Line* (1975).

9. See Engel's own recollection of the premiere, *The American Musical*, pp. 146-49. See also Barbara Zuck, *A History of Musical Americanism* (Ann Arbor: UMI Research Press, 1980). Chapter IX is devoted to Marc Blitzstein. For Blitzstein's expectations, see his article, "Coming—The Mass Audiences!" in *Modern Music*, XIII:4 (May-June, 1936), pp. 23-29.

10. Three performances in 1947 under Leonard Bernstein's direction charmed the music critic Virgil Thomson, to let go a flurry of approving terms: "sweetness, cutting wit, fancy, faith, passion, freshness, prophetic, talent for caricature, a fairy tale with villains and a hero, a morality play. . . ." He also wrote:

In a year when the Left in general, and the labor movement in particular, is under attack, it is important that the Left should put its best foot forward. . . . *The Cradle* is the gayest and the most absorbing piece of musical theatre that America's Left has inspired. Long may it prosper, long may it remind us that union cards are as touchy a point of honor as marriage certificates. *Music Right and Left* (New York: Henry Holt & Co., 1951), pp. 74-75.

11. Engel, *The American Musical*, p. 77. There were other leading men who were less than heroic models. Before Joey, there was Ravenal in *Showboat*, and afterwards, Billy in *Carousel*, Harold Hill in *The Music Man*, the King in *The King and I*, and Professor Higgins in *My Fair Lady*.

12. Gerald Bordman, *American Operetta from H.M.S. Pinafore to Sweeney Todd* (New York: Oxford University Press, 1981), chapter XI. See also Engel, *The American Musical*, chapter IV. Concurrent with this direction in the Broadway theater was the appearance of American operas with social themes.

13. Bordman, *American Operetta*, p. 154.

14. See Engel, *American Musical*, chapter V.

15. The Menotti operas cited here received Pulitzer Prizes for music.

16. Maxwell Anderson, *Knickerbocker Holiday* (Washington, D.C.: Anderson House, 1938), p. v. The text of "September Song" (not titled in the book), pp. 55-56.

CHAPTER 8

The Decade of Protests:
Popular Music in the 1960s

Come gather 'round people, wherever you roam
And admit that the waters around you have grown,
And accept it that soon you'll be drenched to the bone.
If your time to you is worth savin',
Then you'd better start swimmin' or you'll sink like a stone,
For the times they are a-changin'.

Bob Dylan (© 1963 Warner Bros., Inc.
All Rights Reserved. Used by Permission.)

No age group in the 1960s—grandparents, the middle-aged, or their children—was untouched by the social protests of that decade. Most read about the marches, the protest rallies, the voices of anger, and the fires of frustration. Some formed the marches and the rallies, spoke the anger, raised the signs, and gave vent to their frustration. But they all *heard* the protests through the enormous outpouring of songs in the mass media. The period was one of revolution, and it is not remote in history. Many of its advocates are still here, and its movements, social action, and concerns are still stirring emotions and its hurts not yet fully healed. The literary chronicle of that time of general unrest is to be found in its books, newspapers and magazines, some of which are cited in this chapter. It was also a time, like all times of crisis, when events were documented in a torrent of popular songs and verse. In the 1960s, public protest by singing became a daily occurrence. There were hundreds of new songs, and vivid old songs were recalled. Old songs were reworked with new lyrics, and vehement new lyrics that aroused the emotions were written. Poignant melodies and compassionate words comforted the hurt and despairing. The topics that stimulated this decade of protest songs covered an extraordinary range of discontents; individual and group alienation, racial bigotry, an unpopular remote war, civil rights, the abuse of the land, water and air, and the extinction of wildlife for trivial reasons.

These were movements of people; the songs were composed for public hearing and for mass gatherings, with the expectation of a sympathetic response. The protest songs of past generations were spread slowly and often to a limited audience. The potential of the electronic media in the 1960s was of overwhelming power. A song heard on television was a message delivered to millions. To be sure, some of these millions, especially among the older generation and the rulers of society, usually judged the messages as wrong or meaningless. Since so many of the songs were the product of young performers—in the current popular style—the musical and the verbal messages were categorically discounted as the emotional expression of adolescents who could not grasp the realities of modern civilization. Bob Dylan became the spokesman for the younger generation. His was a perceptive mind that addressed the world through descriptive lyrics and a simple, captivating tune with a strong beat, elements that are always present in a genuine folk style. Surely it is no coincidence that he arrived in New York City from Hibbing, Minnesota in the fall of 1960. After a period of trying out his songs on small audiences, in 1963 he wrote the first of several hits, *Blowin' in the Wind* (C, 40).[1] Eventually this song was recorded by some sixty singers, from Peter, Paul and Mary to Duke Ellington and Marlene Dietrich. Next he wrote *The Times They Are A-Changin'* (C, 274).

With the electric guitar—an icon of rock—the "pure" folk singers were replaced by the rock generation, and the social messages continued. The age-old theme of the rejected lover was still necessary, but the vocabulary changed. Significant to that generation was the acute sense of standing alone and powerless. This was expressed by antagonism toward the values established by the older generation. For many, and not only among youth, a person had become one of a nameless mass to be manipulated by an uncaring bureaucracy.

The Beatles, Joan Baez, the Kingston Trio, Johnny Cash, Simon and Garfunkel and many others became the mouthpieces for millions of the under-thirty, who felt bewildered, cynical, and threatened by the prospect of nuclear war and a life likely to be short and frightening. At mammoth concerts such as the festivals in Monterey, California in 1963 and Woodstock, New York in the summer of 1969, enormous gatherings of youth were bonded in imitation of a devoted, caring family for a few days. The Woodstock event was, in its way, a gigantic rally against what many youth saw as the relentless corruption of the nation's ethical standards. The passionate, amplified music was the message, much more than the words sung. A member of that generation, Dave Marsh, in his book about The Who, believed that the heart of the entire Youth movement was the music.

What I'm trusting here is that the reader also has some inkling of how much rock meant to its audiences in the heyday of the Who—of how much some of it still means. Those who know only the cynicism into which popular culture is sunk may find portions of this narrative naive. I can only insist that many of us genuinely shared a dream in those days, that together we imagined that it was possible to create an open and democratic culture. And that the center of that dream was rock & roll.[2]

Joan Baez was the first of this younger generation of politically conscious singers that had followed Pete Seeger, Woody Guthrie and others. She programmed standard folk songs (*Barbara Allen*) along with new and contemporary laments, protests, such as *We Shall Overcome* (D, 24) and *Birmingham Sunday* (G, 175). She sang in an attractive, untrained voice, without slipping out of tune in the style of "authentic" folksingers. By 1962, she had three albums on the hit charts and appeared on the cover of *Time*. She had become a national spokeswoman, as much the articulate, persuasive leader of a large constituency as many contemporary political, religious, or educational leaders. Her preoccupation with social concerns, however, all but buried her activity as a singer. She marched and sang in many civil rights occasions. Eventually she founded a school for nonviolence. When her guitar and voice are heard today, it is at a rally, such as the Pasadena Rose Bowl conclave against nuclear armaments in June, 1982, not at a concert.

The unparalleled attention received by the Beatles made every one of their albums almost a worldwide touchstone of the state of the mind of youth. The Beatles (and other popular artists) told how to view the contemporary world. Or was it the other way around? No matter. As crass as were the production goals of record manufacturers and the managers of the musicians, the younger generation was unmistakably in vociferous rebellion and they craved these songs. But the sound of the folk/rock and rock and roll was the sound of hostility to many parents. This was a rebellion explicitly proclaimed in many of the lyrics. If the fans couldn't understand all the words, they found them published in word books and often on the album covers. Not many parents listened sympathetically. The subject matter, however, expressed with superamplified sound and frenetic physical movement, was of grave concern. The future condition of society, the hope that there would *be* a future, and the despair of the participating age group, was stated, explicitly or implicitly, in song after song. The compassion of many of the composers—so different from the conventional stream of popular music which addressed a singular "you"—now reached out to the many; its empathy was for every person's psyche. The message was a shared concern, and it was gratefully accepted by youth. The price of the newest album was a small cost for solace against the perception of an impersonal world that crowded one's private "space." The Beatles's album, *Sgt. Pepper's Lonely Hearts Club Band*, released in June, 1967, made every attentive listener aware of the profound change that had taken place in the purpose of popular music, rock and folk/rock. The lyrics in this album presented a sympathetic view of individuals, groups, and whole classes of psychologically bruised and buffeted people. The Beatles had identified the fears of contemporary living in *Within You, Without You*. Desperation is admitted in *Good Morning, Good Morning, A Day in the Life*, and *She's Leaving Home*. Whatever the private impetus was for these lyrics, the songs supplied more than light sentimental pleasure for their millions of followers.

The Beatles also chided the unthinking, insensitive person as a *Nowhere Man*, who makes all his "nowhere plans" for nobody, has no point of view, and can't see any at all (F, 14). Some other of the Beatles's songs in the same vein were *Eleanor Rigby* (C, 75) and *Hey Jude* (C, 95). All of these might too simply be categorized as love songs—the old, commonplace theme—but they clearly expressed more than clichés about a romantic twosome. The musical elements of their songs, in the mainstream of early '60s rock, emphasized the Beatles's authority as spokesmen to and for youth: This was youth music, as well as youth consciousness.

Another popular group, Crosby, Stills and Nash, mustered up a wavering courage with *Long Time Gone*. From Simon and Garfunkel came *Bridge Over Troubled Water* (C, 44), *The Sound of Silence* (C, 237), and *The Dangling Conversation*, by Paul Simon. There was a bewitching ballad, *What the World Needs Now Is Love* (C, 306), with words by Hal David and the music by Burt Bacharach, who also wrote *Alfie* (C, 26), the title song of a film.

> What's it all about, Alfie?
> Is it just for the moment we live?
> What's it all about when you sort it out, Alfie?
> Are we meant to take more than we give, or are we meant
> to be kind?
> And if only fools are kind, Alfie, then I guess it is wise to
> be cruel.
> As sure as I believe there's a heaven above, Alfie, I know
> there's something much more.
> Something even nonbelievers can believe in
> I believe in love, Alfie.
>
> [Words: Hal David; Music: Burt F. Bacharach.
> © 1966 Famous Music Corporation.]

Another film song, *Georgy Girl*, portrays a young woman who suppresses her feelings of loneliness (C, 84). Diana Ross sang *Reach Out and Touch Somebody's Hand*, written by Nicholas Ashford and Valerie Simpson (F, 60.)

The widespread introduction of drugs to blot out fear and alienation with a new "heightened awareness" was suggested in some lyrics. Since the use of drugs was an illicit action, this was at once a defiance of "Law and Order." Drugs also became a theme for gossip about several performers. This was also the hour of the "be-ins," and, in San Francisco in particular, the psychedelic experience. The style called acid rock attempted to reproduce the distorted hearing of a person under the influence of LSD. The invention of light shows presumably also induced the illusion of an hallucinogenic state. This discovery of "chemical ecstasy" exploded in San Francisco in the middle of a dance craze in 1965. The music itself was also warped in a way, along with the lyrics, to evoke the strange experience of a drug high. The words were not metaphorical or symbolic; they spoke of sniffing, smoking and popping. The Jefferson Airplane, whose *Surrealistic Pillow* was a hit album, was the first West Coast rock band to capture national admiration. Their free wheeling mix of jazz, folk, blues and rock provided the desired mood for "freaking out." During its instrumental passages, the audience could move around and dance, permitting a participation not offered since the days of jitterbugging in the aisles.[3]

Another San Francisco band was the Grateful Dead, whose *Anthem of the Sun* was supposed to be the suitable accompaniment for an acid trip. The affection of their fans was returned when the group gave free concerts again and again, rejecting the arguments of their managers to make more money—another rebuke to the Establishment.[4] The level of social frustration which rises to violence was displayed in the performances of The Doors, whose ferocious, frightening shows seemed to be carried on under hypnotic trance.

Some bands poetically concealed the pleasures of drugs. The Association's mythical Mary cured the traumas of the world in *Along Comes Mary*; she was whispered to be "Marijuana," the only Mary who could work such wonders! There were double meanings in other songs, and the supposed enigma helped to drive up the sales of records. The Byrds's *Eight Miles High* was banned by some radio stations. The ingenuous tale of *Puff, the Magic Dragon* was later analyzed as a "narc" trip—much to the astonishment of Peter, Paul and Mary, who had sung it innocently enough to audiences of children. *Sgt. Pepper* was also identified as the right background for a trip. Or was it the other way around?

On the East Coast stage taboos also disappeared. The Fugs, a fixture in Greenwich Village in the late 1960s, were outrageous long before outrageousness became the image of rock personalities. They seemed to go out of their way to look, act, write and sound obscene.[5] Their songs included *Marijuana, Slum Goddess, I Couldn't Get High, Group Grope, New Amphet Amine Shriek, Turn On/Tune In/Drop Out, Kill for Peace,* and *I Saw the Best*

Minds of My Generation Rot. Someone called them the Lenny Bruces of music. The Mothers of Invention, whose first album was *Freak Out*, was another group that made a satirical impact through ugliness, in music, lyrics, clothes, gestures and even noises. Its leader, Frank Zappa, became a prototype of defiant youth. Frustration with social custom and defiance of authority erupted in songs by many recording artists: *Midnight Rider* (Joe Cocker), *A Natural Man* (Lou Rawls), *Born to Be Wild* (Steppenwolf), *Eighteen* (Alice Cooper), and *Big Boss Man*, to name a few. The British group, The Who, ended their concerts by smashing their instruments. This sensational recklessness brought them immense publicity, but a recent biographer argued that the purpose was profound: the action symbolized "the fury of rock & roll's attempt to exorcise the world of all its impurities."[6]

Not all the protest was by rock groups. Phil Ochs, rather like Dylan, was a poet-politician-composer and singer, a kind of journalist-critic. Consider the chronicle of events reflected in his album, *All the News That's Fit to Sing: One More Parade, Talking Vietnam, Power and the Glory, Talking Cuban Crisis, Too Many Martyrs, Bound for Glory;* and in the album *I Ain't Marching Anymore* (1965): *In the Heat of the Summer, Draft Dodger Rag, That Was the President, The Men Behind the Guns, Here's to the State of Mississippi.* Another "journalist-critic" was Tom Paxton: *What Did You Learn in School Today?, Daily News, Lyndon Johnson Told the Nation* (A, 207) (anticipating, in 1965, Johnson's unpopular years) and *Talking Vietnam Pot Luck Blues.*

The national anxiety over the prolonged Viet Nam War stimulated one of the most widespread and vehement songs of the period. *Hell, No! I Ain't Gonna Go!* (E, 153) was a vocal banner. There was scarcely a solo singer or a group that did not present a musical statement about the war, excepting, of course, the musicians who were apolitical, or, at least, preferred to keep their music outside the ferment of social and political causes. (On the Viet Nam War the popular English groups were usually outsiders.) Again it was Joan Baez who showed her early and persistent support with *Saigon Bride* and gave emphasis to antiwar songs old and new. She sang Pete Seeger's classic, *Where Have All the Flowers Gone?* (A, 338; C, 310; D, 159) and also featured *I Saw a Vision of Armies, Minister of War* and *In Guernica* in her album, *Baptism: A Journey through Our Time.* The Doors sang *The Unknown Soldier* (E, 32), with its graphic lines derived from watching televised reports from the battle zone. The Fugs's raunchy music has already been noted; their antimilitarism was heard in *Exorcising the Evil Spirits from the Pentagon, October 21, 1967, War Song,* and others. Arlo Guthrie, son of the great folksinger and composer, Woody Guthrie, entered the world of the stars in 1967 with his witty and devastating talk-song, *Alice's Restaurant Massacree* (C, 30), a two-pronged satire on the "Establishment" (the piece fills one side of an LP) about "Law and Order" in terms of one officious village police chief and the hilarious effect of Arlo's arrest for littering on his subsequent draft induction. Another humorous satire was Pete Seeger's rollicking *I Want to Go to Andorra!* (G, 57) with lyrics by Val Shannon [Malvina Reynolds], about the tiny nation which spent only $4.90 on armaments (nobody has ever seen such confidence!). Not humorous, but of chilling effect, was Simon and Garfunkel's simple juxtaposition of pairs of songs to show a tranquil stereotype in contrast with grim current events: *Scarborough Fair/Canticle,* and *7 O'clock News/Silent Night* (in the album *Parsley, Sage, Rosemary and Thyme,* 1966).

The civil rights movement, initiated to draw attention to the unlawful conditions imposed on Blacks in the South, was the most striking protest movement of the time. It attracted the social segments who were concerned about alienation, war, ecology, and religious evangelism and had the salutory effect of bringing the generations together. The energy of the rallies was stimulated by a cultural element. Here was a political movement in which the primary participants, Blacks of all ages, were unified by a common religious and musical experience: a tradition of earnest congregational singing. In particular—as a technique for audience control— there was the call and response style of singing, a heritage from Africa, in which a song leader initiated the first line of each verse or chorus and the audience repeated it. Once started, the leader kept the song moving along by feeding new lines to the audience, interpolating topical and exhortatory phrases during the audience's singing. It was a familiar device, smoothly used by other song leaders like Pete Seeger. Traditional gospel songs, like *This Little Light of Mine,* sparked many rallies. The style offered simplicty, a strong rhythm that inevitably (and traditionally) elicited hand clapping (a tangible unifying gesture), and improvised lines to suit the place and the time.

The most familiar song of the movement, still sung, and one of the most widely known songs of our time, is *We Shall Overcome* (A, 344; C, 196; D, 24; E, 17).[7] It is an old song that has its origin in a Baptist hymn from the turn of the century. The tempo is slow, the tune is easy to sing, and there is much repetition. A skilled song leader (and propagandist) can supply topical lines to a sympathetic audience and make a powerful impact. The effect is rarely to arouse overt hostility, but rather to reinforce the group's conviction that its cause is right, with restrained determination, hope, and, through the tradition of holding hands with the person on either side, the reassurance of numbers. Its fundamental ambiguity (overcome what?) permits great flexibility; it has been put to cohesive purpose in many situations. (For a demonstration by an old master, listen to Pete Seeger gently unify his audience in his record album, *The Bitter and the Sweet* (He chose the song for other albums also).

Another old song, a spiritual, *Ain't Gonna Let Nobody Turn Me 'Round*, was changed to serve the needs of Freedom Marchers in Albany, Georgia in 1962. The word "nobody" was replaced by "Chief Pritchett," "Mayor Kelly," "segregation," and for the final verse, "injunction," the legal obstacle to the march. (A,6). The widely known spiritual, *Joshua Fit the Battle of Jericho*, was used in a version to protest a wall put up by the police in Selma, Alabama, nicknamed *The Berlin Wall* by the Freedom Marchers (A, 23). Martin Luther King's famous speech, "Free at Last," is a line from the spiritual of the same name (A, 114). A new text was *If You Miss Me from the Back of the Bus*, sung to a traditional tune (A, 164). In the popular sphere there was a talking blues by James Brown, soul singer, *Say It Loud—I'm Black and I'm Proud*.

The three-record album produced by the Library of Congress, *Voices of the Civil Rights Movement of the 1960s*, documents this period. It is a source of still other examples, such as *Get Your Rights, Jack*, and *Freedom Song*, a black protest song used in 1906 to protest the Atlanta race riots and again in the 1930s by organizers of the Southern Tenant Farmers' Union.

Some white performers and bands added other kinds of bigotry and bias to their exclamations of protest. Steppenwolf, a hard rock band whose subjects ranged widely, composed *Monster*, an ambitious minihistory of America from its origins as a home for the oppressed seeking freedom to its bigoted or corrupt or warmongering descendants today. They yelled that youth cannot fight the monster alone.

In California, a workers' protest was conducted by the grape pickers, whose four-year strike inspired the song by Luis Valdez, *Huelga en General* (General strike) (A, 152). A cry to rescue another disfranchised group came from Buffy Sainte-Marie, a Cree Indian, with *My Country 'Tis of Thy People You're Dying*, about atrocities suffered by American Indians at the hands of the white settlers. One of her antiwar songs, *Universal Soldier*, was widely sung.

The protests in music were not limited to the under-thirty genera-tion—on either side of the microphone. Along with Seeger, others regularly heard from included Johnny Cash with *What Is Truth*, in which an older man complains about the funny music kids play and receives the reply that the kids are trying to be heard. Joe South sang a song for tolerance, *Walk a Mile in My Shoes* (F, 16).

Malvina Reynolds, an elderly and indefatigable activist, was immediately ready with her rapier pen against any lapse in public responsibility. She ridiculed the uncritical acceptance of uniformity by the younger generation, their bland aspirations for the same education, the same career goals, the same role models. She recorded one of the best known of her many songs *Little Boxes* (A, 202; B, 44; C, 158; E, 190); it describes the uniformity of tract houses and, in effect, of "tract" human beings.

> Little boxes on the hillside,
> Little boxes made of ticky tacky,
> Little boxes on the hillside,
> Little boxes all the same.
> There's a green one and a pink one
> And a blue one and a yellow one,
> And they're all made out of ticky tacky,
> And they all look just the same.
>
> And the people in the houses
> All went to the university,
> Where they were put in boxes
> And they came out all the same,
> And there's doctors and lawyers,

And business executives,
And they're all made out of ticky tacky,
And they all look just the same.

And they all play on the golf course
And drink their martinis dry,
And they all have pretty children
And the children go to school,
And the children go to summer camp,
And then to the university
Where they are put in boxes
And they come out all the same.

And the boys go into business
And marry and raise a family
In boxes made of ticky tacky
And they all look just the same.
There's a green one and a pink one
And a blue one and a yellow one,
And they're all made out of ticky tacky
And they all look just the same.

A fourth theme for the decade was to save the land, air, water, and mankind's bodies. An old word, "ecology," known chiefly by agronomists, was now on everyone's lips. An extensive repertory of ecology songs is the result. These were not limited to the pleas of youth; the authors perceived the ravaged state of the land as further evidence of the selfish directions of the past generation. *Give Me Back my Cool, Clear Water*, by Rick Shaw and Dick Clark, was characteristic of these songs. It enumerates man's destructive practices: cities pump filth into rivers, rusty cans linger along highways, and DDT upsets nature's rhythm (B, 108). The Sierra Club published a volume entitled *Survival Songbook* in 1971 (B). These are the folksongs of our time, like their historic predecessors, springing spontaneously and passionately from current tragedies, threats and fears; they express an emotion that is to be shared with others, as well as a hope that the evil will disappear. There were songs about the endangered species, such as

Beautiful People by Suzanne Harris, describing a lady in Boston who wears a leopard skin, while leopards fall like flies in the jungles (B, 52). Pete Seeger, with his invincible charm, needled the conscience with his song of the last humpbacked whale. He lowered his microphone into the deep and heard the song of the world's last whale, who warns of a similar fate for man (C, 54). Malvina Reynolds sang ironic praise to the omniscient planners of the future society in her *Rand Hymn:*

> The Rand Corporation's the boon of the world,
> They think all day long for a fee.
> They sit and play games about going up in flames,
> For counters they use you and me, Honey Bee,
> For counters they use you and me.
>
> It's so nice to know we have Rand on our side,
> We'll always have good old Rand around;
> A zillion will be fried out, but in some neat hideout
> Rand will be safe under ground, praise the Lord,
> Rand will be safe underground.
>
> They will rescue us all from a fate worse than death,
> With a touch of the push-button hand;
> We'll be saved at one blow from the designated foe,
> But who's going to save us from Rand, Dear Lord,
> Who's going to save us from Rand?

> [Words and music by Malvina Reynolds.
> © 1961 Schroder Music Co. (ASCAP).
> Used by permission. All rights reserved.]

What Have They Done to the Rain? is another song by Malvina Reynolds (B, 104; D, 48). The Pink Floyd recorded *Atom Heart Mother*, a "rock suite." Tom Lehrer had written hilarious satires with similar concerns years before, like *Pollution* in 1954 (A, 167). Jimmy Collier wrote *Lead Poison on the Wall.* Tom Paxton's man from the future asks, *Whose Garden Was This*?—for he knows the charm of living flowers only through old pictures (B, 76).

Ralph Nader, the tireless gadfly, discerned another dangerous subject for protest: noise pollution. "Acoustic trauma from rock and roll music is emerging as a very real threat to the hearing quality of young people who expose themselves to substantial durations of this music by live rock groups with high amplification."[8] He wrote a letter to two congressional committees in May, 1963, urging the government to investigate this increasing hazard. In one of the research studies he cited, a student rock fan approved the high volume level because "it provides people of this age with the opportunity to congregate without having to communicate.[9]

The revival of interest in religion, including exotic experiments with Hinduism and Buddhism and witchcraft, was expressed in various styles. More familiar pious references were voiced in Country and Western music, and these endured. The theme never quite disappeared among Black musicians because of the religious vein of much traditional and popular Afro-American music, including rhythm and blues and the mix of gospel and blues that came to be called Soul. Here Ray Charles led all the rest, but the genre included other stars, such as Aretha Franklin and Otis Redding. The immense anguish that the Black soul singer "owns" could restate a White composer's wistful song into a lament of overwhelming despair. Charles's performance of the Beatles's *Yesterday* is such an example. Perhaps Soul and much other music of Black American musicians was, by definition, protest music, regardless of the literal message.

Biblical names and other scriptural references appeared in the work of several musicians. The Band, who backed Bob Dylan, used the words and names "Nazareth," "the Devil," "Moses" and "St. Luke" in *The Weight*, and "the Golden Calf" and "the crown of thorns" in *To Kingdom Come*. Such references were not expected in rock music. The Beach Boys documented their spiritual study with Maharishi Mahesh Yogi in 1968 with *Transcendental Meditation*. And there was a *Mass in F Minor* by the Electric Prunes!

The current of the decade made it proper for Duke Ellington and his orchestra to perform church concerts in San Francisco and New York in 1965. In the Fifth Avenue Presbyterian Church in New York on Christmas Day, says Edward Fischer, "There in front of the golden oak pews with their burgundy seat pads, there in front of the stained glass windows they praised the Lord in an idiom of the twentieth century.[10] But the idiom would have been inconceivable as the bearer of serious religious expression in that church when the Duke first achieved fame thirty years before. Admittedly, religious expression had not been the focus for his popular successes in the past. But on this occasion, it was. In addition to the several instrumental pieces, all with religious titles, including Ellington's piano solo, *New World A'Coming*, the printed program listed songs by Lena Horne and Brock Peters, and a tap dance by Bunny Briggs, *David Danced before the Lord with All His Might*.

A few years later religion became the story line of musicals in *Godspell* and *Your Arms Too Short to Box with God*, both based on the book of Matthew. The pop style of melody, orchestration and vocal delivery appealed to vast audiences, which may or may not have accepted the precepts of Christianity. But the message came through: Seek for solace in God. When *You Are the Light of the World* is sung in *Godspell*, the cast invites the audience to share a glass of wine, a symbolic reenactment of the Last Supper. But this invitation to share the action of the players, and their very workplace, the stage, was an openhearted gesture that many in the audience found touching and accepted. *Jesus Christ, Superstar* by Andrew Lloyd Webber and Tim Rice took the trappings of the adulation of the rock star who brings inspiration and hope and presented a "relevant" Passion of Christ. The raucous sound of rock for this hallowed material offended many conservative worshippers. Those who listened found the "rock opera" also made use of old-fashioned torch songs, ballads, and even hymn and anthem styles. Like *Godspell*, the message was sincere. Most important, it was effective: The young public did indeed listen, and in huge numbers. It passed from the (British) record medium in 1970 to the Broadway and London stages, and ultimately to a film version in 1973.[11]

The familiar topic of broken romances and unrequited love in popular songs was not quite rejected by this generation of seekers of social reform. Some of the biggest stars and an enormous quantity of pop music, including rock, offered no didactic statements. Barbra Streisand, Janis Joplin, Brenda Lee, Gordon Lightfoot, Stevie Wonder, and—not to be overlooked—Tiny Tim all sang about the age-old lament in their quite varied styles. Into this spirit in the mid-sixties came another English group, Herman's Hermits, whose sweet, winsome manner (like that of the early Beatles) was adored by preteens, much to the relief of their parents. They sang *Mrs. Brown, You've Got a Lovely Daughter, Little Boy Sad, Wings of Love, Mum and Dad, Don't Go out into the Rain (You're Going to Melt)*. Peter Noone, lead singer, "was the Mr.

Clean of rock and the only pop star that Ed Sullivan could cope with painlessly."[12] Meanwhile, the whole world of Country and Western remained virtually unencumbered by edifying messages.

The most sensational hard rock group was the Rolling Stones. Their repeated drug arrests made them the personification of youth in rebellion and the counterculture. But if they supported any of the several protest themes of the decade in their songs, such support was not conspicuous. Is it in these songs? *Confessin' the Blues, Good Times, Bad Times, Everybody Needs Somebody to Love, Under Assistant West Coast Promotion Man, Get Off My Cloud, 19th Nervous Breakdown, As Tears Go By.*

Another British group which achieved a special mark was The Who, who produced a "rock opera," *Tommy*, in 1969. *Tommy* was not an opera; it was not presented as stage drama. The story was a frank and sordid tale of parental tyranny and the hypocritical adulation of the public: The hero is a small boy who witnesses the murder of his mother's lover by his long-lost father, who has returned after a wartime mishap. Tommy is threatened by his parents to hold his tongue and to forget everything he has seen. He retreats into being (psychologically) deaf, dumb and blind, and can see only when he observes himself in a mirror. No one can penetrate this alienation (*See Me, Feel Me, Touch Me, Heal Me*). His only skill is to play, by a remarkable sense of touch, pinball machines, and this success attracts a great following of irrational admirers (*Pinball Wizard*). When he opens a vacation camp for his disciples, he forbids the use of drugs and alcohol; they reject him violently (*We're Not Going to Take It!*). Left totally alone, his senses are at last restored, and he is free. In 1972, The Who made a second album, which was luxuriantly dressed up with a chorus and the London Symphony Orchestra, several of the roles sung by celebrated rock stars, and an extravagant album book (Ode Records).

The several protest movements seemed to crystalize in *Hair*, the off-Broadway show produced for the New York Shakespeare Festival Public Theater in 1966. *Hair* was an impudent, original, unvarnished look at the world (at least in New York's East Village) from the viewpoint of the new generation who couldn't fit into the Establishment's mold. With a brash claim to being all things suitable for the hour, *Hair* was called the "American Tribal Love-Rock Musical." What tribe? A new tribe, the collection of young people who believed they had a culture, a purpose, most certainly a language, and a music identifiable to themselves, and that their culture was significant. They were right. The show jarred the status quo of the musical theater, especially in norms for acceptable language and stage behavior. By word of mouth and, for people who would never see it, through published reviews across the country, it symbolized for the older generation all that was outrageous among "those hippies." The twenty-five musical numbers included some first-rate songs that are tuneful and easy to remember. The authors of the book and lyrics, Gerome Ragni and James Rado, played in the show: Ragni as George Berger, a high school drop-out and Rado as Claude Hooper Bukowski, Berger's best friend and leader of the tribe. Bukowski is about to be drafted and the tribe hopes to save him. (In fact, there was very little plot.) The first number, *Aquarius*, became a hit. The song was a reference to the topical interest in a mystical control of one's destiny and to the coming enlightened age of Aquarius. The full range of contemporary protests was included, one after another: the status of the poor black, turned away from every respectable path (*I'm Black, Colored Spade, Black Boys, Ain't Got No*), civil rights (*Abie Baby*), alienation (*Easy to be Hard*), the alarm over pollution (*Air*), the bigoted adult view of youth's long hair, assumed to indicate the worst of character traits, (*My Conviction*), and the use of drugs (*Hashish* and *Walking in Space*). On draft resistance they were not anti-American, the boys insisted, but their view of the Red, White and Blue included other "colors" in *Don't Put It Down*. Other interests were religious ecstasy (*Hare Krishna* and *Be-In*) and a joyous sharing in the finale, *Let the Sunshine In!* In retrospect, *Hair* now seems an oasis of youthful freshness and spoofing in that harsh, bitter decade compared to the many angry, nasty songs of some groups. It *was* fresh, charming and spoofing, but it was not play-acting; the authors and the performers, like many, if not all, of the big-name recording artists, meant every word.

There were many other rock bands and singers who held the attention of young audiences—Blood, Sweat and Tears, Iron Butterfly, Yardbirds/Led Zeppelin—but here the performers' interest was the music. Some were virtuoso artists and original, exploratory composers. Since this is not a history of rock and roll, they need not be discussed here. The deafening volume and sometimes violent stage action—smashing guitars (The Who) and setting the guitar on fire (Jimi Hendrix)—served as a sublimation for the frustration of thousands of youth who saw themselves as prisoners of an adult society that would not listen to them.

The titles of only a few hit albums from the beginning of this decade, and a recall of the sound of the music, is a startling contrast to the songs just surveyed. In 1960 some of the best-sellers were *Heavenly* by Johnny Mathis, *Theme from Summer Place* by Percy Faith, *Belafonte at Carnegie Hall*, *Nice 'n' Easy* by Frank Sinatra, *Elvis is Back*, by Elvis Presley, and *Sold Out* by the Kingston Trio. In 1964 a new direction became clear: Along with *Blue Velvet* by Bobbie Vinton and *The Second Barbra Streisand Album*, the hits were *Meet the Beatles* (and other Beatles albums), *Blowin' in the Wind* by Peter, Paul and Mary, and *Joan Baez in Concert*. In 1968, *The Graduate: Original Soundtrack*, composed by Simon and Garfunkel, *Lady Soul* by Aretha Franklin, *Johnny Cash at Folsom Prison*, *Magical Mystery Tour* by the Beatles, and the Rolling Stones's answer to the Beatles, *Their Satanic Majesties Request*. A retrospective view from an insider was voiced on the CBS Television Morning News on May 30, 1983. One member of the Kingston Trio remarked that in the '60s they had not sung about drugs because they did not play in rock style, and the theme would not have been taken seriously by their audience.

The radical change in much of the pop and rock music of the 1960s, that is, to be a social message *as well as entertainment*, is unarguable when some of the favorite songs of the previous generation are reviewed. In 1934 everyone hummed *Blue Hawaii* with its lines, "Night and you and blue Hawaii/The night is heavenly and you are heaven to me." (*Blue Hawaii*, Words and Music: Leo Robin and Ralph Rainger. Copyright © 1936 and 1937 by Famous Music Corporation. Copyright Renewed 1963 and 1964 by Famous Music Corporation.) *Love in Bloom* discussed the sensitive man's concern: "Can it be the trees that fill the breeze with rare and magic perfume?" And the convincing explanation: "Oh, no, it isn't the trees, it's love in bloom!" (*Love in Bloom*, Words and Music: Leo Robin and Ralph Rainger. Copyright © 1934 by Famous Music Corporation. Copyright Renewed 1961 by Famous Music Corporation.) It is impossible to imagine these lyrics and the pretty tunes that carried them satisfying the '60s generation.

Twenty years later huge rock or folk/rock concerts are still held, usually in mammoth municipal auditoriums or stadiums, but their purpose is how to generate massive record sales for the artists. The intense energy and social purpose of the '60s has all but vanished. The Simon and Garfunkel "neighborhood concert" in New York City's Central Park in September 1981, attracted about four hundred thousand people—the same number as the historic Woodstock Festival in 1969. Though many of their songs were from the '60s by request, and the crowd (young fans and old) responded to them enthusiastically, it could be observed that the audience was not as passionately involved in the social messages as the original listeners had been. A record album of the concert program was released the following year.

Like the jazz movement before, American (and English) rock music from the '60s passed around the world. Hong Kong, Tokyo, Manila, Singapore, Bangkok and other metropolitan centers eagerly watched their own "Top Ten" and "Top Forty" charts, which paralleled those of the American and European popularity only a few weeks or a few months later. The attractiveness of everything "modern," which usually means Western, to the Third World countries has been a mixed blessing. Along with the intense admiration and need for Western technology, education, and forms of government, the non-West has absorbed our fashions in clothing, films, television shows, sports, and idioms of speech. An American traveler in Asia recognizes the music in local clubs, restaurants and radio. Large cities, such as those noted above, have produced recordings of local bands and developed their own stars—and all in the mold of the "big names" of Western music. Ballads, jazz, rhythm and blues, and, later, rock of most kinds, often with lyrics in a vernacular English, are to be heard on recordings, the pronunciation so close a copy of American speech that it is all but indistinguishable from the products of a Hollywood, Memphis, or Motown studio.

India's film industry (the world's largest after Hong Kong) demands a musical score emphasizing popular song styles (though often with native instruments and elements). The record market is enormous, as in the West. The 1973 film *Purab aur Pachim* (East or West) symbolized the contrast between traditional and "new" India: A conservative young man from India meets an Indian girl who has received a Western education and has been living in Rome, and their meeting of minds comes about by teaching each other the song styles they know. Some of the choices were scarcely contemporary to the American view (Jazz rhythm was fitted to *Twinkle, Twinkle, Little Star*); there was also a rock number. The clash with the Western life style, and particularly the wide range of its moral spectrum, is no less egregious in the parliamentary democracy of India than in the totalitarian regimes of the USSR and the People's Republic of China. The difference, however, is that in India, Western films, plays, books, magazines, and music of all shades are in generous supply and are enjoyed virtually without censorship by large segments of the population.

[Student unrest] is a worldwide phenomenon that represents the growing disillusionment of youth all over the world with the older generation. . . . They do not believe us when we give them advice, which they dismiss as sermonizing. They do not find consistency between our practice and our professions. Fear of an atomic war that may wipe out human civilization hangs like a black cloud that threatens their rising horizon, and they do not understand why the leaders of the world cannot find a way to a state of enduring peace.[13]

These remarks were not from the pen of an American or European writer, but from a distinguished educator and government cabinet minister of India, V.K.R.V. Rao. His alarm, expressed in a national forum, followed the student unrest which had turned India into turmoil in 1966. It is evidence of a youth protest movement which circled the world.

The authoritarian governments found imitation of the West's counterculture on the borderline of sedition. This attitude was especially conspicuous among Third World nations. North and South Korea, Burma, Singapore, and the countries within the Soviet Russian sphere promulgated regulations to shield their youth from recreation which "taught" an unproductive and thus immoral life style. In 1970, during my visit to the National Radio and Television offices of the Republic of Singapore, I read the following notice at the reception desk (where I had to deposit my passport before entering): "You are reminded of the ban on Hippieism in our Republic. . . . Members of the Staff must not

[wear] hippie-type hair or hippie-type clothes on RTS premises nor may persons appearing on television shows or their guests. Receptionists will refuse admittance to such people." Needless to say, such threatening figures were never seen to be on Singapore television. The alarm was not over the counterculture's loud music, though that was discouraged, but over the illicit use of drugs associated with hippieism. In those years male tourists "sporting hair below the collar" might be refused entry. In the Hong Kong *South China Post* in June, 1973 it was reported that the Beijing government considered that a major cause of illegal immigration into the British Colony was the popular music broadcast on the government-run radio station there: "The immigrants seem to get the idea that Hong Kong is a happy place where everyone is dancing in the street." Radio sets in the Cantonese province of Guangdong easily reached this freewheeling enclave on the Asian mainland.[14]

In November 1975, the Korean Broadcasting Ethics Commission in Seoul issued a ban on 137 foreign songs that had tantalized the ears of citizens in recent years, including *Never on Sunday, Kiss Me Quick, House of the Rising Sun, Delilah, Pillow Talk* and *Hippy Hippy Shake*. All songs by Alice Cooper and the Fugs were outlawed. *Master of War* was banned for its antiwar content, not considered an appropriate sentiment in a government perpetually on military alert.[15]

At the end of World War I, Will Marion Cook took his American Syncopated Orchestra of forty-one players to London and Paris, and jazz has fascinated many Europeans ever since. Despite the social injustices imposed on the black musicians who had invented it, jazz always connoted the American way to the rest of the world, which regarded it as a metaphor of free speech, economic opportunity, time for leisure, even luxurious hedonism. In recent years, in tempered amounts, jazz groups have played and made records in the USSR. The albums of the Leningrad Dixieland Band (on Melodiya label), for example, would fool all but the most profound connoisseurs. The amateur group was formed in 1958, and—need it be said—makes no social comment; it is "just for fun." Some celebrated foreign stars received invitations to perform in the USSR—Louis Armstrong, for one.

In the 1960s Willis Conover produced a recorded jazz program over the Voice of America's "Music—U.S.A." six days a week. It was not a political propaganda program, according to Conover, but "soft-sell jazz," generated by his own enthusiasm. He also played recordings of Iron Curtain bands from Estonia, Poland and elsewhere. Conover's popularity in those years was enormous. He was a virtual adopted citizen of Russia and East Europe. Avid fans mobbed him at the airport when he arrived for appearances at jazz festivals.[16]

In a study of the "transmutation" of American jazz in west Europe in the middle 1960s, a German educator, Ekkehard Jost, examined the social and political atmosphere surrounding the younger generation. He observed that many of the younger jazz musicians sympathized with the student revolt in Europe. A general aversion to established authority, even the revered American models, turned them away from "the continuous effort to imitate the creative processes that took place in the United States.[17] This rejection occurred in the face of the striking new directions of the time, Free Jazz, for example. But there was also an anti-American feeling because of the Viet Nam War.

Jazz became conditionally acceptable to some authoritarian regimes in the Soviet bloc and some nations of the Third World. Then rock arrived with its aggressive sound, frequently loaded with hostile lyrics, and an apparent or real alliance with rebellions of many causes. The boisterousness of jazz (the "old" jazz of pre-World War II) received good-humored sufferance by authorities, who regarded it as mindless amusement. Rock was not perceived as amusement or recreation which could exist safely within the fragile democracies of new nations. Nor could it be permitted to threaten the mind control so tenaciously established by the Communist ideologies. The performance of this music in Eastern Europe and Asia—when permitted—intimated an attack on the establishment. The inference of incipient revolution was dangerously close.

The erratic course of Soviet censorship permitted rock music in recent years, reaching a climax of sorts preceding the 1980 Olympics; the intent was to display to the international community that the Russians were as open-minded as the West. Elton John was an enormous hit in Leningrad in 1979, playing to four thousand fans who paid scalpers up to $150 for tickets priced at the equivalent of $9. The flamboyant star played his *Crocodile Rock* and *Goodbye Yellow Brick Road*.[18] Such invitations did not become routine. But once four thousand Russians had heard John, they had become learners. Of what? Of a current musical style of the West, yes, but of much else too: words, ideas, one individual's free statements, and what young people on the other side of the Iron Curtain admired. Leningrad saw the first Soviet rock opera in 1975, *Orpheus and Euridice* by twenty-nine-year-old Alexander Zyurbin. It was performed by the Singing Guitars, a group formed in 1966. A youth journal (*Yunost'*) commented that rock music was now viewed as a "rather stable musical tradition"![19] A Soviet rock band called Time Machine has also survived for several years, adroitly moving between the hazards of losing the affection of Russian youth and snapping the patience of the cultural hierarchy as they sang, "I didn't believe the promises and I won't believe in the future." This negative view did not reinforce the positive and happy line ever proclaimed by the Party. "Wear a mask, wear a mask; only under a mask can you remain yourself." These sentiments went too far. In May 1982 the Communist Party youth newspaper (*Komsomolskaya Pravda*) rebuked the Time Machine for their cynicism: "Even Western groups . . . do not pass over the sharper subjects: the struggle for peace. What have you done for the common good? . . . But here we see vague and bitter dreams, a deliberate escape to pointless grumbling." The news, however, did not announce the group was banned.[20]

It is with astonishment, perhaps, that we recall that in the 1960s a California civic group accused Soviet Russia of utilizing American folk music gatherings—hootenanies—"to brainwash and subvert, in a seemingly innocuous but actually covert and deceptive manner, vast segments of young people's groups." On August 7, 1963, the Fire and Police Research Association of Los Angeles sent a resolution to the United States House of Representatives requesting the Committee on Un-American Activities "investigate Communist subversive involvement in the Folk Music field, that the continued, effective misuse of this media . . . may not be further used as an unidentified tool of Communist Psychological or Cybernetic Warfare to ensnare and capture youthful minds in the United States as it has so successfully and effectively captivated them abroad."[21]

Senator Kenneth B. Keating (New York) made a droll speech on September 26 of that year in which he cited many "deceptive" uses of folk music in United States history which should, according to the same line of thinking be investigated: Elizabethan balladry, English Protestant hymns, Negro spirituals, African rhythms in jazz, *The Star-Spangled Banner*—the tune being an English drinking song (*To Anacreon in Heaven*)—and seditious folksongs against the national defense, for example, the spiritual that declares, "Gonna lay down my sword and shield/Down by the riverside. . . . Ain't gwine study war no more," and another blatant lyric against paying taxes in *Copper Kettle:*

> My pappy he made whiskey,
> My grandpappy he did, too,
> We ain't paid no whiskey tax
> Since 1792.[22]

Senator Russell of Georgia rose to ask Senator Keating to extend his "mantle of tolerance" to include the Confederacy's *Dixie*, inasmuch as it was written "by a constituent of one of (Keating's) predecessors," that is, Dan Emmett, a New Yorker. Senator Pell of Rhode Island also rose to praise the annual Newport Jazz Festival that previous summer: "More people came to it, they were better shaved, and more enjoyment was received by our local citizens than had ever before been the case in any form of public entertainment."[23]

Folk music, popular music, is the direct expression of a people in every epoch and culture. The new songs of this decade conspicuously proclaimed anger, indignation and judgment. They were vehement or beguiling, bitter, sly, droll, or compassionate. Because of cheap and rapid distribution by the electronic media, these topical messages reached a public far more vast than one ever known before. Listeners turned in a radio or television or played a recording for recreation, and purchased albums for personal pleasure. These congenial habits seemed to define this music as entertainment. So it was, but not within the former description of popular songs. The critics, including the older generation, saw the phenomenon as mindless adolescent behavior, and "another noisy style" which would pass. Two decades later we observe that rock has not disappeared, but that the political uses of it have essentially dropped away. The protest songs from the '60s, however, were not simply entertainment, certainly not those uttered in the tense situations of confrontations. The propaganda was in earnest, the objective both immediate and intensely felt. The objectives were not limited to private pleasure, or to supplying a market. The songs achieved the first goal of propaganda: They seized the attention, for a time, of a whole people.

NOTES

1. The words and music of many of the significant songs cited are published in anthologies of the period. Those cited by a letter and page number (C, 40) are found in the anthologies listed at the end of this notes section.

2. Dave Marsh, *Before I Get Old: The Story of the Who* (New York: St. Martin's Press, 1983), Introduction. See also note 6 below.

3. Lillian Roxon, *Lillian Roxon's Rock Encyclopedia* (New York: Grosset & Dunlap, 1971), pp. 262-63.

4. *Ibid.*, p. 210.

5. *Ibid.*, p. 198.

6. Marsh, *Before I Get Old*, p. 125.

7. Eileen Southern, *The Music of Black Americans* (New York: W. W. Norton & Co., 1971), p. 491.

8. Nicolas Slonimsky, *Music Since 1900*, (New York: Charles Scribner's Sons, 1971), fourth edition, p. 1413.

9. *Ibid.*, p. 1416.

10. "Ritual as Communication" by Edward Fischer, in *The Roots of Ritual*, James D. Shaughnessy, ed. (Grand Rapids, Mich.: William B. Eerdmans Publishing Co., 1973), pp. 180-81.

11. The complete text is found in Stanley Richards, *Great Rock Musicals* (New York: Stein and Day, 1979) pp. 246f. This volume also includes the text (and other data) for *Tommy*, pp. 485f, and *Hair*, pp. 386f, discussed in this chapter.

12. Roxon, *Rock Encyclopedia*, p. 232.

13. "Problem of Student Unrest" by V.K.R.V. Rao, in *Youth in Ferment*, Ram Chandra, ed. (Delhi: Sterling Publishers (P), 1968), p. 12.

14. St. Louis *Post-Dispatch*, June 6, 1973.

15. *The Korean Times* (Seoul), November 19, 1975.

16. *Newsweek*, June 5, 1967. See also Boris Schwarz, *Music and Musical Life in Soviet Russia, Enlarged Edition, 1917-1981* (Bloomington: Indiana University Press, 1983), p. 629.

17. "European Transmutations of Afro-American *Avant-garde* Jazz since the Mid-Sixties," in International Musicological Society, *Report of the 12th Congress*, Bonnie Wade and Daniel Heartz, eds. (Kassel: Bärenreiter, 1981), p. 578.

18. *Newsweek*, June 4, 1979, p. 33.

19. Schwarz, *Musical Life*, p. 584. See also Frederick S. Starr, *Red and Hot: The Fate of Jazz in the Soviet Union* (New York: Oxford University Press, 1983).

20. Anthony Barbieri, Jr. (Baltimore *Sun*) in St. Louis *Post-Dispatch*, May 2, 1982, p. 5F. A book of Moscow underground songs of the 1950s and the 1960s has been published in the United States. They were composed by Bulat Okudzhava. A collection was made by a Soviet émigré musician, Vladimir Frumkin, as *Bulat Okudzhava: 65 Songs*, English translations by Eve Shapiro (Ann Arbor: Ardis, 1980).

21. Slonimsky, *Music Since 1900*, fourth edition, p. 1407.

22. I have cited verse three of the traditional song of unknown date. (See Patricia Hackett, *The Melody Book*, Prentice-Hall, 1983, p. 41.) The senator read from a version current in 1963, only slightly different from the traditional lyrics.

23. *The Congressional Record*, September 26, 1963 (vol. 109, No. 154), pp. 18,221-24.

Anthologies Cited

A. Tom Glazer, ed., *Songs of Peace, Freedom, and Protest.* (New York: David McKay Co., 1970. Paperback edition, Fawcett Crest Books, 1972.)

B. Jim Morse, and Nancy Mathews, Eds., *Survival Songbook* (San Francisco: Sierra Club, 1971. Distributed by Belwin-Mills Publishing Corp.)

C. Milton Okun, ed., *Great Songs of the Sixties.* (Chicago: Quadrangle Books, 1970. Distributed by Random House.)

D. Maynard Solomon, ed., *The Joan Baez Songbook.* (New York: Ryerson Music Publishers, 1964.)

E. Jerry L. Walker, ed., *Pop/Rock Lyrics.* vol. 3. (New York: Scholastic Magazines, 1969.)

F. _____, *Pop/Rock Lyrics.* vol. 3. (New York: Scholastic Magazines, 1971.)

G. Wanda Willson Whitman, ed., *Songs That Changed the World.* (New York: Crown Publishers, 1969.)

CHAPTER 9

The Contemporary Composer as Social Critic

The fight must begin in the primary schools and continue in the streets, in the universities, in the media, and in the ancient temples of the muses. No occasion should seem too unimportant to young artists for them to miss the chance to assert an anti-fascist stance. . . . Every verse you write, every painting you paint, every lesson you give, every bar of music you write or play, can be a move against those who want to reverse the wheel of history, to use the power of the police and of blackmail to drag you back into their own sullenness. Don't lose heart.

Hans Werner Henze[1]

Every artist has the right to make his art out of an emotion that really moves him. If Blitzstein, like many other artists in every field, was moved to expression by the plight of the less privileged in their struggle for a fuller life, that was entirely his right. If these works fail in a certain sense, it is not because they are a form of propaganda art, but because the propaganda is not couched in terms that make the pieces valid for audiences everywhere.

Aaron Copland[2]

The composer who grew up during and immediately after World War II was surrounded by the social and political jolts and aftershocks of the world conflict, intensified and made immediate by the facility of worldwide communication. It is rare, perhaps not possible, to find a contemporary composer whose music is totally untouched or unshaped in some way by the public record—if not a private memory—of war, racism, emigration, political trials, poverty or civil disobedience. The major composers of the earlier twentieth century (Stravinsky and Bartók, for example) did not display such a civil awareness by means of their music. And among other prominent figures, perhaps one or two explicit pieces appeared in a lifetime of artistic effort; Britten's *War Requiem* is an example, and Schoenberg's *A Survivor from Warsaw* is another. (This does not exhaust the examples.)

There is, then, but a handful of contemporary composers who have devoted their work conspicuously to social commitment. This commitment arose either by formal (and "official") education, as in the case of the Soviet composers—Dmitri Shostakovich is the significant example—or by personal experiences and self-education. Here the German Hans Werner Henze (b. 1926) is a leader among social critics. Shostakovich lived his whole life within state censorship; Henze never has, except for his youthful years as a schoolboy in Nazi Germany. Shostakovich worked outside the stimulation and competition of European experimental music following World War II; Henze was immersed in it and later discarded the radical methods. Shostakovich worked from the time of his years as a brilliant conservatory student to his status as the leading musician of the USSR as an employee of the state. His objectives and finished works were always subject to the constraints of an official cultural policy. Henze chose his métiers, his aspirations, and his audiences to suit both his philosophical *and* artistic credos. His scope was worldwide, from Tokyo to Havana, from La Scala to the Santa Fé Opera, residing in Berlin, or Greenwich Village, or the ancient Italian town of Montepulciano. History shows that both these creative minds are joined by dedication to music for public service and by efforts that earned genuine public pleasure as well as critical acclaim.

Whether Shostakovich would have explored contemporary new styles if he had lived where Henze did, we shall not know. It is clear that Henze would have produced works with antifascist, anticapitalist, and antimilitaristic messages in one form or another no matter where he chose to live. He chose not to live behind the Iron Curtain. His political persuasion was freely adopted, not directed by the state or education. Even the Brunswick State Conservatory he attended had no political action curriculum. Among the European composers of the same generation there are a few others so committed; Luigi Nono and Sylvano Bussotti were two in Italy. Other notable contemporaries, such as Pierre Boulez and Karlheinz

Stockhausen, were not so politicized in their professional work. The discussion here is not a lament at the apparent lack of social involvement of contemporary composers—that they did not all take up a torch or banner. The purpose is to scrutinize those who did. And those who did eventually faced the old dichotomy of artistic choice versus political dogma.

Shostakovich was born in 1906, twenty years before Henze, and his training was within the Soviet socialist system. He served in the war as a civilian fire fighter in Leningrad, while continuing to teach, and composed his seventh symphony ("Leningrad") during the horrendous siege of the city.[3] (He was evacuated before the siege was ended.) He had long mastered his craft as the postwar period commenced. Henze and other younger Europeans were impatient to put together careers which had been snuffed out by the war. The generation of the 1950s and '60s wanted to regenerate the radical direction of music as begun by Anton Webern, who had been tragically and accidently shot as the war ended. The development of the new serialism was paramount; it was not a nationalistic goal; it embraced all. The centers for research in *musique concrète* and electronic music were in Germany and Paris. Festivals of the new music were held in Darmstadt. Henze tried the highly organized serial method but rejected it as too restrictive to the artist and, importantly, to his potential audience.

Because of the isolationist tenets of the USSR's culture, Shostakovich (and most other Soviet musicians) remained outside these new experiments. In the West, radical artistic movement, by virtue of its esoteric nature, is antipopular; it speaks to an elite. In itself it is not political at all. When Shostakovich spoke against the twelve-tone method, it was to mimic the official aesthetic position of the Soviet Communist party. Because of censorship and control of publications in Russia, it is difficult, if not impossible, to determine all Shostakovich actually believed or wrote and whether his name was added unwillingly to doctrinaire articles.

In the liberal spirit of the 1960s, the American magazine, *Music Journal*, received three articles that had ostensibly been written by Shostakovich.[4] He deplored the decadence, the selfish ends, and the vulgarity of music in the West. Whole paragraphs suggested the rhetoric of official proclamations. "Bourgeois Culture Is Bankrupt!" reads the title of the article in the January 1962 issue.

"Today problems of creative innovation are solved more maturely on the basis of kinship with the people and realism . . . with a clear understanding of the pitfalls of blind imitation of current Western fads." The author declared that serialism and *musique concrète* were not music. "They are founded on dogmas and dogmas can have nothing in common with art." Did Shostakovich, after living fifty years in a dogmatic regime, believe this statement? How dogmatic it was to cut off by ideological fiat the opportunity to explore a new method!

Shostakovich had learned at the beginning of his professional career the instant danger of violating official policy. At twenty-four, he wrote the music for a satiric ballet, *The Age of Gold*, in which a Soviet soccer team bests a Western team on their own field. As a joke, he had included his orchestral arrangement of Vincent Youmans's song, *Tea for Two*, which had been retitled strangely in the Soviet Union as *Tahiti Trot* (Op. 16).[5] The catchy American tune was regarded as subversive! The Commissar of Education, Anatoly Lunacharsky, spoke out against the "fox trot problem," which he saw as the kind of insidious bourgeois threat to young Soviets that the people must reject. This official criticism frightened the young composer, and, as we have seen, other censures followed.

Shostakovich was never arrested, although he was rebuked, and placed on a list of "enemies of the state."[6] Volkov believes that despite the personal intervention by Stalin in 1936 over the opera *Lady Macbeth of Mtsensk*, the composer's genius was recognized as so superior, so incomparable, that Stalin always stopped short of the ultimate order to silence him.[7]

The censure in public print of Shostakovich's "negative" work emphasizes the absolute necessity of controlled art in a dictatorship. No dictator can ignore the arts. Lehmann-Haupt underscores this point in his study of the visual arts:

[The dictator] does not think of art as a luxury or a pastime, a pleasant embellishment of life. . . . He has a very healthy respect for it. That is why he must control it absolutely, must mold it into a completely subservient instrument. He knows that there is hardly a better way of getting hold of a person . . . his inner life, the subconscious, hidden personality—than through art. . . . [Art] must create the illusion of a secure, serene world, that hides the sinister motives and the terror.[8]

Shostakovich regained favor with the regime with his heroic Fifth Symphony (1937), brilliant and assured, which has become one of the symphonic masterpieces of the twentieth century. It offered no patriotic slogan or subtitle, but it was his personal statement. Shostakovich had come to terms with the might of the hierarchy. "This symphony is an artist's practical reply to just criticism . . . a work which displays the reeducation of the human mind . . . under the influence of the new ideals."[9] In his "practical reply" Shostakovich also revealed the psychological complexity of this symphony, much in the mold of Beethoven:

The subject of my Fifth Symphony is the evolution of an individual. . . . The finale resolves on an optimistic plane the tragic tension of the first three movements. The question is sometimes asked whether tragedy should have a place in Soviet art at all; but tragedy is not to be confused with hopelessness and pessimism. It is my belief that Soviet tragedy is entirely valid as a genre. But its essence must be suffused with a positive ideal, as in the life-asserting pathos of Shakespeare's tragic plays.[10]

Shostakovich's finale is not the uninterrupted triumph of Beethoven's Fifth. It admits struggle, some reassurance, again anxiety, and finally a calm, perhaps in a time to come. Yet a review of the premiere by a Soviet music critic described this finale as "an energetic, bright and joyful march."[11] This review, written for the American magazine, *Modern Music*, breathed with relief that Shostakovich had done what was needed to be rehabilitated. When Leonard Bernstein conducted a performance with the New York Philharmonic in Moscow in 1959, the reviewers were enthusiastic, yet puzzled. The "complete absorption" of the Americans in the work astonished everyone. But some complained that Bernstein had "deprived the finale of its characteristic festivity and solemnity."[12] Without the hand of the Soviet ministry on his shoulder, the American conductor could bring to life what is in the score (as he saw it) without the preconceptions evoked by dogma.[13]

What was not presented for approbation in 1937 was Shostako-vich's Fourth Symphony. After ten rehearsals by the Leningrad Philharmonic, it was withdrawn by the composer and stored away for twenty-five years. On its premiere in 1961 it was discovered to be a very long, involved and extremely emotional work.[14] Presumably the "just criticism" assuaged with the Fifth might have been recalled against this sprawling Fourth, and Shostakovich was prudent enough not to expose himself to further censure. It was not music which stated the positive, extroverted attitudes that Stalin wanted proclaimed. Number Four was withheld and the composer wrote his Fifth. Twenty-five years later, under the looser controls of the Khruschev period, Shostakovich released the Fourth, and it was hailed as another masterpiece.[15]

In his carefully documented history of Soviet music, Boris Schwarz cautions that it is wrong to see Shostakovich as "a misunderstood rebel oppressed by an inimical regime. . . . It is important to remember that Shostakovich never posed as an 'ivory tower' artist nor as a misunderstood futurist. He had a vital need to communicate with his audiences and with his performers, and nothing seemed to frighten him more than a possible alienation from his surroundings. This might explain his apparent submissiveness to official criticism."[16] Shostakovich's name never joined the international roster of emigrants. "He said in 1931, 'I consider that every artist who isolates himself from the world is doomed. . . . I think an artist should serve the greatest possible number of people. I always try to make myself understood as widely as possible, and, if I don't succeed, I consider it my own fault.'"[17] In an interview by Harrison Salisbury in 1954, Shostakovich insisted that the Soviet composer is no mere automaton. There is a "line" established by the party to guide artists, clearly stating that art must appeal to the people and that it be rendered with "depth and perfection." He referred to himself as an often-criticized composer, but declared: "Who can say that my works suffered from this criticism? My works are played all over Russia. Just because one work is criticized, does not mean that orchestras stop playing others. And I go on writing and the Government goes on supporting me, and generously too."[18]

Under the still more tolerant monitors of the Brezhnev administration, Shostakovich's work revealed a recurring disenchantment with his life, for which he offered no justification. The emphasis on works with texts from 1962 to his death makes this direction in his thought distinct,[19] as more and more explicitly he became a social critic. The Thirteenth and Fourteenth Symphonies are cantatas rather than in the traditional orchestral form. Each thus permits a clearly stated message in words of protest, or despair, or political imprisonment or death. For the Thirteenth (1962), a bass soloist and bass men's chorus sing words of the dissident poet Yevgeny Yevtushenko. The opening section is the poet's censure of the Soviet death camp for Jews, *Babyi Yar*. The premiere earned an ovation from the audience, with shouted bravos for the composer and the poet.[20] The next morning a one-sentence review in *Pravda* indicated the government's cool opinion. Some lines of the text—not the music—had to be changed, particularly to remove the identification of the Jews as the principal victims. There now exist the altered version in the USSR and the original version (published by Leeds, Canada). The elimination of certain words in this vocal piece was an absurd bureaucratic decision; Yevtushenko's poem had been published the year before and was known everywhere.

In his Fourteenth Symphony (1969), solo soprano and solo bass sing the verses of four poets: Apollinaire, Rilke, Garcia Lorca, and the only Russian, Wilhelm Küchelbecker (from Pushkin's generation). Küchelbecker spent the last twenty years of his life in prison for his participation in the Decembrist revolt of 1825.[21] Possibly his lines are the most trenchant: "What comfort is there for talents among villains and fools?" (Poem No. 9.) Strangely, this work was not censored; indeed, it was recorded by the Moscow Chamber Orchestra, immediately permitting a nationwide audience.[22] Perhaps Shostakovich had reached the status of the untouchable national artist. But the arrival of this composition in 1969 was an oblique slap at the regime. It was the one hundredth anniversary of the birth of Lenin, a year jammed with glowing celebrations extolling the advances since the great leader's death. In the middle of this festival year the country's most distinguished composer presented his newest symphony: not a joyous tribute to Soviet life, but a meditation on tyranny and death. The gloom of these works continued into the last years of the composer's life in the *Michelangelo Suite* (1974) for voice and piano (later orchestrated), the Viola Sonata, and the six adagio movements of his Fifteenth (and last) String Quartet. But such was Shostakovich's multifaceted personality that his Fifteenth Symphony (1971) is good-natured, even rambunctious, tantalizing the listener with quotations from Haydn's Symphony No. 104, the *William Tell* Overture, Siegfried's Funeral March, the "Fate" motive from *Die*

Walküre, and flashes from five of his own symphonies. The Fifteenth Symphony appears to be autobiographical, or possibly it is self-mockery; at the least it includes his "favorite tunes."

The Eighth String Quartet of 1960 is similar in the use of self-quotation. There is a two-note motto in the second movement that is said to represent his long feared knock at the door, the terrifying summons from the KGB. The suggestion is strengthened (or corroborated) by a quote from the *Dies irae* by the cello immediately following the motto. Shostakovich clearly connected the feared knock to himself by his use here (as in the third movement of his Tenth Symphony and the opening of the Fourteenth Symphony) of his monogram in musical letters: D., S. (in the German style, Es, that is, E-flat), C, and H (the German note B)—"D. Sch."[23] This is sounded near the beginning of the quartet. It is also the essence of the fugue subject in the last movement. There are also quotations from his First and Fifth Symphonies, and a Russian song, *Languishing in Prison,* an autobiographical piece, followed by music from Katerina's aria on self-sacrifice in *Lady Macbeth.*[24]

The intimate, introspective style of the string quartet may offer insignificant public service by a Socialist Realist musician. Volkov reports Shostakovich's ruse to allow himself such a private, self-directed act:

You say that you're planning such-and-such composition, something with a powerful, killing title. That's so they don't stone you. And meanwhile you write a quartet or something for your own quiet satisfaction. But you tell the administration that you're working on the opera, "Karl Marx" or "The Young Guards" and they'll forgive you your quartet when it appears.[25]

If we survey but one genre of Shostakovich's works—for example, the symphonies, which are his most significant mark on twentieth-century music history—we can see that he has enlarged the horizons of the form as freely as Beethoven and Mahler. Like the symphonic works of these masters, Shostakovich's several symphonies range from an abstract working with musical materials, like the most frequently heard First, Fifth and Tenth, to the frankly programmatic style of No. 2, "To October," and No. 3, "The First of May," both patriotic works with choral finales.

Others are purely instrumental, but they contain extramusical elements, such as the bombastic but moving No. 7, written during the turmoil of the war in Leningrad, and its counterpart, No. 8, which depicts the darker side of the war, shorn of heroics and promises of peace ever after. There are others with dutiful subtitles of socialist content, such as the Eleventh, "The Year 1905," with each of its movements also subtitled, and the Twelfth, "The Year 1917," with the references more sublimated.[26]

The musical revolutionists, the anarchists of art in this century of radical political systems, flourished in the open societies of the Western democracies. Soviet curiosity about the mid-century developments of total serialism, electronic music, aleatoric music, *musique concrète*, and even jazz developments after the 1920s, was actively discouraged, and scant repertoire was extant in scores or recordings for the young composer to study and perhaps to imitate. The kind of brash individualism that John Cage or Karlheinz Stockhausen or Luciano Berio practiced could not and did not arise in the collective state. The one Western, humanist concept that modern Communism cannot tolerate is liberalism, individual or group. Earlier chapters have noted the vigilance of the authoritarian states against deviation from the cultural norms and against artistic statements that hint at independence, and therefore criticism of the establishment.[27]

In a brief chapter in *The New Music*, Reginald Smith Brindle noted the paradox of the pro-Communist Italian composers who tried to bring radical art to the radical politicians of northern Italy, where the Communist Party is strong. Unlike the committed composers of Russia or China, their counterparts in the West used "an advanced language, incomprehensible to the masses."[28] Brindle cites the dozen concerts of music by Luigi Nono in 1970, supported by the Communist Party, who replaced the aristocratic patrons of the past! Sylvano Bussotti's opera, *Lorenzaccio*, dedicated to the Communist Party (rather than to a prince) "was guaranteed performance at several provincial opera houses before it had been heard; no small accomplishment." The workers dutifully attended their opera, and surely went away baffled at what they heard.[29]

The leaders of the avant-garde—Boulez, Stockhausen, Berio, Mauricio Kagel, Gyorgy Ligeti, Bruno Maderna, and in America, Cage, Steve Reich, Earle Brown, Milton Babbitt—have not shown a commitment to clarifying world problems through their music. In the West, where they and their audiences dwell, this is not judged a failing. Rather, they are usually admired for their imagination, concentration, and daring, and for their efforts to sustain the viability of the art. Cage said, "Our proper work now if we love mankind and the world we live in is revolution."[30] But his musical expression could not but create confusion and anxiety, a veritable anarchist's bomb, if it were offered as the "voice" of a political party.

New music and the avant-garde has largely avoided real concern for the ills of this world. . . . In mitigation, it may be said that it is by no means fashionable in artistic circles [in the West] to be positively involved or concerned. It is certainly not fashionable to be patriotic. It is not even fashionable to be a rebel. . . . The truth is that we cannot expect an artist to crucify himself forever for the sorrows of this world.[31]

In explaining his position of commitment, Henze quoted an unreconcilable view of Theodor Adorno. "If one takes composing with deadly seriousness, one ultimately has to ask whether, today, it is not becoming totally ideological. Therefore, without the consolation that it can't go on like this, one must unmetaphorically come face to face with the possibility of falling silent."[32] And Henze, who saw "that Hitlerism lived on after the fall of Hitler, wearing a mask," could not believe that a composer, a creative mind, might be a fascist, give support to racism and tyranny of the mind.[33]

Henze's Fifth Symphony (1958), however, was a paean of the artist's delight in New York City and its shiny skyscrapers, its "avenues that all end in the ocean, [its] salt breeze," the bohemian scenes in Greenwich Village, and so on. The New York "program" was inspired by a commission for this work, the opening of Philharmonic Hall. But where was an admonition to watch out for the booby traps and flimflam of this metropolis of Big Business? Did he succumb to it? Was this symphony his practical demonstration of art for the American masses, or, in this case, for the small mass fitted into Philharmonic Hall?

Henze had turned away from the esotericism of Boulez and Stockhausen. In turn, they found his eclectic style regressive. For

Henze, the ultrarationality of total serialism was needlessly confining and not productive. An accessible language was the only route by which to reach the masses. When the civic-minded composer cries for social change in his music, he must change his artistic medium very slowly, in order not to lose the ears and minds of his constituency. Henze also believed Cage's random, aleatoric music to be antihistorical. It certainly did not rise from the stream of tonality-chromaticism-atonality of Schoenberg's viable method. For Henze, the elimination of a historical direction was unMarxist and undialectical and, hence, wrong: "For one who is fighting, all music that has accompanied those who have fought before him— and that has preceded him in history—has subversive significance. One can find subversion in Mozart, in Beethoven; in both one can find a utopian conception of freedom."[34]

It is also telling that Henze considers the most important composer of this century not the spiritual father of the New Music, Anton Webern, but Gustave Mahler:

It is true that he made little contribution to freeing music from its grammatical impasse, and did little to invent new systems; yet he was a witness to his time. His portrayal of frustration and suffering, in an unmistakable and direct musical language, seems to be more interesting and more important than the achievements of the Viennese School. . . . One might think that the difference lies in the techniques employed, but I would maintain the difference lies in the effect which the composer wanted to make.[35]

The proof of Henze's artistic criteria—for a propagandist—is that his eclectic tonal style resulted in frequent, usually early, and prestigious performances of every new work. His several operas were performed on leading stages. As his career matured, the theater works became more and more conspicuously social criticism. *Boulevard Solitude* (written in 1951 at age 25) is antibourgeois. *The Bassarids* (1965), with a libretto by W. H. Auden and Chester Kallman, is an anti-Nazi message. Similar polemics are heard in his hybrid cantata-opera-streetmusic works: *El Cimarrón* (1970), the elaborate *Raft of the Medusa* (1968), and the "show," *The Tedious Way to Natascha Ungeheurer's Flat* (1971)[36], which included prerecorded tape sounds of street noise, popular music styles, a chord from his Sixth Symphony, a flexa-tone, and a fourteen-part tone cluster. *We Come to the River*, an opera of 1976, is another powerful antiwar statement, grimly dramatizing many atrocities of contemporary society.

Henze had witnessed the brutal conduct of Nazi soldiers as a child. At the Brunswick State Music School, he recalled, a few people had dared to talk about the loss of personal freedom; they had also whispered about the composers who could no longer be performed: Hindemith, Stravinsky, Schoenberg.[37] In the middle of the war a resistance group, the White Rose, sprang up in Munich. They openly resisted Nazi rule, but their numbers were small and they were soon rounded up and executed. In 1965 Henze recalled their integrity and courage in a piece composed as a contribution to the Congress of European Antifascist Resistance held in Bologna, *In Memoriam: die weisse Rose*. As a practical requirement, the music was scored for a chamber orchestra, but the chamber style seems symbolic here: One player alone bears the responsibility for each portion of the whole.

His overt politicization as a composer, however, grew slowly. In 1967 in New York, he was sharply aware of the bitterness over the Viet Nam War, the riots in Washington and Newark, and the problems of the Blacks (memorialized in a 1979 piece, *El Rey de Harlem*). In that year he also began to study the radical left, and, still later, its antecedents, Marx and Lenin.[38] He had joined the election campaign of Willy Brandt in 1965 and had befriended the German SDS and the student leader Rudi Dutschke. In 1969 he was an official guest in Cuba, where he says he began to learn how his music and political beliefs could give strength to each other.[39]

Cuba was the source of a solo cantata, *El Cimarrón* based on the recollections of a runaway slave, Estebán Montejo, that was published in 1963 in Cuba. With a translation into German, Henze composed a work for solo baritone (the voice of the slave), flute, guitar and percussion, with all four performers required to play a variety of instruments. When the piece was produced, it was perceived as a militant political piece at the Berlin Festival of 1970. "The Mediterranean lyricism and dreamy removal from reality . . . have since his Piano Concerto, yielded to a new musical directness, an immediacy of expression."[40]

Two years earlier, Henze had been commissioned to write a work for the North German Radio System. When he announced the work as a requiem for Che Guevara, the premiere was assured of being a political affair. And so it was; such a commotion arose in the hall that the concert was stopped before the first note was struck. The performance was scheduled for Hamburg, December 11, 1968. The audience was composed of the unusual mix of well-to-do patrons of the arts and contingents from the Hamburg and Berlin wings of the SDS. After the chorus, soloist and, orchestra assembled on stage, but before Henze appeared to conduct, some students hung a large portrait of Guevara on the podium. When this was immediately torn down by the program director of the Radio System, the students returned with a red flag. The Radio Chamber chorus shouted that they would not sing under a red flag. Bedlam broke out and the police were called. Henze strode to the stage and announced that the intervention of the police made the performance physically and morally impossible, and he left. The scandal of the premiere, unlike the historic one over that of Stravinsky's *Rite of Spring* in 1913, was unfortunately an uproar not over the music, or the subject of the text (the nineteenth-century scandal of the French navy shipwreck, the inspiration for Géricault's famous painting of 1818). A political confrontation had prevented the hearing of the work.[41] Subsequently the producer of the Nuremberg City Opera, Wolfgang Weber, persuaded the composer that the highly theatrical work would be more effective as an opera, because the cantata staging required the singers to pass from one side of the stage to the other (a metaphor of life and death). In this operatic version, *The Raft of the Medusa* was seen and heard in the less sensitive city of Nuremberg April 15, 1972. The dedication to Che, however, remained, and the story of death claiming the abandoned survivors one by one was termed a "compelling stage experience."[42] The theater may be the most effective means of presentation for Henze's purpose. In listening to a recording of this work in its original form (Deutsche Grammophon), one hears long stretches of recitative, with occasional outbursts: shouting by the chorus and the massing of percussion and winds. The growing tragedy of the drama is not grasped by the armchair listener.[43] The notoriety of the non-premiere turned many producers away from Henze's works for a time.

Henze has enjoyed throughout his career the performing talent of some of the most distinguished institutions and artists of his time: the English National Opera, the Berlin German Opera, La Scala, Covent Garden, the New York Philharmonic, the Berlin Philharmonic, and the Chicago Symphony; singers Dietrich Fischer-Dieskau, Peter Pears, and Elisabeth Söderström; ballerina Margot Fonteyn; conductors von Karajan, Bernstein, Britten, and Solti; librettists W. H. Auden and Chester Kallman; stage directors Sellnar and Visconti. He has received an honorary doctorate from the University of Edinburgh, the Robert Schumann Prize of the city of Dusseldorf, membership in the West Berlin Academy of the Arts (he resigned in 1968 and became a corresponding member of the East Berlin Academy), and is an honorary member of the Royal Academy of Music, London. He has been a visiting professor at Dartmouth College, the Salzburg Mozarteum and other institutions in Europe.[44] His *vita* thus looks like that of an eminent member of the old establishment, and a darling of the capitalist cultural elite. Yet he is demonstrably the most performed musical foe, on philosophical grounds, of all the capitalist elite stands for.

A third contemporary who deserves inclusion here as an overt social critic or commentator is the Polish composer Krzysztof Penderecki (b. 1933). His childhood experience is similar to that of Henze; he grew up under Nazi authority. In the direction of his compositional method, however, he is one of the boldest experimenters. He is not associated with the total serialists, nor with nontraditional sounds of the electronic media. He uses the standard symphony orchestra with unorthodox performance instructions. Penderecki splits the spectrum of the orchestral sound into dozens of separate tones, clustered together, especially at the highest extremes of pitch. "Clouds" of mysterious, unidentified tones in varying timbres and volume shift throughout the piece. His music is arresting, even upsetting, especially at first hearing, but it is emotionally coherent. It requires listeners to be unusually open-minded and imaginative.

Nonetheless, Penderecki communicates his social concerns: Each work bears a title or dedication that uncovers a painful wound, a moral tragedy of broad significance from the past, which brings with it the fear and warning of its return. The intellectual anguish is made visceral by a strange texture of sounds.

In his *Threnody—to the Victims of Hiroshima* (1960), fifty-two solo string players produce tones (not precise pitches) that are stacked from very low to very high and wrap the listener in an awesome curtain of sound. It sounds electronic, but it is not. With the textual reminder of the explosion of the first atomic bomb before the audience, the terrifying occurrence is aurally suggested: a horrifying experience never known before. The astonishing effect, however, might convey a quite different—though disturbing— emotion if it were given a different title. This piece was, in fact, composed without a title, or rather, as *8'26"*.[45]

The tone clusters, or *clouds*, are used both instrumentally and chorally in the same composer's remarkable oratorio, that borrows (after a long disuse) the Baroque Lenten form of the Passion of Christ. In 1969 Penderecki composed his *Passion According to St. Luke* for three soloists, narrator, multiple choirs, and orchestra. The text is in scriptural and liturgical Latin, and the form and the familiarity with the subject matter signal a composer of Roman Catholic background. The multiple-pitch clouds Penderecki uses create a powerful representation of the unruly mobs who cried out during the trial of Jesus. He also composed a setting of the *Stabat Mater* in 1963.

Some of Penderecki's religious works which infer political thrusts are his *Dies irae*, written for the unveiling of the International Monument to the Victims of Fascism at Auschwitz-Birkenau, Poland; *Te Deum* for Pope John II; and *Lacrymosa* (from the Requiem liturgy), commissioned by Lech Walesa and the Solidarity Labor Movement for the unveiling of the monument to honor the twenty-eight Polish workers killed in the riots of 1970 at Gdansk (1981). The theme of his opera, *The Devils of Loudun*, is persecution. Penderecki has also written many purely instrumental works without suggestive titles.[46]

Poland's government is Communist, yet the Roman Catholic religion is a vital aspect of the society. The daily news records persistent dissension between the two creeds. A new composition rising from the Christian liturgy is not banned, though such a work proclaims an allegiance which defies the paramount authority expressed in a Communist system. This composer's stand as a propagandist is not that of a nationalist or socialist, nor does he show an exclusive political stance. He is a humanist. His compassion springs from other sources; religion is one. His works clearly ask the listener to share his personal creed, which is not apolitical.

One more composer deserves a place here: Luigi Nono (b. 1924), who was a prominent figure in the *avant garde* of the 1950s and was at one time a pointillist whose early works were chiefly abstract.[47] He is also one of the few politically committed composers who pursued an experimental technique and still won general audiences. He is an active Communist in a capitalist system, Italy. A glance at his works shows his progress from antifascism in *Epitaph to Garcia Lorca*, his rebuke of Nazi atrocities in *Il Canto Sospeso* and *Ricorda quello che ti han fatto ad Auschwitz*, the anti-American *A Floresta*, and his overtly pro-Communist opera, *Intolleranza 1960*, which attacks several contemporary social ills, including the atom bomb, and ends with the annihilation of the world. In memory of Luciano Cruz, Chilean leader of the Movement of the Revolutionary Left, in 1971 he wrote *Como una ola de furza y luz* (Like a wave of power and light), with words by an Argentine poet, Julio Huasi. It was scored for soprano, piano, tape and orchestra.

In 1975 Nono brought to the opera stage his second opera, *Al Gran Sole Carico d'Amore*, and his musico-political confrontations won public acclaim at La Scala, Edinburgh, and Frankfurt. The title is derived from a line from a poem by Arthur Rimbaud ("In the great sun charged with love") which recalled the conflict of the Communist rebellion in Paris in 1870. The libretto was loaded with other polemical texts, including lines from Marx, Lenin and Brecht. The opening chorus proclaimed Che Guevara's "*La belleza no está reñida con la revolucion.*" It is a thought which any artist firmly committed to art, however politicized, might support: "Beauty is not a denial of the revolution." The scenes of the opera move from the Paris Commune to Russia in 1905, Turin, Italy in the 1940s and '50s, and the attack on the Moncada Barracks in Cuba in 1953. The conclusion assails the listener with other war scenes such as Vietnamese mothers in mourning who sing lines from actual letters. Then follow words of hope from prisoners of past wars, including Fidel Castro. Two phrases from *The Internationale* close the curtain. The texts sound inspiring or outrageous, depending on one's politics. But one astute reviewer (Andrew Porter) freely admitted it was highly expressive, powerful and convincing theater.[48]

Beethoven's audience for *Fidelio*, more than 150 years before Nono's *Al Gran Sole*, was made up of a similar conservative, fashionable public, far more ready for sophisticated entertainment than for political polemics. Each of these audiences came to hear the new work of an established composer, and remained, held by the music and, most certainly, goaded by the allusions to living problems—goaded, offended, perhaps outraged, perhaps consoled, spurred on, given hope, and compelled to think.

This book has attempted to demonstrate that composers in many times and places have consciously used their craft to change the world outside their studio: the world which also nourished or eroded, directed or arrested, encouraged or stifled, their artistic striving. For some, art could attain the supreme goal only if it carried with it the victory, or the promise of victory, of the good in society, as the artist recognized the good. It is the purpose of propaganda to persuade, to beguile, and to instruct. This is a record of such propaganda by means of the universal art of music, more varied, more pervasive, more seductive, and more persistent a vehicle than music history has recognized in the past.

NOTES

1. Hans Werner Henze, *Music and Politics: Collected Writings, 1953-81*, tr. by Peter Labanyi (London: Faber & Faber, 1982), p. 276.

2. *The New Music, 1900-1960*. (New York: W. W. Norton Company, 1968, rev. edition), pp. 143-44.

3. Read Harrison Salisbury, *The 900 Days: The Siege of Leningrad* (New York: Harper & Row, 1969).

4. The articles appeared in the issues of January, March and September, 1962. It appears they are translations of articles concurrently printed in *Pravda*. See Boris Schwarz, *Music and Musical Life in Soviet Russia, Enlarged Edition, 1917-1981* (Bloomington: Indiana University Press, 1983), p. 346, n. 72; p. 516 on Shostakovich's published praise of Scriabin, whose music in fact did not please him; and the remarks of Maxim Shostakovich, p. 645; and also *Testimony, the Memoirs of Dimitri Shostakovich*, as related to and edited by Solomon Volkov (New York: Harper & Row, 1979), pp. xiv-xv. Note: Volkov's work is yet to be

authenticated (by the appearance, for instance, of original notes or the tapes he refers to), but it offers a rich store of commentaries that are plausible, (if rather too persistently negative), whether or not they are all word-for-word from the composer. For further views on the usefulness of Volkov's *Testimony*, see Christopher Norris, ed., *Shostakovich: The Man and His Music* (Boston: Marion Boyars, 1982), pp. 8-10, 174, 186, 216 (n. 2.). See also Schwarz's interview of Maxim Shostakovich, in *Musical Life*, p. 645.

5. "Tahiti Trot" by Solomon Volkov, in *The Musical Quarterly*, April 1978 (volume LXIV, No. 2), pp. 223-28.

6. Volkov, *Testimony, passim*, especially p. 115; Schwarz, *Musical Life*, pp. 119f, 195.

7. To read how a prizewinning composer of lesser talent, Herman Zhukovsky, found his career crushed before it began, see Schwarz, *Musical Life*, p. 263.

8. *Art Under a Dictatorship* (New York: Oxford University Press, 1973), pp. xviii-xix.

9. Dmitri and Ludmilla Sollertinsky, *Pages from the Life of Dmitri Shostakovich*, tr. by Graham Hobbs and Charles Midgley (New York: Harcourt Brace Jovanovich, 1980),   p. 83. See note 10. For a Soviet historian's evaluation, see Ivan Martynov, *Dmitri Shostakovich: The Man and His Work* (written in 1942), tr. by T. Guralsky (New York: Greenwood Press, 1960), pp. 59-87. Shostakovich later deleted his "apology" from the score.

10. Nicolas Slonimsky, *Music Since 1900*, (New York: Charles Scribner's Sons, 1971), fourth edition, p. 658.

11. Grigori Schneerson, *Modern Music*, Vol. XV (March-April 1938), pp. 174-75. See also Slonimsky, *Music Since 1900*, pp. 657-58.

12. Translated in the jacket notes for the Columbia recording No. MS6115 by Bernstein and the New York Philharmonic.

13. A concise analysis of the Fifth Symphony, and its association with the Fourth, is provided in "The First Twelve Symphonies" by Robert Dearling, in *Shostakovich: The Man and His Music*, Christopher Norris, ed. (Boston: Marion Boyars, 1982), pp. 55-61.

14. See Schwarz, *Musical Life*, pp. 130-31, 170-73. For this and other works Shostakovich held back for several years, see p. 244.

15. Schwarz, *Musical Life*, pp. 328. It was in this same year (1961) that Shostakovich joined the Communist Party. His candidate's address affirmed the Party principles: "artists must be in the thick of life, to relate their creative work to the needs of the times." Cited in "Dmitry Dmitrievich Shostakovich" by Alan Bush, in *Shostakovich: The Man and His Music*, Norris, ed., p. 224.

16. Schwarz, *Musical Life*, pp. 130-31.

17. From an interview by Rose Lee, "D. Szostakovitch," in *The New York Times*, December 20, 1931; cited in Schwarz, *Musical Life*, p. 130.

18. *New York Times Magazine*, August 8, 1954, p. 9.

19. See "Words and Music in Late Shostakovich" by Malcolm MacDonald in *Shostakovich: The Man and His Music*, Norris, ed., pp. 125-33.

20. Schwarz was present for the premiere. See *Musical Life*, pp. 365-69. The Thirteenth Symphony in the historical context of Shostakovich's work is found in "Shostakovich and the Soviet System, 1925-1975," by Robert Stradling, *Shostakovich: The Man and His Music*, Norris, ed., pp. 208-9, 211-16.

21. The Decembrists were a young elite who rebelled against the Czar's policy in 1825. This revolutionary historical subject was thus acceptable for Soviet art. Yuri Shaporin (b. 1887) spent many years composing a major opera about it, and *The Decembrists* was given its premiere in 1953. See Stanley D. Krebs, *Soviet Composers and the Development of Soviet Music* (New York: W. W. Norton Company, 1970), pp. 177-84.

22. Schwarz, *Musical Life*, pp. 492-93.

23. See Dearling, "The First Twelve Symphonies," pp. 71-72, in *Shostakovich: The Man and His Music*, Norris, ed.

24. Stradling, "Shostakovich and the Soviet System" in ibid., pp. 211, 213.

25. Volkov, p. 257. See Schwarz, *Musical Life*, p. 136, on Shostakovich seeking "refuge" in writing film music throughout his career.

26. In his preface to *Testimony*, p. xi, Volkov gives me the impression that the Eleventh, "written after the 1956 Hungarian uprising," is a hidden assault on the Soviet regime despite its title. But the Eleventh was planned for the fortieth anniversary (1957) of the Bolshevists' October Revolution, which had succeeded, whereas the 1905 people's uprising had been crushed by the Czarist government. The timing of the symphony may have resulted in an ironic statement but it was no covert plan on the part of Shostakovich. Similarly the companion Twelfth, which also memorialized 1917, coincided with the opening of the Twenty-second Party Congress in October, 1961. (See Schwarz, *Musical Life*, p. 337.)

27. There has been an *avant-garde* movement for over twenty years, but little of the music has appeared for us to judge in the West. Innovators—"rebels"—included Arvo Pärt and Alfred Schnittke (both born in the 1930s) working as (apparently) minimalists, and Vladimir Zagortsev (born 1945) of Kiev, who wrote under the influence of Boulez and Stockhausen. His piece, *Gradations* (1966), was played by the New York Philharmonic in 1980. See *Stereo Review*, March 1982, p. 90, on the first two names; *The*

New Yorker, February 4, 1980, p. 110, for a review of *Gradations*. Elliott Carter saw "several bus loads" of Moscow Conservatory students at the 1962 Warsaw Festival. "They reacted pro and con to advanced scores." *Perspectives of New Music*, Spring 1963, pp. 202-3. Shostakovich told Slonimsky in 1935 that he had "tried his hand" at the twelve-tone method but found he could do nothing with it. He also showed Slonimsky his copy of Varèse's landmark percussion piece of 1931, *Ionisation*. "Russia Revisited" in *Modern Music*, XIII:1 (November-December, 1935), pp. 21-22. Slonimsky found experiments in Shostakovich's early Second Symphony. See "Dmitri Dmitrievitch Shostakovitch" in *The Musical Quarterly*, XXVIII:4 (October, 1942), p. 424.

28. Reginald Smith Brindle, *The New Music: The Avant-garde Since 1945* (London: Oxford University Press, 1975), p. 183.

29. The sympathy toward Leftist musicians in the North Italian Communist town halls logically rebounds to a hostility toward non-Leftists. The American conductor, Henry Lewis, learned this political criterion was an obstacle to his receiving engagements in some of the provincial opera houses in the region. Quoted in the St. Louis *Post-Dispatch*, June 10, 1983.

30. *A Year from Monday* (New York: Middletown, Ct.: Wesleyan University Press, 1967).

31. Brindle, *The New Music*, p. 185.

32. Henze, *Music and Politics*, p. 196.

33. Ibid., p. 275.

34. Ibid., p. 170. In Cage's *Imaginary Landscape No. 4*, for example, the music is produced by tuning in twelve radios and listening to the random collage of sounds in a deliberately nonrational (and Zen influenced) manner. Cage reported he once walked out of a concert in which Stockhausen electronically and consciously manipulated the sounds of live musicians, because he (Cage) viewed this control of one person by another a violation of individual integrity. See "On Radical Culture" by Trevor Wishart, in John Shepherd, et al., *Whose Music? A Sociology of Musical Languages* (London: Latimer New Dimensions, 1977), p. 247.

35. Henze, *Music and Politics*, pp. 170-71.

36. In German the two titles are *Das Floss der Medusa* and *Das langwierige Weg in die Wohnung der Natascha Ungeheuer*.

37. Henze, *Music and Politics*, pp. 32, 178, also 28-30.

38. Ibid., p. 179f.

39. Ibid., p. 56.

40. *The Musical Quarterly*, LVII:2 (April, 1971), p. 314.

41. *High Fidelity Magazine*, December, 1969, pp. 106-7; Henze, *Music and Politics*, pp. 61-62, 167-68.

42. *Musical Times*, CXIII (1972), pp. 588-89.

43. See Henze's comments in *Music and Politics*, pp. 161-62, 167-68, 254.

44. Ibid., pp. 15-23; *passim*.

45. Ray Robinson, *Krzysztof Penderecki: A Guide to His Work*. (Princeton: Prestige Publications, 1983), p. 12.

46. Ibid., pp. 7, 9-14. A recommended general study is in B. M. Maciejewski, *Twelve Polish Composers* (London: Allegro Press, 1976), pp. 165-94.

47. Brindle, *The New Music*, pp. 17-19.

48. Andrew Porter, *The New Yorker*, October 16, 1978. For other vocal works with social messages, see Istvan Anhalt, *Alternate Voices: Essays on Contemporary Vocal and Choral Compositions* (Toronto: University of Toronto Press, 1984), Chapter VI, "Deep themes, not so hidden," esp. pp. 176-86, 199-205.

Bibliography

CHAPTER 1: MESSAGES IN THE MUSIC

Ballantine, Christopher. *Music and Its Social Meanings*. New York: Gordon & Breach, 1984.

Baxandall, Lee, and Stefan Morawski, eds. *Karl Marx and Frederick Engels on Literature and Art*. New York: International General, 1974.

Beaumarchais, Pierre Caron de. *Théâtre complet*. 3 volumes. d'Heylli, G., and E. de Marescot, eds. Genève: Slatkine Reprints, 1967. Originally published 1870.

Beethoven, Ludwig van. *Beethoven: Letters, Journals and Conversations*. Tr. and ed. by Michael Hamburger. Garden City, N.Y.: Doubleday & Co., 1960.

————. *The Letters of Beethoven*. 3 volumes. Tr. and ed. by Emily Anderson. London: Macmillan 1961.

Biancolli, Louis, ed. *The Mozart Handbook*. New York: Grosset & Dunlap, 1962.

Chase, Gilbert. *America's Music*. Rev. ed. New York: McGraw Hill, 1966.

Forbes, Elliot, ed. *Thayer's Life of Beethoven*. 2 volumes. Princeton: Princeton University Press, 1964.

Geiringer, Karl, and Irene Geiringer. *Haydn: A Creative Life in Music*, second revised and enlarged edition. Garden City, N.Y.: Doubleday & Co., 1963.

Greenway, John. *American Folksongs of Protest*. New York: Octagon Books, 1970.

Grendel, Frédéric. *Beaumarchais: The Man Who Was Figaro*. Tr. by Roger Greaves. London: Macdonald & Jane's, 1973.

King, Alexander. *Mozart in Retrospect*. Westport, Ct.: Greenwood Press, 1976. Reprint of 1970 edition.

Landon, H. C. Robbins, comp. and ed. *Beethoven: A Documentary Study*. New York: Macmillan & Co., 1970
_____. *The Life of Haydn: Chronicle and Works*. 5 volumes. Vol. II. *Haydn at Esterháza, 1766-1790*. Bloomington: Indiana University Press, 1978.

Lomax, Alan, ed. Introduction by Woody Guthrie. *Hard Hitting Songs for Hard-Hit People*. New York: Oak Publications, 1967. [Songs of the 1930s.]

Lawrence, Vera Brodsky. *Music for Patriots, Politicians and Presidents: Harmonies and Discords of the First Hundred Years*. New York: Macmillan, 1975.

Nettl, Paul. *Mozart and Masonry*. New York: Da Capo Press, 1970. Reprint of 1957 edition.

Okun, Milton, ed. *Great Songs of the Sixties*. New York: Quandrangle Books, 1970.

Sadie, Stanley, ed. *The New Grove Mozart*. New York: W. W. Norton & Co., 1983.

Scheff, Thomas J. *Catharsis in Healing, Ritual and Drama*. Berkeley: University of California, 1979.

Silber, Irwin, ed. *Songs American Voted By*. Harrisburg, Penn.: Stackpole Books, 1971.

Sloboda, John A. *The Musical Mind: An Introduction to the Cognitive Psychology of Music*. New York: Oxford University Press, 1984.

Sonneck, O. G., ed. *Beethoven: Impressions by His Contemporaries*. New York: Dover Publications, 1954.

Thomson, Katherine. *The Masonic Thread in Mozart*. Atlantic Highlands, N.J.: Humanities Press, 1977.

Whitman, Wanda Willson, ed. *Songs That Changed the World*. New York: Crown Publishers, 1969.

CHAPTER 2: PEOPLE WITHOUT POWER
A Brief Bibliography of Musical Nationalism

Bohemia (Czechoslovakia)

Abraham, Gerald. *Slavonic and Romantic Music*. New York: St. Martin's Press, 1968.

Bartos, Frantisek. *Bedřich Smetana: Letters and Reminiscences*. Prague: Artia, 1953.

Clapham, John. *Antonín Dvořák*. London: St. Martin's Press, 1966.

Sourek, Otakar. *The Orchestral Works of Antonín Dvořák*. Tr. by Roberta Finlayson Samsour. Prague: Artia, n.d.

Finland

Johnson, Harold E. *Jean Sibelius*. New York: Alfred A. Knopf, 1959.
Levas, Santeri. *Sibelius: A Personal Portrait*. London: tr. by Percy M. Young. J. M. Dent & Sons, 1972.

Hungary, Romania

Bartók, Béla. *Letters*. Collected, selected, edited and annotated by Janos Demény. Tr. by Peter Balabán and István Farkas. Tr. revised by Elisabeth West and Colin Mason. London: Faber & Faber, 1971.
Lesznai, Lajos. *Bartók*. Tr. by Percy M. Young. London: J. M. Dent & Sons, 1961.
Stevens, Halsey. *The Life and Music of Béla Bartók*. Rev. ed. London: Oxford University Press, 1964.
Walker, Alan, ed. *Franz Liszt: The Man and His Music*. New York: Taplinger Publishing Co., 1970.

Poland

Walker, Alan, ed. *Chopin*. New York: Barrie & Rockliff, 1966.

Russia

Abraham, Gerald. *Essays on Russia and East European Music*. New York: Oxford University Press, 1984. See "Satire and Symbolism in *The Golden Cockerel*" [Rimsky-Korsakov's last opera].
_____. *Studies in Russian Music*. New York: Books for Libraries, 1968.
Evans, Edwin. *Tchaikovsky*. New York: E. P. Dutton & Co., 1940.
Lakond, Wladimir (Walter Lake). *The Diaries of Tchaikovsky*. New York: W. W. Norton & Company, 1945.
Leyda, Jan, and Sergei Bertensson, eds. *The Musorgsky Reader: A Life of Modeste Petrovich Musorgsky in Letters and Documents*. New York: Da Capo Press, 1970. [Reprint of 1947 edition.]
New Grove Encyclopedia of Music and Musicians. Sixth edition. Stanley Sadie, ed. London: Macmillan, 1980. [Mussorgsky (vol. XII) and others.]
Salem, Walter, ed., *The Social Status of the Professional Musician from the Middle Ages to the 19th Century*. Tr. by Herbert Kaufman and Barbara Reisner. New York: Pendragon Press, 1983. Chapter IX.
Seroff, Victor I. *The Mighty Five: The Cradle of Russian National Music*. Freeport, New York: Books for Libraries Press, 1948.

CHAPTER 3: WAGNER, HITLER AND THE GERMAN "RACE"

Adorno, Theodor. *In Search of Wagner.* Tr. by Rodney Livingstone. London: NLB, 1981.

Barzun, Jacques. *Darwin, Marx, Wagner.* Boston: Little, Brown & Co., 1941.

Deathridge, John, and Carl Dahlhaus, eds. *The New Grove WAGNER.* New York: W. W. Norton & Co., 1984. [The collected articles on Richard Wagner and his music from the *The New Grove Dictionary of Music and Musicians,* Stanley Sadie, ed., 1980.]

DiGaetani, John Louis, ed. *Penetrating Wagner's Ring: An Anthology.* Cranbury, N.J.: Associated University Presses, 1978. [For George G. Windell on Hitler and Wagner.]

Goldman, Albert, and Evert Sprinchorn. *Wagner on Music and Drama.* London: Victor Gollancz, 1964.

Grunberger, Richard. *A Social History of the Third Reich.* London: Weidenfeld & Nicolson, 1971.

Herzstein, Robert Edwin, ed. *Adolf Hitler and the Third Reich.* Boston: Houghton Mifflin & Co., 1971.

Hitler, Adolf. *Mein Kampf.* Tr. by Ralph Manheim. 2 volumes. Boston: Houghton Mifflin & Co., 1943.

Josserand, Frank B. *Richard Wagner: Patriot and Politician.* Lanham, Md.: University Press of America, 1981.

Kerman, Josef. *Opera as Drama.* Westport, Ct., Greenwood Press, 1981. Originally published in 1956.

Kubizek, August. *The Young Hitler I Knew.* Tr. by Emily V. Anderson. Cambridge, Ma.: Houghton Mifflin & Co., 1953.

Large, David C., and William Weber, eds. *Wagnerism in European Culture and Politics.* Ithaca: Cornell University Press. In press 1984.

Lehmann-Haupt, Hellmut. *Art Under a Dictatorship.* New York: Octagon Books, 1973. Originally published in 1954.

Miller, Barbara Land, and Leila J. Rapp, eds. *Nazi Ideology before 1933: A Documentation.* Austin: University of Texas, 1978.

Norman, Gertrude, and Miriam L. Shrifte, eds. *Letters of Composers.* New York: Grosset & Dunlap, 1946.

Rather, L. J. *The Dream of Self Destruction.* Baton Rouge: Louisiana University Press, 1979. [On Norse mythology in eighteenth- and nineteenth-century Europe, and Wagner's use of the Nibelung tales, the Oedipus myth, and theories of racism.]

Rolland, Romain. *Musicians of Today.* Second edition. New York: Henry Holt & Co., 1915.

Shaw, George Bernard. *The Perfect Wagnerite.* New York: Dover Publications, 1967. Reprint of the 4th edition.

Shirer, William. *The Rise and Fall of the Third Reich*. New York: Simon & Schuster, 1960.

Stein, Leon. *The Racial Thinking of Richard Wagner*. New York: Philosophical Library, 1950.

Škvorecký, Josef. *The Bass Saxophone*. Tr. by Káča Poláčková-Henley. New York: Alfred A. Knopf, 1979.

Viereck, Peter. *Meta-politics: The Roots of the Nazi Mind*. New York: Capricorn Books, 1965.

Wagner, Cosima. *Cosima Wagner's Diaries*. Two volumes. Ed. by Martin Gregor-Dellin and Dietrich Mack. Translated with an Introduction by Geoffrey Skelton. Vol. I, 1869-77. London: William Collins & Sons, 1978. Vol. II, 1878-83. New York: Harcourt, Brace, Jovanovich, 1980.

Wagner, Friedelind, and Page Cooper. *The Royal Family of Bayreuth*. London: Eyre & Spottiswoode, 1948.

———. *Heritage of Fire*. New York: Harper Brothers, 1945.

Wagner, Richard. *The Diary of Richard Wagner 1865-1882*. Annotated by Joachim Bergfeld. Tr. by George Bird. [The family nickname was "The Brown Book."]

———. *Prose Works*. 12 volumes. Tr. by William Ashton Ellis, New York: Broude Brothers, 1966. Reprint of 1897 edition.

Wolman, Benjamin B., ed. *Psychoanalytic Interpretation of History*. New York: Basic Books, 1971. [For the references by Robert G. L. Waite on Hitler and Peter Loewenberg on Herzl.]

CHAPTER 4: MUSIC FOR THE TOTALITARIAN STATE

Abraham, Gerald. *Eight Soviet Composers*. Westport, Ct.: Greenwood Press, 1970. Reprint of the 1943 edition.

Antonov-Ovseyenko, Anton. *The Time of Stalin: Portrait of Tyranny*. Tr. by George Saunders. New York: Harper & Row, 1981.

Baxandall, Lee, and Stefan Morawski, eds. *Karl Marx and Frederick Engels on Literature and Art*. New York: International General, 1974.

Boelza, Igor. "Communication from Moscow, I: On Oriental Culture in Soviet Music," in *The Musical Quarterly*, XXIX:4 (October, 1943), pp. 517-20.

Brown, Malcolm H. "The Soviet Russian Concepts of 'Intonazia' and 'Musical Imagery,' " in *The Musical Quarterly*, LX:4 (October, 1974), pp. 557-67.

Cassinelli, C. W. *Total Revolution: A Comparative Study of Germany under Hitler, the Soviet Union under Stalin, and China under Mao*. Santa Barbara, Calif.: Clio Books, 1976.

Ehrenburg, Ilya. *Memoirs 1921-1941*. Tr. by Tatania Shebunina in collaboration with Yvonne Kapp. New York: Grosset & Dunlap, 1966.

_____. *Post-War Years 1945-1954*. Tr. by Tatania Shebunina in collaboration with Yvonne Kapp. Cleveland: World Publishing Co., 1967.

Krebs, Stanley D. *Soviet Composers and the Development of Soviet Music*. W. W. Norton & Co., 1970.

Kubalkova, V., and A. A. Cruickshank. *Marxism-Leninism and the Theory of International Relations*. London: Routledge & Kegan Paul, 1980.

Lenin, V. I. *Collected Works*. English edition. Vol. X. Moscow: Progress Publishers, 1962, [1905-6.]

_____. *Culture and Cultural Revolution*. Moscow: Progress Publishers, 1966.

_____. *On Literature and Art*. Moscow: Progress Publishers, 1967.

Leyda, Jay. *Eisenstein: Three Films*. New York: Harper & Row, 1974.

Lipman, Samuel. *The House of Music: Art in an Era of Institutions*. Ch. IV. "The New Wave of [USSR] Émigrés" (1980), pp. 106-19. Boston: David R. Godine, Publisher, 1984.

Martynov, Ivan. *Dmitri Shostakovich: The Man and His Work*. Tr. by T. Guralsky. New York: Greenwood Press, 1969. [Written in 1942. Reprint of 1947 edition.]

Medvedev, Roy A. *Let History Judge: The Origins and Consequences of Stalinism*. David Joravsky and Georges Haupt, eds. Tr. by Colleen Taylor. New York: Alfred A. Knopf, 1971.

Norris, Christopher, ed. *Shostakovich: The Man and His Music*. Boston: Marion Boyars, 1982.

Prokofiev, Sergei. *Autobiography, Articles, Reminiscences*. Tr. by Rose Prokofieva. London: Central Books, 1960. [Note: the translator is not a relative.]

_____. *Materials, Articles, Interviews*. English edition. Compiled by Vladimir Blok. Moscow: Progress Publishers, 1978.

_____. *Prokofiev by Prokofiev: A Composer's Memoir*. David H. Appel, ed. Tr. by Guy Daniels. Garden City, N.Y.: Doubleday & Co., 1979. [His youthful years.]

Roseberry, Eric. *Shostakovich, His Life and Times*. New York: Midas Books, 1982. [Good photos and quotations, but no footnotes to verify or locate the sources.]

Salisbury, Harrison E. *The 900 Days: The Siege of Leningrad*. New York: Harper & Row Publishers, 1969.

Schwarz, Boris. *Music and Musical Life in Soviet Russia. Enlarged edition, 1917-1981*. Bloomington, Ind.: Indiana University Press, 1983.

Shostakovich, Dmitri. *Testimony: The Memoirs of Dmitri Shostakovich*. As related to and edited by Solomon Volkov. Tr. by Antonina W. Bouis. New York: Harper & Row, 1979.

Slonimsky, Nicolas. "Dmitri Dmitrievitch Shostakovitch," in *The Musical Quarterly*, XXVIII:4 (October, 1942), pp. 415-21.

_____. *Music Since 1900*. First edition. New York: W. W. Norton & Co., 1937. Fourth edition. New York: Charles Scribner's Sons, 1971.

Sollertinsky, Dmitri, and Ludmilla Sollertinsky. *Pages from the Life of Dmitri Shostakovich*. Tr. by Graham Hobbs and Charles Midgeley. New York: Harcourt, Brace, Jovanovich, 1980. [The Russian version was published in 1979.]

Solzhenitsyn, Aleksandr I. *The First Circle*. Tr. by Thomas P. Whitney. New York: Harper & Row, 1968.

Vishnevskaya, Galina. *Galina: A Russian Story*. Tr. by Guy Daniels. San Diego: Harcourt, Brace, Jovanovich, 1980. [The autobiography of a former Bolshoi Opera singer and the wife of Mtislav Rostropovich.]

Werth, Alexander. *Musical Uproar in Moscow*. Westport, Ct.: Greenwood Press, 1973. Reprint of the 1949 edition.

White, Stephen. *Political Cultures and Soviet Politics*. London: St. Martin's Press, 1980.

Wolman, Benjamin B. *The Psychoanalytic Interpretation of History*. New York: Basic Books, 1971. [For the reference by Gustav Bychowski on Stalin.]

Zhdanov, Andrei. *Essays on Literature, Philosophy and Music*. English edition. New York: International Publisher, 1950.

CHAPTER 5: MORE TOTALITARIAN MUSIC

Anonymous. *Decision of the Central Committee of the Chinese Communist Party Concerning the Great Proletarian Cultural Revolution*. Peking: Foreign Languages Press, 1966.

Barnstone, Willis. *The Poems of Mao Tse-tung*. New York: Harper & Row, 1972.

Baxandall, Lee, and Stefan Morawski, ed. and tr. *Karl Marx and Frederick Engels on Literature and Art*. New York: International General, 1974.

Beijing Review. English edition. Weekly. Beijing, China. [Before 1979 *Peking Review*).

Chai, Winberg. *Essential Works of Chinese Communism*. Rev. ed. New York: Bantam Books, 1972.

Ch'en, Jerome. *Mao and the Cultural Revolution*. New York: Oxford University Press, 1965.

_____. *Mao Papers*. New York: Oxford University Press, 1970.

Chiang Ch'ing. *On the Revolution of Peking Opera*. Peking: Foreign Languages Press, 1968.

Committee of Concerned Asian Scholars. *China! Inside the People's Republic*. New York: Bantam Books, 1971.

Crozier, Ralph C., ed. *China's Cultural Legacy and Communism*. New York: Praeger Publishers, 1970.

DeWoskin, Kenneth J. *A Song for One or Two: Music and the Concept of Art in Early China*. Ann Arbor: Michigan Papers in Chinese Studies No. 42. Center for Chinese Studies, University of Michigan, 1982.

Domes, Jürgen. "China in 1977: Reversal of Verdicts," in *Asian Survey*, XVIII:1 (January, 1980).

Granet, Marcel. *Festivals and Songs of Ancient China*. Tr. by E. D. Edwards. New York: E.P. Dutton, 1932.

Gulik, Robert H. van. *The Lore of the Chinese Lute*. Second edition. Rutland and Tokyo: Charles E. Tuttle, 1969.

Han, Kuo-Huang. "The Chinese Concept of Program Music," in *Asian Music*, X:1 (1978), pp. 17-38.

_____. "The Modern Chinese Orchestra," in *Asian Music*, XI:1(1979), pp. 1-8.

Hsin Chi. *The Rise and Fall of the Gang of Four*. New York: Books New China, 1977.

Huang, Siu-Chi. "Musical Art in Early Confucian Philosophy," in *Philosophy East and West*, XIII:1 (April, 1963), pp. 49-60.

Judd, Ellen R. "New Yangge: The Case of 'A Worthy Sister-in-Law,' " in *Chinoperl Papers*, X pp. 167-86. Ithaca, N.Y.: China-Japan Dept., Cornell University.

Legge, James. *The Chinese Classics*. 5 volumes. Third edition. Hong Kong: Hong Kong University Press, 1960. Originally published in 1872.

Legge/Chai, Ch'u, and Winberg Chai. *Li Chi* (The Book of Rites). 2 volumes. New Hyde Park, N.Y.: University Books, 1967. [Based on Legge's work.]

Levis, John Hazedel. *The Foundations of Chinese Musical Art*. Second edition. New York: Paragon Book Reprint Corp, 1963. Originally published in 1936.

Liang, David Ming-Yueh. *The Chinese Ch'in: Its History and Music*. San Francisco: Chinese National Music Assn., San Francisco Conservatory of Music, 1972.

Lieberman, Fredric. "Texted Tunes in the Mei-An Ch'in P'u," in *Asian Music*, VI:1, 2 (1975), pp. 114-46.

Mackerras, Colin. *The Chinese Theater in Modern Times from 1840 to the Present Day*. Amherst: University of Massachusetts Press, 1975.

_____. ed. *China: The Impact of Revolution: A Survey of 20th Century China*. New York: Longmans, 1976.

Mao Zedong (Mao Tse-tung). *Selected Works*. 5 volumes, 1965-1977. English edition. Peking: Foreign Languages Press.

_____. *Poems*. Peking: Foreign Languages Press, 1976.

Marx, Karl. *Marx on China*. London: Lawrence and Wishart, 1951. [Contains the author's articles for the New York *Daily Tribune*.]

McDougall, Bonnie S. *Mao Zedong's "Talks at the Yan'an Conference on Literature and Art": A Translation of the 1943 Text with Commentary*. Ann Arbor: Michigan Papers in Chinese Studies No. 39. Center for Chinese Studies, University of Michigan, 1980.

Mowry, Hua-Yuan Li. *Yang-Pan Hsi: New Theater in China*. Berkeley: Center for Chinese Studies, University of California, 1973.

Oxsenberg, Michel. *China, the Convulsive Society*. New York: Foreign Policy Association, 1970.

Oxsenberg, Michel, and Gail Henderson. *Research Guide to People's Daily Editorials, 1949-1975*. Ann Arbor: Center for Chinese Studies, the University of Michigan, 1982.

Peyrefitte, Alain. *The Chinese: Portrait of a People*. Tr. by Graham Webb. New York: Bobbs-Merrill Co., 1977.

Pian, Rulan Chao. *Sonq Dynasty Music Sources and Their Interpretation*. Cambridge: Harvard University Press, 1967.[Sung Dynasty]

Plato. *Protagoras*. Tr. by W.R.M. Lamb. Cambridge: Loeb Classical Library. Harvard University Press, 1924.

_____. *The Republic* Tr. by Paul Shorey. Cambridge: Loeb Classical Library. Harvard University Press, 1930.

Pusey, James R. *Wu Han: Attacking the Present through the Past*. Cambridge: Harvard University Press, 1969.

Schram, Stuart R. *The Political Thought of Mao Tse-tung*. New York: Praeger Publishers, 1969.

_____. *Chairman Mao Talks to the People 1956-1971*. New York: Pantheon Books, 1974. [Published in England as *Mao Tse-tung Unrehearsed: Talks and Letters*.]

Scott, A. C. *An Introduction to Chinese Theater*. New York: Theatre Arts Books, 1959.

Snow, Edgar. *Red Star over China*. New York: Grove Press, 1961. Originally published in 1944.

Snow, Lois Wheeler. *China on Stage*. New York: Random House, 1972.

Steegmuller, Frances, and Norbert Guterman. *Sainte-Beuve: Selected Essays*. Garden City, N. Y.: Doubleday & Co., 1963.

Terrill, Ross, ed. *The China Difference*. New York: Harper & Row, 1979.

Thomas, Hugh, comp. and tr. *Comrade Editor: Letters to the People's Daily*. Hong Kong: Joint Publishing Company, 1980.

Thrasher, Alan R. "The Sociology of Chinese Music: An Introduction," in *Asian Music*, XII:2 (1981), pp. 17-53.

Waley, Arthur. *The Nine Songs: A Study of Shamanism in Ancient China.* London: Allen & Unwin, 1955.

Wan Kung. "How Our Revolutionary Operas Were Produced" in *Chinese Literature*, V-VI, 1977, pp. 66-72. Peking: n.p.

————. "What Chiang Ch'ing Did to Culture,"*China Reconstructs*, XXVI:5 (1977). [Peking.]

Witke, Roxane. *Comrade Chiang Ch'ing.* Boston: Little, Brown & Co., 1977.

Wu Han. *Hai Jui Dismissed from Office.* Tr. by C. C. Huang. Honolulu: University of Hawaii Press, 1972.

Wu, Zuguang; Huang Zuolin; and Mei Shaowu. *Peking Opera and Mei Lanfang.* Beijing: New World Press, 1981.

CHAPTER 6: SACRED OR PROFANE

Arberry, Arthur J. *The Koran Interpreted.* 2 volumes. London: Allen & Unwin, 1955.

Augustine. *Saint Augustine's Confessions.* Tr. by William Watts (1631). 2 volumes. Reprinted in the Loeb Classical Library. Cambridge: Harvard University Press, 1961.

Bammate, N. "The Islamic Cultural Tradition and the West," in Charles A. Moore, ed., *Philosophy and Culture East and West: East-West Philosophy in Practical Perspective.* Honolulu: University of Hawaii Press, 1962.

Banerji, Sures Chandra. "Influence of Tantra on Indian Music and Dance," in *Journal of the Indian Musicological Society*, X:3, 4 (September, December, 1979), pp. 19-22.

Barzun, Jacques. *Berlioz and the Romantic Century.* 2 volumes. Third edition. New York: Columbia University Press, 1969.

Bharatamuni (attributed to). *The Nāṭyaśāstra.* Volume II. Manomohan Ghosh, ed. and tr. Calcutta: The Asiatic Society, 1961. [With a commentary by the editor.]

Bhattacharya, Somnath. "Psychoanalysis and Creativity: With Special Reference to Musical Creativity," in *Journal of the Indian Musicological Society*, XI:1, 2 (March, June, 1980), pp. 90-104.

Brown, Howard Mayer, and Joan Lascelles. *Musical Iconography.* Cambridge: Harvard University Press, 1972.

Burnim, Mellonee. "The Black Gospel Music Tradition: Symbol of Ethnicity." Unpublished Ph.D. dissertation. Indiana University, 1980.

Cambridge Medieval History. Volume IV. *The Byzantine Empire.* Part 2.

Government, Church and Civilisation, ed. by J. M. Hussey. London: Cambridge University Press, 1967.

Code of Maimonides. Book 8. *The Book of the Temple.* Tr. by Mendell Lewittes. New Haven: Yale University Press, 1957.

Daniélou, Alain. *Hindu Polytheism.* New York: Pantheon Books, 1964.

———. *Northern Indian Music.* New York: Frederick A. Praeger, 1969.

Deva, B. Chaitanya. *An Introduction to Indian Music.* New Delhi: Publications Division, Ministry of Information and Broadcasting, 1973.

Deva, B. C., and K. G. Virmani. "A Study in the Psychological Response to Ragas," in *Journal of the Indian Musicological Society,* XI:1, 2 (March, June, 1980), pp. 33-36. [Abstract.]

Edgerton, Franklin. *The Beginnings of Indian Philosophy.* Cambridge: Harvard University Press, 1965.

Encyclopaedia Judaica. New York: Macmillan 1971.

Epstein, Dena. *Sinful Tunes and Spirituals.* Chicago: University of Illinois, 1977. [Chapters XI and XII.]

al Faruqi, Lois [Lamya'] Ibsen. "Tartīl al-Qur'ān al-Karīm," in *Islamic Perspectives: Studies in Honour of Sayyid Abul A'la Mawdudi.* Leicester, U. K.: The Islamic Foundation, 1979.

———. "Factors of Continuity in the Musical Cultures of the Muslim World." Paper read at the Annual Meeting of the Society for Ethnomusicology, College Park, Maryland, 1982.

———. "What Makes 'Religious Music' Religious?" in *Sacred Sound: Music in Religious Practice,* ed. by Joyce Irwin. Journal of the American Academy of Religion. Thematic Studies, L:1. Chico, Calif.: Scholars Press, 1983, pp. 21-34.

Fischer, Edward. "Ritual as Communication," in *The Roots of Ritual,* ed. by James D. Shaughnessy. Grand Rapids, Mich.: William B. Eerdmans Publishing Co., 1973.

Frazer, James George. *Folklore of the Old Testament.* 3 volumes. London: Macmillan, 1919.

Goldron, Romain [A. Louis Burkhalter]. *Minstrels and Masters: The Triumph of Polyphony.* New York: H. S. Stuttman Co./Doubleday & Co., 1968.

Hornell, James. *The Indian Conch and Its Relation to Hindu Life and Religion.* London: William & Norgate, 1915.

Howard, Wayne. *Sāmavedic Chant.* New Haven: Yale University Press, 1977.

Jones, Jafran. *The 'Isāwīya of Tunisia and Their Music.* Ph.D. dissertation, University of Washington, 1978.

Lang, Paul, and Otto Bettmann. *A Pictorial History of Music.* New York: W. W. Norton & Co., 1960.

Lesure, François. *Music and Art in Society*. University Park: Pennsylvania State University Press, 1968.

Müller, F. Max, ed. *The Sacred Books of the East Series*, Vols. XII and XXVI. *The Śatapatha-Brāhmana*. Tr. by Julius Eggeling. Reprinted from 1885 edition. Delhi: Motilal Banarsidass, 1963.

The New Grove Dictionary of Music and Musicians. Sixth edition. Stanley Sadie, ed. London: Macmillan 1980.

O'Connell, Robert J. *St. Augustine's Confessions: The Odyssey of Soul*. Cambridge: Harvard University Press, 1969.

Pal, Pratapaditya. *The Ideal Image*. New York: The Asia Society, 1978.

Papal Documents on Sacred Music. Third edition. New York: St. Gregory Society of America, 1939.

Pereira, José, ed. *Hindu Theology: A Reader*. New York: Image Books/ Doubleday & Co., 1976.

Pirrota, Nino. "Music and Cultural Tendencies in 15th-Century Italy," in *Journal of the American Musicological Society*, XXI:2 (1966), pp. 127-61; especially 134-35, 152-54.

Pius XII. Encyclical letter, "Musicae Sacra Disciplina." Washington, D.C.: National Catholic Welfare Conference, 1956.

Prajñānānanda, Swāmī. *A Historical Study of Indian Music*. Calcutta: Ānandadhārā Prakāshan, 1965.

Raboteau, Albert J. *Slave Religion*. New York: Oxford University Press, 1978.

Rimmer, Joan. *Ancient Musical Instruments of Western Asia in the British Museum*. London: British Museum, 1969.

Rothmüller, Aron Marko. *The Music of the Jews: An Historical Appreciation*. New and revised edition. Tr. by H. S. Stevens. South Brunswich, N. J., London: Thomas Yoseloff, 1967.

Sharif, M. M. "Islam and Spiritual Values," in Charles A. Moore, ed., *Philosophy and Culture East and West: East-West Philosophy in Practical Perspective*. Honolulu: University of Hawaii Press, 1962.

Singh, Jaidev. "Nāda in Indian Tradition" in *Journal of the Indian Musicological Society*, XI:1, 2 (March, June, 1980), pp. 37-43.

Southern, Eileen. *The Music of Black Americans*. New York: W. W. Norton & Co., 1971.

Strunk, Oliver. *Source Readings in Music History*. New York: W.W. Norton & Co., 1950.

Vanarase, Shyamala. "Modernity and Musical Taste: Some Psychological considerations," in *Journal of the Indian Musicological Society*, X:1, 2 (March, June, 1979), pp. 5-9.

Van der Meer, Frederik. *Augustine the Bishop*. New York: Sheed and Ward, 1961.

Van der Leeuw, Gerardus. *Sacred and Profane Beauty: The Holy in Art.* New York: Holt, Rinehart & Winston, 1963.

Weiss, Piero. *Letters of Composers through Six Centuries.* Philadelphia: Chilton Book Co., 1967.

Wellesz, Egon. *A History of Byzantine Music and Hymnography.* Second edition. London: Oxford University Press, 1961.

Werner, Eric. *The Sacred Bridge: The Interdependence of Liturgy and Music in Synagogue and Church during the First Milennium.* New York: Columbia University Press, 1959.

Winternitz, Emmanuel. *Musical Instruments and Their Symbolism in Western Art.* New York: W. W. Norton & Co., 1967.

Zaehner, R. C., ed. and tr. *Hindu Scriptures.* London: J. M. Dent & Sons, 1966.

CHAPTER 7: THE HIDDEN ROSTRUM OF OPERA AND THE BROADWAY MUSICAL

Abraham, Gerald. *A Hundred Years of Music.* Third edition. London: Methuen & Co., 1964.

Blitzstein, Marc, "Coming—The Mass Audiences!" in *Modern Music,* XIII:4 (May-June, 1936), pp. 23-29.

Boardman, Gerald. *American Musical Comedy from Adonis to Dreamgirls.* New York: Oxford University Press, 1982.

_____. *American Operetta from HMS Pinafore to Sweeney Todd.* New York: Oxford University Press, 1981.

Budden, Julien. *The Operas of Verdi.* 3 volumes. Volume I. *From Oberto to Rigoletto.* New York: Praeger Publishers, 1973.

_____. Ibid. Volume II. *From Il Trovatore to La Forza del Destino.* London: Cassell, 1978.

_____. Ibid. Volume 3. *From Don Carlos to Falstaff.* New York: Oxford University Press, 1981.

Crosten, William L. *French Grand Opera: An Art and a Business.* New York: King's Crown Press/Columbia University Press, 1948.

Engel, Lehman. *The American Musical Theater: A Consideration.* New York: Macmillan, 1967.

Graf, Herbert. *Opera for the People.* Minneapolis: University of Minnesota Press, 1951.

Grieb, Lyndal. *The Operas of Gian Carlo Menotti, 1937-1972: A Selective Bibliography.* Metuchen, N. J.: Scarecrow Press, 1974.

Jacobi, Frederick. "WPA Shows in Music," in *Modern Music,* XIV:1 (November-December, 1936), pp. 42-44.

Tawa, Nicholas. *Serenading the Reluctant Eagle: American Musical Life, 1925-1945.* New York: Schirmer Books, 1984.

Thomson, Virgil. *Music Right and Left.* New York: Henry Holt & Co., 1951.

Weaver, William, ed., and tr. *Verdi: A Documentary Study.* London: Thames & Hudson, 1977.

Zuck, Barbara. *A History of Musical Americanism.* Ann Arbor, Mich.: UMI Research Press, 1980.

CHAPTER 8: THE DECADE OF PROTESTS

Andre, Don A. "Leonard Bernstein's *Mass* as Social and Political Commentary on the Sixties." D. M. A. dissertation. University of Washington, 1979.

Beatles, The. *Things We Said Today: The Complete Lyrics and a Concordance to the Beatles' Songs, 1960-1970.* Ann Arbor, Mich.: Pierian Press, 1980.

Belz, Carl. *The Story of Rock.* Second edition. New York: Oxford University Press, 1972.

Booth, Mark W. "Popular Music," in *Handbook of Popular Culture.* vol. I. Ed. by M. Thomas Inge. Westport, Ct.: Greenwood Press, 1978. [A summary of the subject currently with a survey of the literature.]

Bowden, Betsy. *Performed Literature: Words and Music by Bob Dylan.* Bloomington: Indiana University Press, 1982.

Dane, Barbara, and Irwin Silber, eds. *The Vietnam Songbook.* New York: The Guardian, 1969.

Dylan, Bob. *The Songs of Bob Dylan from 1966 through 1975.* New York: Alfred A. Knopf, 1976.

Etzkorn, K. Peter. "Popular Music: The Sounds of the Many," in *Music in American Society 1776-1976.* New Brunswick, N. J.: Transaction Press, 1977.

Fischer, Edward. "Ritual as Communication" in *The Roots of Ritual.* Ed. by James D. Shaughnessy. Grand Rapids, Mich.: William Eerdmans Publishing Company, 1973.

Hoffmann, Frank. *The Literature of Rock, 1954-1978.* Metuchen, N. J.: Scarecrow Press, 1981. [A sequel is planned.]

Hopkins, Jerry, and Danny Sugerman. *No One Here Gets Out Alive.* New York: Warner Books, 1980. [On rock musicians.]

Marsh, Dave. *Before I Get Old: The Story of The Who.* New York: St. Martin's Press, 1983.

"Performers and Audiences," in *Popular Music 4* (Yearbook for 1984), pp. 261-77. Cambridge: Cambridge University Press, 1984. [See especially part 5, "Rock Music and Politics."]

Reynolds, Malvina. *The Malvina Reynolds Songbook.* Berkeley: Schroder Music Company, 1974.

Starr, S. Frederick. *Red and Hot: The Fate of Jazz in the Soviet Union.* New York: Oxford University Press, 1983.

Wallis, Roger, and Krister Malm. *Big Sounds from Small Peoples: The Music Industry in Small Countries.* New York: Pendragon Press, 1984. [Studies of countries of the Caribbean, Africa, Europe and South Asia.]

Williams, Paul. *Outlaw Blues: A Book of Rock Music.* New York: E. P. Dutton & Co., 1969. [The author's recollections; he was twenty years old at the time of Bob Dylan's appearance.]

CHAPTER 9: THE CONTEMPORARY COMPOSER AS SOCIAL CRITIC

Anhalt, Istvan. *Alternate Voice: Essays on Contemporary Vocal and Choral Compositions.* Toronto: University of Toronto Press, 1984. [See especially Chapter VI, "Deep Themes Not So Hidden," and "Rituals," pp. 176 ff.]

Casals, Pablo. *Joys and Sorrows: Reflections.* As told to Albert E. Kahn. New York: Simon and Schuster, 1970. [By the celebrated cellist and Spanish civil rights spokesman.]

Henze, Hans Werner. *Music and Politics: Collected Writings.* Tr. by Peter Lebanyi. London: Faber & Faber, 1982.

Kemp, Ivan. *Michael Tippett: The Man and His Work.* New York: Da Capo Press, 1984. [A contemporary English composer with a political and social outlook conspicuous in many of his compositions. See also White, Eric Walter.]

Lehmann-Haupt, Hellmut. *Art Under a Dictatorship.* New York: Octagon Books, 1973. Originally published in 1954. [On Hitler's regime.]

Lipman, Samuel. *The House of Music: Art in an Era of Institutions.* Boston: David R. Godine, Publisher, 1984. ["Shostakovich in Four Parts," pp. 17-30.]

Maciejewski, B[oguslav] M. *Twelve Polish Composers.* London: Allegro Press, 1976. [Chapter III is on Witold Lutoslawski, Chapter X on Krzysztof Penderecki.]

Norris, Christopher, ed. *Shostakovich: The Man and His Music.* Boston: Marion Boyars, 1982.

Robinson, Ray. *Krzysztof Penderecki: A Guide to His Work.* Princeton, N. J.: Prestige Publications, 1983.

Salisbury, Harrison E. *The 900 Days: The Siege of Leningrad.* New York: Harper & Row, 1969.

_____. "Visit with Dmitri Shostakovich," *New York Times Magazine,* August 8, 1954, pp. 9, 44. [Shostakovich's argument for the artistic freedom and financial security of the Soviet artist. See p. 45 for a "rebuttal" by a Moscow musician, Julie Whitney, now the wife of a U. S. citizen.]

Schoenberg, Arnold. *Style and Idea.* Leonard Stein, ed. Tr. by Leo Black. Berkeley: University of California Press, 1975. [Part 10, "Social and Political Matters," pp. 491-512.]

Shepherd, John; Graham Vulliamy; and Trevor Wishart. *Whose Music? A Sociology of Musical Languages.* London: Latimer New Dimensions, 1977.

Shostakovich, Dmitri. *Testimony: The Memoirs of Dmitri Shostakovich.* As related to and edited by Solomon Volkov. Tr. by Antonina W. Bouis. New York: Harper & Row, 1979.

Slonimsky, Nicolas. "Dmitri Dmitrievitch Shostakovitch," in *The Musical Quarterly,* XXVIII:4 (October, 1942).

_____. "Russia Revisited," in *The Musical Quarterly,* XIII:1 (November-December, 1935).

Smith-Brindle, Reginald. *The New Music 1900-1960.* Revised edition. New York: W. W. Norton & Co., 1968.

Sollertinsky, Dmitri, and Ludmilla Sollertinsky. *Pages from the Life of Dmitri Shostakovich.* Tr. by Graham Hobbs and Charles Midgeley. New York: Harcourt, Brace, Jovanovich, 1980.

Schwarz, Boris. *Music and Musical Life in Soviet Russia. Enlarged edition. 1917-1981.* Bloomington: Indiana University Press, 1983.

White, Eric Walter. *Tippett and His Operas.* New Introduction by Andrew Porter. London: Barrie & Jenkins, 1979.

Index

About the Author

ARNOLD PERRIS is Associate Professor of Music at the University of Missouri, St. Louis. He holds degrees in political science and musicology. His articles have appeared in *Ethnomusicology, Imago Musicae,* and other journals.